Contents

Acknowledgements

Text

The authors and publishers would like to thank the following organisations for permission to reproduce text.

p13 & p17 – © National Readership Survey Ltd. (NRS); p14 – © Broadcasters' Audience Research Board (BARB); © Radio Joint Audience Research Limited (RAJAR).

Photographs

The authors and publishers would like to thank the following individuals and organisations for permission to reproduce photographs.

p10 © Alamy Images/SBDPhoto Travel; p12ff – © Harcourt Ltd/Gareth Boden; p14ff – © Getty Images/PhotoDisc; p15 – © Rex Features/Martin Lee; p16 – © Harcourt Ltd/Chrissie Martin; p17 – © Image Courtesy of The Advertising Archives; p18 – © Rex Features; p19 – © Rex Features/Jonathan Hordle; p21ff – © Photos.com; p23 – © Corbis/Bob Sacha; p25 – © Corbis/Rune Hellestad; © Aquarius Collection/ABC; P26ff – © Photos.com; p27 – © Harcourt Ltd/Debbie Rowe; p32 – © Harcourt Ltd/Jules Selmes; p33ff – © Photos.com; p36 – © Rex Features/VM/KOMM/Keystone US; p37 – © Rex Features/Sipa Press; p38 – © Digital Vision; p39ff – © Getty Images/PhotoDisc; p43ff – © Getty Images/PhotoDisc; p46 – © iStockphoto/Joseph Justice; p49 – © BIPP; p53 – © ASA; © BBFC; © ICSTIS; © Ofcom; p54 – © PCC; p65 – © iStockphoto/Lise Gagne; p78 – © Alamy Images/Jason Smalley; p82 – © RAJAR; © BARB; © ELSPA; p84 – © Harcourt Ltd/Arnos Design Ltd; p96 – © iStockphoto/Jane Diederich; p103 & p108 – © iStockphoto / Justin Horrocks; p126, p127, p130 & p138 – © Arnos Design Ltd; p142 – © Corbis / Reuters; p143 & p144 – © BBC Photo Library; p146 – © Arnos Design Ltd; p149 – © Alamy Images/Martin Bond; p152 – © Emap Performance Ltd; p153 – © Zooid Pictures Ltd; p155 – © Corbis; p158 – © BBC Photo Library; © Rex Features; p165 – © Rex Features Ltd; p174 – © The Kobal Collection / Working Title; © The Kobal Collection/Miramax; © The Kobal Collection/Dreamworks LLC; p176 – Paul Bayliss, p182 – © Zooid Pictures Ltd; p190 – © Virgin; p197 – © SONY; p198 – © Virgin; © Paramount; © Viacom; p206 – © Skillset; © BECTU; p210 – © NUJ; p211 – © Philip Holmes; p215 – © Arnos Design Ltd; © PA Photos/Kurt Strumpf/AP; p222 – © Alamy Images/Barry Lewis; p224, p225 & p227 – © Philip Holmes; p228 – © Turtle Studios; © Tin Pan Alley Studios; p230 – © Harcourt Education; © Philip Holmes; p231 & p232 – © Philip Holmes; p234 – © Game Republic.

Every effort has been made to contact copyright holders of material reproduced in this book. Any omissions will be rectified in subsequent printings if notice is given to the publishers.

Introduction

Welcome to the National Award, Certificate and Diploma in Media Production. This is a qualification that has recently been revised and updated, and this book reflects these changes. The revisions mean that the qualification reflects some of the very latest developments in media production practices and technology in the dynamic and exciting media industries. Understanding how the media industries work, the job roles you might find, and the way that media producers make their products is an important part of this qualification.

The Nationals in Media Production might lead you straight into a career in the media or to Higher Education. However, this qualification is not just for people who want to work in the media industry. Many of the techniques and skills you will develop are transferable to a variety of other work situations. You will learn to communicate with a team and a client, present yourself and your work, deal with interview situations and use the latest technology to produce reports, programmes and presentations. The planning, research and organisational skills you will learn will be invaluable in almost any career or profession. Being able to present information in a lively and engaging way, such as by using a video, audio, interactive or printed product, can be a real asset to a person's skills portfolio.

You may want to move on from this qualification to Higher National Diploma, Foundation Degree or a Degree programme at university. The skills you will develop in your National in Media will be an excellent starting point for a career in the media or further study.

Media plays an important part in everyone's life. In your work for this qualification you will be looking at what media producers make and how their output is influenced by what people want. You will be able to investigate particular sectors of the media industry and where you might fit into this industry.

How to use this book

You will see that this book is divided, like the qualification, into units. These are the Core Units for this National Award, Certificate and Diploma in Media Production. These Core Units provide you with the underpinning understanding, knowledge and skills required for the qualification.

The National Award, Certificate and Diploma in Media Production provide an opportunity to study media production to a level that reflects professional practice. This is undertaken through the Specialist Units and these units will be covered in a separate publication.

You should see this qualification as being an opportunity to seamlessly produce a range of media products while developing an understanding of the media industry, research techniques and media audiences. You will also be able to demonstrate professional practice in these units and the specialist production units.

Your teacher will advise you on the best approach to developing your understanding, knowledge and skills depending on the pathway you are taking. The pathways in this qualification are:

BTEC National Award in Media Production (Television and Film)

BTEC National Award in Media Production (Radio)

BTEC National Award in Media Production (Sound Recording)

BTEC National Award in Media Production (Print and Publishing)

BTEC National Award in Media Production (Interactive Media)

BTEC National Award in Media Production (Games Development)

BTEC National Certificate in Media Production

BTEC National Certificate in Media Production (Television and Film)

BTEC National Certificate in Media Production (Radio)

BTEC National Certificate in Media Production (Sound Recording)

BTEC National Certificate in Media Production (Print and Publishing)

BTEC National Certificate in Media Production (Interactive Media)

BTEC National Certificate in Media Production (Games Development)

BTEC National Diploma in Media Production

BTEC National Diploma in Media Production (Television and Film)

BTEC National Diploma in Media Production (Radio)

BTEC National Diploma in Media Production (Sound Recording)

BTEC National Diploma in Media Production (Print and Publishing)

BTEC National Diploma in Media Production (Interactive Media)

BTEC National Diploma in Media Production (Games Development)

At the start of each unit you will see a list of learning outcome. These state exactly what you should 'know, understand or be able to do' as a result of completing the unit. Your teacher will provide suitable assignments to enable you to complete work in the Core Units and to achieve a Pass, Merit or Distinction grade. You must bear in mind that to achieve a Pass grade for a unit you have to complete all the assessment criteria at Pass level. In order to achieve a Merit grade you must achieve all the Pass criteria and all the Merit criteria. In order to achieve a Distinction grade you must achieve all the Pass, Merit and Distinction criteria. Your teacher will provide you with guidance on how you might improve your work in order to achieve an appropriate final unit grade.

Getting a higher grade depends on you doing your best to follow the guidance in this book. You should look carefully at the assessment criteria for the Core Units, study the information provided in the unit, use the 'Theory into practice' activities to develop your understanding, knowledge and skills and use the 'Preparation for assessment' section to demonstrate these.

We have tried hard to make this book appealing and engaging, so that you will want to learn more. We hope you find this book helpful and we wish you good luck in working on the Core Units for this qualification.

Philip Holmes
Guy Starkey
Paul Baylis

Guide to learning and assessment features

This book has number of features to help you relate theory to practice and reinforce your learning. It also aims to help you gather evidence for assessment. You will find the following features in each unit.

Your teacher or tutor should check that you have completed enough activities to meet all the assessment criteria for the unit, whether from this book or from other tasks.

Teachers/tutors and students should refer to the BTEC standards for the qualification for the full BTEC grading criteria for each unit (www.edexcel.org.uk).

Case studies

Interesting examples of real situations or companies are described in case studies that link theory to practice. They will show you how the topics you are studying affect real people and businesses.

Knowledge checks

At the end of each unit is a set of quick questions to test your knowledge of the information you have been studying. Use these to check your progress, and also as a revision tool.

Grading icons

Throughout the book you will see the **P**, **M** and **D** icons. These show you where the tasks fit in with the grading criteria. If you do these tasks you will be building up your evidence to achieve your desired qualification. If you are aiming for a Merit, make sure you complete all the Pass **P** and Merit **M** tasks. If you are aiming for a Distinction, you will also need to complete all the Distinction **D** tasks. **P1** means the first of the Pass criteria listed in the specification, **M1** the first of the Merit criteria, **D1** the first of the Distinction criteria, and so on.

Case study

Applying research methods and techniques

Let's take a look at how a group of BTEC National Diploma Media Production students applied some of the research methods and techniques they learned about in this unit to their practical production work.

John's research
Remember John? He was producing a series of radio adverts aimed at 14–18-year-olds for Unit 44 and needed some information about his target audience.

John decided to produce a questionnaire that asked people in the 14–18 years age group about their hobbies and interests. It included a mixture of open and closed questions. These aimed to get both quantitative and qualitative information that would help John to produce more effective adverts that appealed to the target audience.

John decided to ask students in his own school to complete the questionnaire, but also asked some young people in the street and in a local college, so that he didn't just get responses from his friends at school.

Alice's research
Alice was working with a group of students on a video project. Like John, Alice and her team produced a questionnaire for a representative sample of their target audience as part of their research. They also decided to organise a focus group so that they could ask some more in-depth questions and find out what people really thought about their proposed product.

Alice's group also looked at a range of different programmes and videos that were aimed at their target audience. They hoped this would give them a better understanding of the sorts of codes and conventions and production techniques that would appeal to this age group.

Shilpa's research
Shilpa and her team decided to develop their design and journalistic skills by producing a promotional magazine. As part of their research they examined a range of printed products aimed at their target audience as well as different forms of printed promotional material, to get additional design ideas.

To extend their vocational knowledge they also decided to visit a local newspaper office to find out more about the actual process of putting together and printing a print product.

Bilal's research
Bilal sees interactive media as the future and decided to design and produce a website as his main production project. He conducted a great deal of secondary research on the Internet, looking at what did and did not work in website design, and then used this information to produce a series of sample pages which he tested on his audience via email.

Bilal used the results of this research to help him fine-tune his ideas for his website.

- **Which research methods and techniques are you going to use in your research?**
- **What skills will you need to develop to make sure your research is a success?**
- **Do you have a clear idea of what the timescale is for your research project?**

Knowledge check

1. Explain the four main methods of research. **p**

2. Explain, using specific examples from your own work, what factors need to be considered when planning, designing and carrying out a survey using a questionnaire. **m d**

3. Explain what a focus group is. **p**

4. Explain clearly what issues you would need to consider when undertaking your own secondary research. **m d**

1.3 Be able to present results of research

After you have completed a substantial research project, or a number of smaller linked research tasks, you will need to present the results of this research.

In fact, the name of this final section is a little misleading as you need to do more than simply present the results that you obtained from your research. The content of your presentation should include the following key elements:

- an introduction to your research in which you outline its purpose and aims
- an explanation of the methods and techniques that you have used
- the research data itself, presented in a suitable form (such as tables, charts, graphs or diagrams)
- a summary of your main findings (the results)
- the conclusions that you can make from these findings
- any proposals that you are making based on these conclusions.

This information can be presented in the form of a written report, as an oral presentation or as a combination of the two, with a presentation to the class backed up by a written report and accompanying notes, logs and data.

If you choose to present your findings in the form of an oral presentation then you must make sure that this is recorded so that your mark can be checked by the moderator towards the end of the course.

However you decide to present your findings, you will need to think carefully about the structure and content of what you produce as well as the language that you use.

For your work in this unit you may have been working with a real client, and in this case it would be better if this client was in the audience for your presentation. If not, then it is more likely that your audience will be comprised of your tutor and fellow members of your class.

Planning your presentation in advance is crucial to its success. You will also need to practise it and do some run-throughs so that it goes as smoothly as possible on the day.

Think it over 7

Oral presentations are often used in the media industry to pitch new ideas to a potential client or backer, and these pitches will often include details of research that has been carried out to support the proposals being made.

The sorts of people who would be in the audience for such a presentation would be those who would have the final say as to whether your idea would go into production or not. These people could include a commissioning editor, producer, exhibitor, broadcaster, publisher or potential purchaser of the final product.

■ Presentation skills

Conducting an effective presentation is not an easy task. You will need to identify which presentation and communication skills you already have, and which ones you need to develop further.

Theory into practice 16

Think about your own communication skills. Are you confident when speaking to other people? What can you do to improve the way in which you get your ideas across? **P**

Key Terms

Intrapersonal communication refers to communication within you, and includes all of the thoughts, fears and anxieties that you may have about your presentation. Control these and your presentation is more likely to go well.

Interpersonal communication is face-to-face communication between two or more people, and includes aspects of spoken and non-verbal communication.

Preparation for assessment

Each unit concludes with a full unit assessment, which taken as a whole fulfils all the unit requirements from Pass to Distinction. Each task is matched to the relevant criteria in the specification.

Think it over

These are points for individual reflection or group discussion. They will widen your knowledge and help you reflect on issues that impact on media production.

Theory into practice

These practical activities allow you to apply theoretical knowledge to media production tasks or research. Make sure you complete these activities as you work through each unit, to reinforce your learning.

Key terms

Issues and terms that you need to be aware of are summarised under these headings. They will help you check your knowledge as you learn, and will prove to be a useful quick-reference tool.

Research techniques for the media industries

Introduction

Media production is a complex process and research is the starting point for productions of any scale. The films and television programmes that we watch, the radio programmes and podcasts that we listen to, the newspapers and magazines that we read and the websites and computer games that we interact with have all been thoroughly researched and planned in the pre-production stages.

In the first part of this unit you will learn about the different purposes of research within the media industries. For example, research is used to assess the financial viability of a planned production, to gather a range of information relevant to the content of the production, or to allow for the effective planning of a production schedule. There are also media companies which conduct extensive market research in order to gather data about audience consumption of media products and services.

In the second part of this unit you will have the opportunity to further develop your research skills and apply them to your own media production work. You will also learn how to use market research intelligence to further improve the effectiveness of your media products.

The final part of the unit will show you different ways in which you can present the results of your research.

After completing this unit you should be able to achieve the following outcomes:

- Understand the purposes of research in the media industries.
- Be able to apply a range of research methods and techniques.
- Be able to present results of research.

Think it over

Media products are often very expensive and time-consuming to produce, and there is a lot of pressure on the people who plan and make them to get them right. A major Hollywood film such as *King Kong,* which cost over $200 million to produce and a further $50 million to promote, needs to attract a large cinema audience to begin to recover these costs and also earn additional revenue from DVD rental and purchase. Can you think of any other ways in which the producers of the film can earn extra revenue?

Similarly, the companies who have paid money to have their products and services advertised in a glossy lifestyle magazine or prime-time soap expect and demand a quality product that will reach their desired audience.

Because of these pressures and demands, media companies put a lot of time and effort into thoroughly researching a product to ensure that it will attract the right audience and that this audience will react to it in the appropriate way. They also plan the production process thoroughly, and make use of the latest technology and techniques to ensure that their product has the desired values to compete effectively in the media marketplace.

As you learn about the different research methods and techniques that are used, you should be thinking about the relevance that they have to your own production work. You should also think about how you can use both market research and production research to improve the quality and effectiveness of your own media products.

Purposes of research

There are two main forms of research undertaken by the media industries. The first is called **market research** and the second **production research**. It is important that you understand the purposes of each of these forms of research and what they involve.

Key Terms

Market research is the collection and analysis of information about the market within which a particular product will compete with other products for an audience and for revenue.

Production research is related to the production process itself.

Market research

Effective and successful media products target the right audience and communicate to them in an effective way. As the media industry becomes more fragmented so competition for a share of the audience becomes more intense. Knowing who your target audience is, and what makes them tick, is therefore increasingly important.

Market research involves looking at:

- statistical data about audience size and composition for a particular media product (for example, how many people read *The Sun* newspaper and what sort of people they are)
- the extent to which a potential audience is aware of a media product or service (for example, how many people are aware of new digital radio channels that are available)
- what people think about particular products and services and what their patterns of behaviour are (for example, what people think about broadband Internet technology and what they use it for)
- market competitors who are competing for a share of the audience and revenue with similar products

(for example, a company launching a new lifestyle magazine will want to be fully informed about other similar magazines).

The media marketplace is highly competitive and media producers will often undertake detailed research into their target market or, more commonly, commission other companies to undertake research on their behalf.

Think it over 1

Why do you think media producers employ other companies and organisations to carry out research on their behalf? What are the advantages and disadvantages of this approach?

■ Market research organisations

There are various organisations whose main role is to undertake market research on media audiences and products. The findings of their research often become a commercial product in its own right that is then sold on to media companies.

Some of this information is also freely available to the public. You can find examples by visiting the websites of the organisations listed below, as well as by looking in the media pages of newspapers such as *The Guardian* and *The Independent*, and in specialist magazines such as *Broadcast*.

Key Terms

National Readership Survey (NRS) provides information to the industry on who reads what publication.

Audit Bureau of Circulation (ABC) provides circulation information to the newspaper and magazine industry.

Key Terms

Broadcasters' Audience Research Board (BARB) provides estimates of the number of people watching television programmes.

Radio Joint Audience Research Limited (RAJAR) provides estimates of the number of people listening to radio programmes.

The **National Readership Survey (NRS)** is a non-profit-making organisation that provides the industry with estimates of how many people read different newspapers and magazines and the type of people they are (see Figure 1.01). These estimates are based on interviews with a representative sample of the population, a total of some 36,000 such interviews every year. NRS provides a breakdown of the readership of each title according to such factors as gender, age, social class and many other demographic and lifestyle characteristics. This information is invaluable to publishers and advertising agencies planning, buying and selling advertising in the print medium, as the data allows them to select the titles that reach a given target market more effectively.

NRS publishes data for over 250 newspapers, newspaper supplements and consumer magazines. These data are made available to NRS subscribers for detailed analysis via specialised computer bureaux.

The **Audit Bureau of Circulation (ABC)** also provides circulation information to the newspaper and magazine industry and includes directories, leaflets, exhibitions and websites in its range of products researched. It was launched in 1931 in response to demands from the advertising industry for independent verification of the circulation and readership claims made by the sales teams of newspapers and magazines.

The **Broadcasters' Audience Research Board (BARB)** is used by the BBC and independent broadcasters to provide estimates of the number of people watching their programmes. The data produced includes which channels and programmes are being watched at a specific time, and a breakdown of the type of people who are watching a particular programme. BARB provides television audience data for all analogue and digital channels received within the UK. The information is obtained from panels of viewers from selected television-owning households, representative of each ITV and BBC region. The data produced by the research represents the viewing behaviour of over 25 million households within the UK.

Radio Joint Audience Research Limited (RAJAR) was established in 1992 to operate a single audience

Title	Readers 000s	%	ABC1 000s	%	C2DE 000s	%	Age 15–44 000s	%	Age 45+ 000s	%	Male 000s	%	Female 000s	%
Population	48 314	100	26 638	100	21 676	100	24 201	100	24 112	100	23 448	100	24 866	100
Take a Break	3209	6.6	1199	4.5	2010	9.3	1651	6.8	1559	6.5	445	1.9	2764	11.1
OK!	2398	5.0	1396	5.2	1003	4.6	1834	7.6	564	2.3	367	1.6	2031	8.2
Radio Times	2810	5.8	2122	8.0	689	3.2	988	4.1	1822	7.6	1332	5.7	1478	5.9
Nuts	1286	2.7	599	2.2	687	3.2	1219	5.0	67	0.3	1106	4.7	180	0.7
Auto Trader	1394	2.9	654	2.5	740	3.4	1111	4.6	284	1.2	1089	4.6	305	1.2
The Sun	7840	16.2	2928	11.0	4912	22.7	4707	19.4	3133	13.0	4537	19.3	3303	13.3
Daily Mail	5253	10.9	3355	12.6	1898	8.8	1643	6.8	3610	15.0	2511	10.7	2742	11.0
The Guardian	1239	2.6	1124	4.2	115	0.5	682	2.8	556	2.3	689	2.9	550	2.2

Figure 1.01: Market breakdown of the readership of a selection of publications April 2006–March 2007. (Source: *NRS*)

measurement system for the radio industry, including all BBC, UK-licensed and other commercial stations. The company is owned by the RadioCentre and the British Broadcasting Corporation (BBC).

In addition to these organisations, there is a growing number of commercial agencies that offer research and analysis services to media producers, advertisers and regulators.

	Average weekly viewing per person		Share of total viewing	
	February (Hrs:Mins)	January (Hrs:Mins)	February (%)	January (%)
ALL TV	27:27	28:06	100.0	100.0
BBC 1	6:10	6:15	22.5	22.3
BBC 2	2:25	2:27	8.8	8.8
TOTAL BBC 1/2	8:36	8:42	31.3	31.0
ITV	5:24	5:23	19.7	19.2
Channel 4/S4C	2:30	2:58	9.1	10.6
Five	1:30	1:30	5.5	5.3
TOTAL Terrestrial TV	9:24	9:51	34.3	35.1
Other viewing	9:27	9:31	34.5	33.9

Figure 1.02: Share of viewing times of the different terrestrial TV channels in January/February 2007. (Source: BARB)

Station	Weekly reach of adults		Average hours	Share of listening
	000s	% of population		
All radio	45,045	90	23.5	100
All BBC	32,810	66	17.5	54.4
All BBC Network	28,711	58	16.2	44.0
BBC local/regional	10,262	21	10.7	10.4
All commercial	31,346	63	14.6	43.2
All national commercial	13,318	27	8.3	10.5
All local commercial	25,772	52	13.4	32.8
BBC Radio 1	10,262	21	10.0	9.7
BBC Radio 2	13,269	27	12.6	15.8
BBC Radio 3	2,028	4	7.1	1.4
BBC Radio 4	9,342	19	12.5	11.1
BBC Radio Five Live	5,846	12	8.0	4.4

Figure 1.03: Summary of radio audience figures for the quarter ending December 2006. (Source: RAJAR)

Grading tips

To reach Merit level, you should explain, rather than simply describe, the range of services offered. Use well-chosen examples, express your ideas with clarity and use the correct subject terminology.

To reach Distinction level, fully explain the range of services offered. Use supporting arguments to justify what you have written. Use technical and specialist language correctly.

■ Audience segmentation

Segmenting the audience into different categories makes it easier for media producers to identify and target groups of people with the same needs and wants. Those undertaking research within, or on behalf of, media organisations therefore look for categories they can use to divide up the potential audience.

Common classifications include:

- age
- gender

▲ Figure 1.04: The BBFC put an age category on all films, videos and DVDs that are shown and offered for sale and rent in the UK, and are now classifying many video and computer games.

- culure and ethnicity (ethnographic classification)
- income and social class (socio-economic classification).

Age

One of the most significant and often-used categories within the media is that of age. A common division used by media researchers is: 15 years or younger, 16–24 years, 25–44 years, 45–64 years, 65 years and over. However, individual pieces of research will use age divisions that are most appropriate for the task.

For example, research into the impact of advertising on young children will need to sub-divide the 15 years or younger category. Also, a company who is looking at the so-called 'grey' market of over-55s may find it useful to know what people in the 55–60 years category think about a particular product compared to those who are aged 65–70 years.

Other more general age-related categories can also be used (such as pre-school children, school children, teenagers, pensioners). The regulatory framework can also sometimes be a factor, as in the different age categories used by the British Board of Film Classification (BBFC).

Many advertisers are also interested in what different age groups are reading, listening to, watching and playing, as they can then decide whether or not to advertise their products and services via these media.

Theory into practice 2

Conduct some research of your own to find examples of advertising that is clearly targeted at a specific age group. Try to include a range of different media.

For printed media you could look in a selection of comics, newspapers and magazines to see if there is a clear relationship between the types of products advertised and the target readership.

You could also record a selection of different television programmes from a commercial station to see what advertising and sponsorship they attract, and look at the pop-ups and banner advertising within a range of different websites.

p₂

Gender

Gender (whether a person is male or female) is also a significant category for audience segmentation as many media products are targeted at a specific gender group. This is perhaps most clearly seen within the magazine market, which has specific products targeted at men and others targeted at women. Of course, this does not mean that men do not read *OK!* magazine or that no women read *Four Four Two* football magazine – we should be careful of outdated gender stereotypes.

Culture and ethnicity

Today's media industries operate in a global marketplace. Newspapers, magazines, radio and television programmes from all over the world are readily available to people living in the UK.

Media producers will also try and sell their products to audiences all over the world. There is also a growing production base in the UK for media products that target different cultures and ethnic groups.

Theory into practice 3

Look at a range of magazines and identify some of the ways in which they try to target men and women.

Assess how successful you think they have been. **P**

▲ Figure 1.05: It is often clear from the front cover of a magazine which gender it is trying to attract.

Case study

UK Bollywood

'Bollywood' is a term used to describe the Indian film industry and is a play on the term 'Hollywood'. It is the largest and most productive film industry in the world; in 1990 it produced over 800 films. Bollywood's cinema-going audience, in India, Pakistan and elsewhere, is also one of the biggest in the world.

Just like Hollywood, Bollywood has large production studios and huge stars, capable of making expensive, commercial movies. Although the output from these studios can be very diverse, the characteristics that are commonly associated with Bollywood films include epic romances that involve mythological and theological characters, and extensive use of song and dance sequences with elaborate costumes.

The UK market for Bollywood films is expanding. The Leicester-based organisation *FilmPur* has developed into a widely recognised gateway for the industry that connects Britain and the Indian sub-continent. It provides Bollywood film producers who are looking to shoot within the UK and Europe with details and contacts for locations, crew and services, thereby serving as a 'one-stop-shop' for all production requirements. Further information can be found on their website (www.filmpur.com).

- **What are the main conventions of a Bollywood film?**
- **Why have Bollywood films become more popular in the UK in recent years?**
- **What other media products have been influenced by Bollywood?**

Income and social class

The potential audience can also be segmented according to annual salary or type of job and social class. Establishing a person's disposable income can be important, particularly for advertisers who need to target the relevant income group as precisely as possible. It is no good advertising a top-of-the-range sports car to households that have a low disposable income.

Most organisations involved with media research and production use the socio-economic groups A, B, C1, C2, D and E to identify and describe the different audience groupings according to income and social class. If you have studied the media before then you will already be familiar with these socio-economic groupings. The table below (Figure 1.06) describes what these categories stand for.

Sometimes the different categories are combined to simplify the data produced. For example, the table showing readership profiles produced by the NRS (Figure 1.01 on page 13) has segmented the readership into two distinct groups: ABC1 and C2DE.

■ Advertising

Advertising is an important source of income for many of the media products that we watch, listen to, read and interact with. You only have to look at a popular lifestyle magazine such as *Marie Claire* to see the amount of pages that are dedicated to advertising. Each of these pages is a valuable source of income for the publishers.

Turn on any commercial television station and tune into any commercial radio station and you will soon notice the amount of advertising space that is available.

Theory into practice 4

Explain why advertising has become such an important part of the media products that we consume.

Do you think advertising is more or less effective than it used to be?

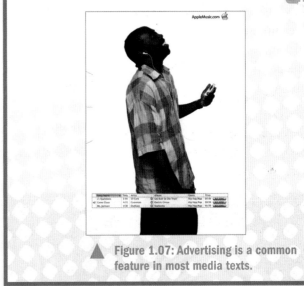

▲ Figure 1.07: Advertising is a common feature in most media texts.

Social grade	Social status	Chief income earner's occupation
A	Upper middle class	Higher managerial, administrative or professional
B	Middle class	Intermediate managerial, administrative or professional
C1	Lower middle class	Supervisory or clerical and junior managerial, administrative or professional
C2	Skilled working class	Skilled manual workers
D	Working class	Semi-skilled and unskilled manual workers
E	Those at the lowest levels of subsistence	State pensioners or widows (no other earner), casual or lowest grade workers

Figure 1.06: Commonly used categories for segmenting an audience according to social class. (Source: NRS website)

Reaching an audience

Advertisers are attracted to media products such as newspapers, magazines, broadcast programmes and websites because they deliver a ready-made audience to them. A popular programme such as *Coronation Street* is watched by around 12 million people, and this is clearly of interest to companies such as Cadbury's, which has sponsored the programme for over 10 years.

However, sponsors are also very sensitive to public opinion and will withdraw their money and support if they believe that the media product is unsuitable. One of the most infamous examples of this in recent years was in January 2007 when the company Carphone Warehouse withdrew its sponsorship of *Celebrity Big Brother* halfway through the series. This was in response to public criticism of the programme for allowing allegedly racist comments to be broadcast.

Predicting accurately how many viewers and listeners a particular programme is going to attract, and knowing how many actually did view or listen, is clearly very important information to the companies who are buying advertising space and time within the programmes and products. The same goes for magazines, newspapers, comics, websites and other commercial media products that rely on advertising revenue. Predicting and then verifying circulation, readership and rating figures is clearly a very important purpose of much media research.

▲ Figure 1.08: *Celebrity Big Brother* lost its makers a lucrative sponsorship deal in 2007 following allegations of racism.

Theory into practice 5

Find examples of different sorts of advertising within a range of media texts. Consider how effectively these advertisements get their message across to the intended audience. **p**

Finding the right audience

However, advertisers are not only interested in the size of the target audience but also, and perhaps more importantly, the demographic make-up of that audience. It is no good advertising Saga holidays for the over-50s to an audience of children and teenagers, however large that audience may be. And the advertising agency charged with promoting holidays for the 18–30 age group would probably not choose to advertise within a religious broadcast targeted at the 35s and over. Finding out detailed, demographic information about the audience is therefore an important purpose of media research.

Knowing your competitors

If a media organisation is planning the launch of a new product then they will also require information on how existing products compare with each other, how successful they are and what the target audience thinks about these products. Investigating and comparing existing media products within the competitive marketplace is another key purpose of media research.

It is not only commercial media organisations that undertake and commission media research. The BBC derives the bulk of its income from the licence fee since it does not have any advertising revenue to support its terrestrial broadcasting services. However, it is still in competition with commercial broadcasters. The BBC therefore needs research data to demonstrate its continued popularity, to show that it is providing a service to the public, and to support the political argument for its continued status as a public service broadcaster in an increasingly competitive and market-driven world.

Theory into practice 6

Research and compare the latest viewing and listening figures for a range of commercial and BBC programmes. What do the figures tell you about the different programmes?

Think it over 2

Consider the future of the BBC in an increasingly competitive marketplace.

The future of the BBC is always a hot topic of conversation and you should be able to find a range of different viewpoints in the newspapers and on the Internet.

Consider the different points of view and try to understand the various ideas and positions about what the role of the BBC is and how it should operate. For example, should the BBC be allowed to carry advertising on its terrestrial services?

▲ Figure 1.09: The BBC has a unique status in the competitive media market.

Production research

The second main type of research is that related to the production process itself.

When planning a new media product the company making the programme, film, magazine, website or game will need to undertake a great deal of product research. This is in order to:

- provide content and gather material to allow them to write and develop the new product
- research the commercial viability of actually making the product
- throughly research and plan the production and post-production stages to ensure that it all runs as smoothly as possible.

Some of this research will be generic, but much of it will depend on the type of product being planned.

For example, a journalist asked to write an article about a new piece of government legislation and its impact on people might have to do some very quick research to be able to write the copy. He or she might use secondary research to find out more specific information about the legislation and the background issues, as well as conducting some primary research in the form of interviews with politicians and sample members of the population to try to understand the potential impact. The information gained can then be used to inform the writing, with some of the quotes used in the article itself. Some form of picture research might also be undertaken to find a suitable image to accompany the article.

A documentary filmmaker will also undertake both primary and secondary research but may have a little more time to do so. As well as researching for the content of the documentary, he or she may also have to undertake research into the cost of hiring equipment and personnel to shoot the documentary as well as the post-production and distribution services required. In addition, the filmmaker will almost certainly have to undertake some location research (called a recce) to identify suitable venues for filming to take place, assist in the planning of specific shots, and assess any problems or health and safety issues that the crew might face.

The amount of information that is gathered during the process of production research can often be huge, particularly if the production is a complex one that involves many different aspects. It is therefore important that all of the information is carefully logged, organised and stored to ensure it is secure, while also allowing easy access and cross-referencing.

Theory into practice 7

Write a list of the problems a crew might face when out on location. How might a recce help to overcome some of these? **p**

Grading tips

To reach Merit level, you should explain, rather than simply describe, the problems a crew might face when out on location and how a recce would help to overcome some of these.

To reach Distinction level, fully explain the problems and the ways in which a recce can help overcome them, using clear examples to support what you are saying. Express your ideas fluently using correct subject terminology.

■ The role of a researcher

Some radio and television productions employ researchers as part of their pre-production team.

The role of a researcher on a television programme such as the talk show *Trisha* is to find out background information about the themes that are going to be covered in a particular show, and to contact and interview potential guests to find out what their stories are and whether they would be suitable for the show.

The reality programme *Big Brother* employed a team of researchers and research assistants to sift through and interview potential housemates.

Researchers are also employed on radio programmes, such as *Today* on Radio 4 and *Newsbeat* on Radio 1, to find out information about the stories of the day, make contact with potential sources of information and arrange interviews.

■ Viability

Another important purpose of production research is to demonstrate that your planned product is viable (workable).

You need to test the viability of your product at a number of different levels:

- Is the product financially viable?
- Do you have the necessary skills to undertake the production process?
- Do you have the right equipment and technology available to you?
- What help and support will you require?
- Have you got enough time to produce the product?

Income

In terms of financial viability, you will need to explore the different ways in which you can fund or generate income from your product and then balance the amount of income that it is likely to generate against the costs of production and distribution. This will show to what extent your proposed product would be viable were it to be launched into the competitive media market.

As we noted earlier, advertising is a crucial source of income for many of the media products that we watch, listen to, read and interact with. Turn on any commercial radio or television station and open any magazine or newspaper and you will soon notice the amount of advertising space that is available. Many websites also have advertising within them – perhaps you are familiar with the plague of 'pop-ups' that seems to be growing in number.

Theory into practice 8

Write a list of the potential sources of income that are available to your type of media product.

How much income do you think you could generate from these sources?

What would you need to do to try to get this income? **p**

Sponsorship of individual products by commercial companies is becoming increasingly popular and should be seen as a potential income source.

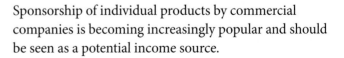

Case study

Careers in research

There are hundreds of market research agencies in the UK, from large international companies to smaller consultancies. The largest market research agencies now commonly take on graduates every year; some have year-round recruitment procedures but places are much sought-after so you have to make sure you are right for the job. Get some work experience in a firm before you apply – it will give the impression that you are really keen!

As a researcher in an agency you will oversee a number of client accounts, working on a variety of projects in, quite possibly, a range of different industries. Most people in the agency will be pursuing the same career path as you and you may have the opportunity to move between different research sectors, giving you a broad experience of research techniques.

Virtually every company in the UK uses market research. As a result, many of these companies, particularly the larger ones, will employ their own researchers, usually one or two.

In this role, you will be expected to keep the company in touch with its customers and informed of its investment and marketing decisions. You will commission researchers in external agencies to work on behalf of your company, as well as organising internal research among staff and customers. You will gain a close knowledge of your company's overall way of working and play a key role in shaping its future development.

Day-to-day role
You'll start off as a Research Executive, overseeing the day-to-day smooth running of specific projects, from the commissioning stages right through to the final presentation to the client.

Your role is likely to include: designing the best way to fulfil a client's need; managing the budget; advising on questionnaire design; briefing interviewers (the people who hold the clipboards); monitoring the conduct of the research process; checking and analysing data; and writing a results and recommendations paper for your client, which you may also have to present to them.

The type of research you are involved in will determine the specific tasks you undertake, but your days will definitely be full and varied.

Career path
Market research is far from a desk-bound career. As you progress you'll be expected to have increasing levels of client contact. Depending on your clients, this could involve a fair amount of national and international travel. You'll also have to make presentations to clients, meet interviewers and respondents, and visit appropriate research venues.

Career progression in market research can be very rapid! As a general rule, you can expect to be a Research Executive for 18 months, after which time you will become a Senior Research Executive. From then on, most companies base promotion on merit, so you can progress as quickly as the quality of your work and opportunities permit. It wouldn't be unusual for you to be holding responsibility for accounts and managing a team by the time you are 30 years old.

Once you've gained a range of experience, you could find yourself making the brave move of going it alone and setting up your own agency. This is a popular route and will allow you to pick and choose the projects you work on and the hours you put in – something to bear in mind during the long months of summer.

- **What skills do you need to be a successful researcher?**
- **What tasks does a researcher undertake?**
- **Why is the role of researcher such a good introduction to working in the media?**

Think it over 3

The Guardian newspaper has a dedicated sponsorship team who offer a range of sponsorship solutions within its newspapers and websites. These include the sponsorship of supplements, advertisement promotions and microsites.

Money from the direct sale of the product to the consumer is also an important source of income that you need to explore. Most newspapers and magazines have a cover price, and some television programmes and websites have a subscription fee or are operated on a pay-per-view basis. Films, television programmes and radio shows can also earn income from the sale and rental of video, DVD and CD copies.

Think it over 4

Pixar, the company that made the animated film *The Incredibles*, reported that it had sold almost 18 million copies on DVD by the end of 2005. Sales of the DVD helped the company to triple its annual profits.

Other potential sources of income for a media product include merchandising, running competitions, and the income generated through premium phone lines.

You should also research the availability of grants, loans and commissions that might be available to help support the costs of media production. There are a number of public and private schemes that are designed to support creative production, including those run by the Arts Council, the British Film Institute and the National Lottery.

Theory into practice 9

Carry out some research to find current information about potential sources of production funding. **p**

Costs

The costs of producing your product also need careful researching.

Some of the different sources of expenditure will depend on the product you are making, but many are common to all forms of media production. For example, if you were going to launch a new media product onto the market, whether a newspaper, magazine, television programme, audio product, game or website, you would need to employ people to get your product off the ground and up and running.

- **Staffing**

You would need creative people to help research and develop your ideas, technical expertise to assist in the production stages, and then marketing people to help sell your product and generate income from advertising, sales and merchandising.

Theory into practice 10

Write down the different roles that you would need people to undertake if you were to launch your proposed product onto the market. **p**

- **Production equipment**

Staffing is only one of the costs of course, and any media product will require the use of some form of production equipment.

Audio and moving image products will require the use of various types of recording and editing equipment. A range of hardware and software options are available for print and multimedia production.

For the production work that you complete as a student for this qualification you will probably be able to borrow the necessary equipment from your school or college. However, if you were working as an independent producer then your equipment would have to be purchased or hired for the duration of the production process. You would therefore have to research the costs in advance so that you could budget for them.

Think it over 5

If you were producing a print-based product such as a newspaper or magazine, then you would need to employ a team of journalists to produce the copy and perhaps a photographer to provide the pictures. You would also need some editing and sub-editing staff, and a designer or two to make sure it looked good and attracted the right audience.

For moving image products, the size of your crew would depend on the size and scale of the production itself and the funds that you have available.

Many small independent production houses will employ only a handful of people who are multi-skilled and able to undertake a number of different roles. Most of these will be employed on a freelance basis and hired only to do a specific role on a specific project.

Broadcast television programmes are likely to have larger crews, and as a result higher production costs and the need to secure a higher budget.

▲ Figure 1.10: A production team needs to work together, with each individual knowing his or her own role inside out.

- **Skills audit**

Having access to the right equipment is essential, but you also need to have the necessary skills to be able to use it effectively.

An important first step is to assess your initial skill level. You will then be able to plan what skills you need to develop further and how you will be able to do this. This process can also help identify any skills gaps you have and those areas in which you might require extra help and support from other people.

Theory into practice 11

Carry out an initial skills audit.

To do this you will need to do the following:

1. List all the equipment you already have experience of using.
2. Describe the level of media production skills and techniques you already have for each item of equipment.
3. Identify any gaps and any areas that you need to develop further.
4. Draw up an action plan to further develop your existing skills and to fill any gaps that you have identified.

Try to use **SMART** targets in your action plan. This means they need to be **S**pecific, **M**easurable, **A**chievable and **R**ealistic, and carried out within an appropriate **T**imescale.

You might wish to use a **SWOT** analysis when doing your initial skills audit. Here you identify the *strengths* that you already have and the *weaknesses* that you will need to improve. You can then identify the *opportunities* that are available to you (resources, workshops, support) and any *threats* (barriers) that might get in the way. **p**

- **Copyright**

When planning your product and drawing up the budget, you also need to take account of the potential costs of using **copyright** material.

Key Terms

Copyright is a type of intellectual property that cannot normally be used without the permission of the owner.

Like other forms of intellectual property, copyright can be bought and sold. Copyright owners can choose to licence others to use their work while retaining copyright ownership over the rights themselves.

Much of your material will probably be original material that you and your team produce yourself. However, you may also want to use some copyright material, such as a still from a feature film or a clip from a song.

One of the ways of using material that is under copyright is to write to the copyright holder and ask permission to use the material. You will often have to make a payment for the right to use the material.

You can find more information on copyright and other forms of intellectual property, such as logos and trademarks, on the UK Patent Office website (www.patent.gov.uk).

• Distribution costs

Having budgeted for the production costs associated with your product, you will also need to research the costs of distribution or placing your product within the market.

It is one thing paying for the production of a radio, television or print-based advert, but you also have to research the costs of buying space and air-time within a specific media form.

Again, the budget you have available to you will dictate what you can and cannot do. For example, to buy a 30-second slot within a drive-time local commercial radio show would cost around £20, so you could get a solid campaign for a few hundred pounds a week. Larger regional and national stations are more expensive and a similar campaign could cost between £1500 and £2000 a week. Similarly, a full-page monotone advert in a local newspaper such as the *Nottingham Evening Post* would cost around £5000, compared to over £20,000 for a full-colour advert in a national magazine such as *Cosmopolitan*.

Case study

Budgeting for copyright

John, a student on a BTEC Media Production course similar to your own, needed to research the viability of an audio product for Unit 44.

He researched the cost of purchasing the right to use a range of different songs in the product. He found that using a current top-10 track would cost several thousand pounds and was therefore way outside his budget.

John then found some cheaper music that was produced by a relatively unknown artist and which would cost a much more realistic £100 for permission to use in the product.

However, John also found some copyright-free music on a CD that came with a music technology magazine. He decided to go with this option instead since it meant that he then had more money to spend on the production.

- **What else is covered by copyright?**
- **What do you need to do if you want to use copyright material?**
- **What does the copyright symbol look like?**

Theory into practice 12

Do some research of your own to find out the different costs of buying advertising time/space in a range of different media products.

To what extent do you think they provide good value for money?

p

- **Marketing and promotion**

Your budget also needs to include the money you will need for marketing and promoting your product. This is often over looked by students who are costing a production, but it is no use having a really good product if you then have no money to promote and market it.

Depending on who you are producing the product for, the marketing and promotion may not be your responsibility. However, you should demonstrate that you have some understanding of the need for effective marketing and promotion, and that you have also undertaken some research into the relative cost of different options.

Advertising is only one aspect of what is called the 'marketing mix' – you might also want to consider such things as:

- sponsorship of an event at which your target audience will be present
- organising a publicity stunt to get your product in the news
- using a celebrity to endorse and promote your product
- producing merchandising items such as badges, T-shirts, pens and hats.

- **Timescale**

As with all aspects of the media industry, you will have a specified timescale to work to and a deadline by which your work must be completed.

Your deadlines are likely to be considerably longer than those you will be faced with if you gain employment within the media industry. For example, the team who put together the *BBC Six O'Clock News* must have all news items ready by the specified time every single day.

Figure 1.11: Bobby Charlton and Alex Ferguson attend a book launch for *The Manchester United Opus*.

Think it over 6

The weekly television series *Lost* had around 250 people working on it and each episode had a three-week production schedule. This comprised:

- five days of planning and preparatory work by the director and his team

- a further three days for getting all of the technical aspects in place

- nine full days for shooting, with most of this taking place on location in Oahu, Hawaii

- four days for post-production work in Burbank, Los Angeles, which included editing, scoring the music and adding visual effects.

Figure 1.12: The producers of *Lost* had to work to a tight schedule.

1. Describe the two main forms of research undertaken by the media industries. **p₁**

2. a) State the full name of the following research organisations: NRS, ABC, BARB, RAJAR. **p₁**

   b) Explain what each organisation does and include an example of the research data produced. **m₁ d₁**

3. Describe the different ways in which a media audience can be segmented. **p₁**

4. Explain the importance of advertising to media production. **m₁ d₁**

5. Summarise the role of a researcher. **p₁**

6. Explain, using clear examples, how the viability of a media product can be assessed. **m₁ d₁**

7. What is a SWOT analysis? **p₁**

8. Explain what the term copyright means and why it is an important factor in media production. **m₁ d₁**

1.2 Be able to apply a range of research methods and techniques

In the previous section we looked at the different purposes of research in the media industries. For whatever purpose research is undertaken, it is likely that many of the methods and techniques used will be the same. In this section you will be able to apply your knowledge and skills to a range of different situations.

The four main methods of research that you need to understand are:

- primary
- secondary
- quantitative
- qualitative.

Primary and secondary research

One of the basic distinctions to be made is between **primary** and **secondary** research.

Primary research is original research that is carried out for a specific purpose. It involves the use of a range of different techniques to obtain new data.

Key Terms

Primary research – Research to obtain original data using such methods as interviews, questionnaires, focus groups and observation.

Secondary research – Research based on the use of pre-existing data and information that has already been gathered by other people or organisations. It is often available in books, journals or via the Internet.

Quantitative research – Type of research that is based on measurable and quantifiable facts and information, producing numerical and statistical data.

Qualitative research – Type of research that is based on opinions, attitudes and preferences rather than hard facts.

▲ Figure 1.13: Conducting a survey in the street can be an effective method of undertaking primary research.

Conducting a survey in the street, interviewing people over the phone and running a focus group are all examples of techniques used to undertake primary research.

Secondary research involves the use of data and information that has already been published or is already available within an organisation. Looking in books, journals and on the Internet for information that already exists are all examples of secondary research.

Many media organisations will also use data and information that has already been gathered and analysed by another company to add to and support, or sometimes even to replace, their own primary research.

▼ Figure 1.14: A media researcher at work using a range of secondary sources.

Quantitative and qualitative research

Another important distinction is between research that produces **quantitative** and **qualitative** types of information and data.

Quantitative research produces data and information that is measurable and quantifiable. The data can usually be represented numerically and is often presented in the form of tables, charts and diagrams.

Both primary and secondary research techniques can produce quantitative data. This includes such things as ratings, circulation figures and market analysis, as well as the counting and measuring of items or space in a content analysis of a media product.

Qualitative research produces information on people's opinions, views and preferences about something. Again, both primary and secondary research techniques can produce qualitative data, and it is often very important within the media industry as it is used to find out what individuals and groups think and feel about a particular advertisement, film or television programme, for example.

Depending on the nature of the research and the types of questions asked, it is not always possible to analyse the resulting information statistically, particularly if the responses are personal and subjective.

Undertaking your own research

You will gain a greater understanding of the different research methods and techniques by applying them to your own research projects. As part of your course you will be working on a number of different practical productions and this is a good opportunity to undertake both market research and production research that is linked to them.

■ Undertaking primary research

Planning your research well in advance is an important factor, particularly when undertaking primary research.

When planning primary research it is important to:

- think carefully about what you are trying to find out
- choose an appropriate sample

- decide upon an appropriate research technique
- be aware of the size, scope and timescale of the task.

Interviews and questionnaires

One of the main methods used in primary research is asking people questions, and it is likely that you will use some form of questioning technique for the research tasks that you undertake.

In undertaking this form of primary research you may decide to:

- conduct one-to-one interviews with a selected number of people
- produce a questionnaire to survey a larger group
- organise a focus group.

Undertaking a series of one-to-one interviews can be a very effective method for getting reliable, qualitative data from selected individuals, but it can also be very time consuming. Also, if you are asking very personal or sensitive questions then the respondent may not feel happy to disclose such information in a face-to-face situation.

The use of a questionnaire is perhaps the most popular form of primary research, but its presentation, and the form and structure of the questions, need careful consideration if the results that you obtain are going to be both reliable and valid.

Questionnaire design

If you are going to send your questionnaire to the respondents for them to fill in, it is important that the questionnaire itself looks attractive and professional and does not put people off.

An appropriate title or theme for the study should be at the top of the page and you should include a brief introduction so that people are clear about who you are, what the purpose of the survey is and what the results will be used for.

You should also include clear instructions for how the survey should be completed. This is particularly important if respondents are to complete the questionnaire by themselves, as you will not be there to explain anything that they do not understand.

You also need to tell them where to return the completed questionnaire to. See figure 1.15.

Key Terms

Open questions allow the person answering to give his or her own views and opinions on a particular subject. They often start with the following words:
- what
- why
- when
- how
- who.

Closed questions are more limited in terms of the potential answers that can be given. They are often answered with *Yes*, *No* or *Don't know*, or an answer picked from a range of given options.

The questions

As a general rule you should start your questionnaire with some straightforward **closed questions** that are easy to answer.

Asking people their age, sex, occupation and marital status, for example, should get them into the process of completing the questionnaire, and will also provide you with some basic demographic information when analysing your results. This will also allow you to check that you have covered a representational sample of people, and to include some more respondents in the survey if you need to.

When using closed questions it is often easier to include the potential answers on the questionnaire itself, with a tick-box for people to select the answer. If you use this method it is important that you include all of the potential answers. You will also need to decide whether to include an 'Other' or 'Don't know' option.

Closed questions, and other types of questions where the potential number of responses is limited and specified in the questionnaire, are good in this form of survey as they are relatively easy for the respondents to complete. They will provide you with quantifiable data which you can represent in the form of graphs, charts and diagrams.

However, more **open questions,** where you might be asking people to write down a personal response to something, often provide you with more qualitative information that can give a more meaningful insight.

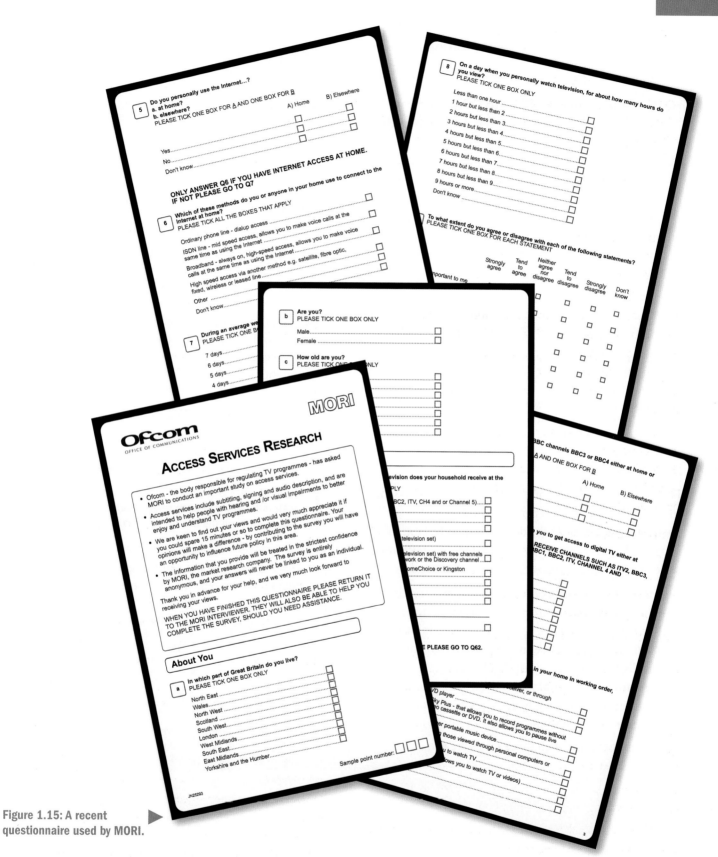

Figure 1.15: A recent questionnaire used by MORI.

Q7a: Do you use the website *Youtube*?

Yes ☐   No ☐

Q7b: If you answered Yes to Q7a, describe your experience of using *Youtube* in the space below.

[ ]

Figure 1.16: A paired question containing both open and closed elements.

Both open and closed questions are sometimes used together in a paired question – see Figure 1.16.

■ Using a scale

For some questions you might want to gauge the extent to which the respondents agree or disagree with a particular statement, or the degree of their feelings on a subject. Here you can use a rating system or a response scale of some kind. Types of scale include the following:

- A **Likert scale** asks the respondent how strongly he or she agrees or disagrees with a series of statements.
- **Rank order scales** ask the respondent to indicate the order of preference from a list of given answers, usually through the use of numbers.
- **Semantic differential scales** use a sliding scale between two opposing words and ask respondents to indicate where on the scale their opinions lies.

Examples of the use of all three scales are shown in Figures 1.17–1.19.

	Strongly agree	Agree	Neither agree nor disagree	Disagree	Strongly disagree
The magazine is informative.		✓			
The magazine is good value for money.				✓	
The front cover is attractive.	✓				

Figure 1.17: A Likert scale asks respondents how strongly they agree or disagree with a series of statements.

Where do you get your news from? Rank the following sources of news in their order of importance to you, with 1 being the most important and 5 being the least important.

Television [1] Internet [3]

Radio [4] Local newspaper [5]

National newspaper [2]

Figure 1.18: Rank order scales ask respondents to indicate their order of preference from a list of given answers, usually through the use of numbers.

Place a cross on the scale below to show what you feel about the product in the advert.

Looks attractive ....X.............. Looks unattractive

Healthy ....X........ Unhealthy

Good value ......X............ Poor value

Tasty ..X................ Tasteless

Figure 1.19: Semantic differential scales use a sliding scale between two opposing words. Respondents indicate where on the scale their opinions lie by marking with a cross.

You might also want to group specific questions together into different sections, perhaps with a separate heading. This can make the questionnaire look more attractive and appealing. It may also give people a sense of achievement when they have completed a section, so the questionnaire does not seem so long.

Theory into practice 13

If you were completing a questionnaire for somebody else, which features would encourage you to answer truthfully and which would put you off?

In formulating the questions themselves, you should avoid ambiguity and keep the language as simple as possible. You should also try to avoid asking leading questions that suggest a particular answer to the respondent, and the use of emotive language (which can cause strong feelings) that again might prejudice the response.

Questions that are too vague or too complex are unlikely to be answered with any validity, if they are answered at all.

Figure 1.20: A badly designed questionnaire is unlikely to be completed by many people.

What is perhaps most important, though, is that you think very carefully about the form and structure of the questions that you are asking. You need to make sure that people will be able to understand and respond to the questions you are asking, and that their responses will provide you with the information you require.

Figure 1.21: A simple tally chart for closed questions may be more efficient than a questionnaire for each respondent.

■ Presenting your questionnaire

There are four main ways in which you can present your questionnaire to your sample audience. You can:

- stop and ask people the questions face-to-face
- telephone them
- post or email the questionnaire to them
- include the questionnaire in a magazine or newsletter and ask respondents to post it back or hand it in.

Theory into practice 14

What do you think the advantages and disadvantages are of the different ways of presenting your questionnaire?

The first three ways will enable you to identify and select specific respondents, so you can target your questionnaire at a selected audience. You can therefore be sure that you are covering a representative range of people according to age, gender, culture and other demographics.

Asking people face-to face or via the telephone can be very time consuming, particularly if you are covering a large sample of people. However, it does allow you to explain any questions that respondents might not fully understand. If you use either of these methods you will also need to think carefully about how you are going to record people's responses.

Using a tally chart (see Figure 1.21) or data recorder might be more efficient than simply filling out an individual questionnaire sheet for each respondent.

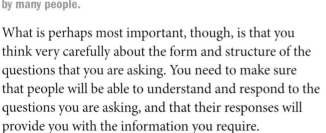

Q	Answers	Responses	Total
Q1	15 years or younger	III	3
	16–18 years	TTTT III	8
	19–21 years	TTTT I	6
	22 years+	III	3
Q2	Male	TTTT IIII	9
	Female	TTTT TTTT I	11

If you post or email the questionnaire, or include it within a publication of some sort, then people can answer the questions in their own time and in their own environment. This means that some people may be more inclined to give you confidential information, though of course you have little control on how many people will actually complete the questionnaire or return it to you.

Pre-testing

Pre-testing your questionnaire on a small sample of your audience before you conduct your full survey is a very good idea. It will allow you to identify any potential problems with specific questions, or the design and layout of the questionnaire itself, in good time for you to make any changes. You may also be able to identify some responses under the 'Other' option that may be better to include as one of the specified options.

Theory into practice 15

1. Design a simple questionnaire that uses a mixture of both open and closed questions as well as at least one of the scales you have learned about in this section. **P₂**

2. Use the questionnaire to survey a chosen group of people. **P₂**

3. Analyse the results and write up the findings in a short report. **P₃**

Grading tips

To achieve Merit level for question 2, you should undertake the survey competently and with only occasional assistance.

To reach Distinction level for question 2, you should undertake the survey to near-professional standards and work independently.

■ Focus groups

Focus groups are pre-selected panels of people who are seen to represent the target audience. They tend to be used by marketing and advertising agencies to test the likely response of the target audience towards the product that is being advertised, as well as to the advert itself.

Film studios also use focus groups in preview screenings of major films prior to release. This is to ensure that the audience reaction is the desired one. There are many examples of studio executives changing the ending of a film, often against the wishes of the director, because the audience in the preview screening didn't like it.

If you are going to use a focus group as part of your research you will need to think carefully about who you invite to be in the group, where you will hold it, how you are going to manage the discussion and what you will use to record what is said.

▲ Figure 1.22: Focus groups are often used in market research.

■ Undertaking secondary research

There is a wealth of information and research data already available in books, journals and on the Internet, and you will probably undertake some form of secondary research to supplement and perhaps support your own primary research.

It is worth noting that simply collecting pages of information from the Internet does not in itself constitute secondary research. Any information that you print off from the Internet, or photocopy from books and journals, needs to be read and understood, perhaps annotated, and then used to inform or supplement your own primary research.

When undertaking secondary research it is important that you clearly understand what the original purpose of the research was, who commissioned it and when it was conducted. Not every piece of research that you come across will necessarily be reliable or valid.

For example, if you were researching the effects of advertising on young people you might discover a piece of research that concludes that there is no evidence to show that cigarette advertising encourages young people to smoke.

What you would need to know before using this secondary information is that the research is very dated (from the 1960s), was conducted in the USA and not the UK, and was sponsored by a leading cigarette manufacturer of the time!

Remember!

It is important that you clearly reference any work that you use and take account of any copyright issues that may apply.

Interpreting results

Once you have collected all of your primary and secondary research data, you need to sort through and collate it then evaluate and summarise the findings.

Sorting and collating

The amount of information that is gathered when undertaking a research study can often be extensive, particularly if it is linked to a complex production that involves various different aspects.

An important step at this stage is to sort through the information you have gathered and select and use the material that is of value to your needs. Teachers and

moderators report that far too many students simply put all of the primary and secondary research they have produced and found into a folder and expect to receive a good mark for it. You need to think carefully how to collate your research material into relevant and logical categories that will be useful and will allow you and others to access it again at a later date.

Remember!

It is not the size or amount of the research that you have undertaken that is important but the methods and techniques you have employed and the way in which you have analysed and used the results.

Storing information

Once you have sorted out the information that you require, and discarded the information that you do not, you need to ensure that all of the relevant information is carefully logged, organised and stored to guarantee it is secure, while also allowing you easy access to it.

It is best if you create a research folder at this stage if you do not already have one, in which you can store all of your relevant research material. This research folder needs to have a clear index system so that you can easily find a relevant piece of information. Any secondary material that is stored should also be highlighted and annotated in some way so it is clear what you have selected from it and what it has been used for.

It is also best to include some form of written commentary in your file that explains to the tutor and moderator what is in there, how it was obtained, why it has been included, and how it has or is going to be used.

You may of course also store some or all of your information electronically. Copies of your questionnaire and any questions that you used in an interview or for your focus group are best stored on a computer and backed up on an appropriate disc or storage device. You may find it worthwhile to store your hard data on a spreadsheet or database as well as the paper versions that you may have produced while carrying out the research.

Case study

Applying research methods and techniques

Let's take a look at how a group of BTEC National Diploma Media Production students applied some of the research methods and techniques they learned about in this unit to their practical production work.

John's research
Remember John? He was producing a series of radio adverts aimed at 14–18-year-olds for Unit 44 and needed some information about his target audience.

John decided to produce a questionnaire that asked people in the 14–18 years age group about their hobbies and interests. It included a mixture of open and closed questions. These aimed to get both quantitative and qualitative information that would help John to produce more effective adverts that appealed to the target audience.

John decided to ask students in his own school to complete the questionnaire, but also asked some young people in the street and in a local college, so that he didn't just get responses from his friends at school.

Alice's research
Alice was working with a group of students on a video project. Like John, Alice and her team produced a questionnaire for a representative sample of their target audience as part of their research. They also decided to organise a focus group so that they could ask some more in-depth questions and find out what people really thought about their proposed product.

Alice's group also looked at a range of different programmes and videos that were aimed at their target audience. They hoped this would give them a better understanding of the sorts of codes and conventions and production techniques that would appeal to this age group.

Shilpa's research
Shilpa and her team decided to develop their design and journalistic skills by producing a promotional magazine. As part of their research they examined a range of printed products aimed at their target audience as well as different forms of printed promotional material, to get additional design ideas.

To extend their vocational knowledge they also decided to visit a local newspaper office to find out more about the actual process of putting together and printing a print product.

Bilal's research
Bilal sees interactive media as the future and decided to design and produce a website as his main production project. He conducted a great deal of secondary research on the Internet, looking at what did and did not work in website design, and then used this information to produce a series of sample pages which he tested on his audience via email.

Bilal used the results of this research to help him fine-tune his ideas for his website.

- **Which research methods and techniques are you going to use in your research?**

- **What skills will you need to develop to make sure your research is a success?**

- **Do you have a clear idea of what the timescale is for your research project?**

Knowledge check

1. Explain the four main methods of research. **p₂**

2. Explain, using specific examples from your own work, what factors need to be considered when planning, designing and carrying out a survey using a questionnaire. **m₂ d₂**

3. Explain what a focus group is. **p₂**

4. Explain clearly what issues you would need to consider when undertaking your own secondary research. **m₂ d₂**

After you have completed a substantial research project, or a number of smaller linked research tasks, you will need to present the results of this research.

In fact, the name of this final section is a little misleading as you need to do more than simply present the results that you obtained from your research. The content of your presentation should include the following key elements:

- an introduction to your research in which you outline its purpose and aims
- an explanation of the methods and techniques that you have used
- the research data itself, presented in a suitable form (such as tables, charts, graphs or diagrams)
- a summary of your main findings (the results)
- the conclusions that you can make from these findings
- any proposals that you are making based on these conclusions.

This information can be presented in the form of a written report, as an oral presentation or as a combination of the two, with a presentation to the class backed up by a written report and accompanying notes, logs and data.

If you choose to present your findings in the form of an oral presentation then you must make sure that this is recorded so that your mark can be checked by the moderator towards the end of the course.

However you decide to present your findings, you will need to think carefully about the structure and content of what you produce as well as the language that you use.

For your work in this unit you may have been working with a real client, and in this case it would be better if this client was in the audience for your presentation. If not, then it is more likely that your audience will be comprised of your tutor and fellow members of your class.

Planning your presentation in advance is crucial to its success. You will also need to practise it and do some run-throughs so that it goes as smoothly as possible on the day.

Think it over 7

Oral presentations are often used in the media industry to pitch new ideas to a potential client or backer, and these pitches will often include details of research that has been carried out to support the proposals being made.

The sorts of people who would be in the audience for such a presentation would be those who would have the final say as to whether your idea would go into production or not. These people could include a commissioning editor, producer, exhibitor, broadcaster, publisher or potential purchaser of the final product.

■ Presentation skills

Conducting an effective presentation is not an easy task. You will need to identify which presentation and communication skills you already have, and which ones you need to develop further.

Theory into practice 16

Think about your own communication skills. Are you confident when speaking to other people? What can you do to improve the way in which you get your ideas across? **p3**

Key Terms

Intrapersonal communication refers to communication within you, and includes all of the thoughts, fears and anxieties that you may have about your presentation. Control these and your presentation is more likely to go well.

Interpersonal communication is face-to-face communication between two or more people, and includes aspects of spoken and non-verbal communication.

Key Terms

Non-verbal communication (NVC) – This term refers to all of the features of body language that occur during interpersonal communication. It includes such features as the clothes that you wear, your posture, facial expression and hand and arm movements.

Paralanguage – This is not what you say but the way that you say it. It includes features such as pitch, tone, pace and volume, as well as the fillers and hesitations that are used in everyday language, for example 'ummm' and 'y'know'.

Visual aids – The props, objects and examples that you include in your presentation. Also includes slides, images and posters that can help to structure what you say.

Non-verbal communication

It is said that first impressions count. Certainly, the way in which you present yourself to your audience, how you dress, your posture, orientation, hand and arm movements and facial expressions are all important aspects to consider.

Paying careful attention to these aspects of your non-verbal communication can make your presentation look more professional and be more effective. It can also make you feel more confident.

▲ Figure 1.23: Body language is an important form of communication.

Think it over 8

It is thought that up to 70 per cent of interpersonal communication occurs through body language.

Dress and appearance

When presenting your ideas you need to dress to impress. What you say and do will look and sound more authoritative if you present yourself in a professional manner.

When deciding what to wear and how to present yourself, you need to think carefully about who will be in your audience and their likely expectations, as well as the context and location of the presentation. Jeans and a T-shirt topped off with a highly gelled hairstyle may look fashionable, but the people who you are hoping will invest money in your project might expect a more formal and business-like approach.

▲ Figure 1.24: The way you dress can have an impact on how you communicate.

It is also important that you feel comfortable in what you are wearing and practise in your presentation clothes beforehand.

Posture and orientation

The way in which you hold and position your body can also communicate a lot of information to your audience.

Case study

Creating the right impression

When planning her presentation, Shilpa was very aware of the need to create a good first impression. She thought carefully about her clothes and overall appearance.

▲ Figure 1.25: Shilpa makes a good impression.

She decided that she would try to communicate professionalism and organisation to her audience by treating it like an interview and dressing in a smart and business-like manner.

The audience was made up of her friends and class mates, and Shilpa felt more comfortable presenting a very different image to them on the day rather than the more casual image of baggy jeans and T-shirts that they were familiar with.

This strategy worked, and the feedback she received on the day was very positive.

- **How do you think you should dress to impress?**

You need to demonstrate that you are a confident, professional person who is in control and that you know what you are doing.

Your audience will not appreciate looking at the back of your head while you talk to the screen behind you. Neither will they think positively about you if you are slumped in a chair or have your arms folded across your body in a defensive manner.

Hand and arm movements

You will probably be nervous when you are presenting to your audience and tell-tale signs of these nerves can 'leak out' and distract from what you are trying to communicate. An audience can end up focusing on the presenter who paces up and down and waves his or her hands and arms around too much, rather than listening and trying to understand what he or she is proposing.

Theory into practice 17

Look carefully at the way in which skilled politicians present themselves to an audience and to the camera. Consider the hand and arm movements they use. How do these make them look decisive and in control of the situation? **p**₃

How does this allow them to communicate clearly? **m**₃

How does this help make their meaning clear? How does it help them to maintain the attention of the audience? **m**₃

▲ Figure 1.26: Politicians are trained to use body language to communicate power and authority.

Facial expressions and eye contact

Facial expressions are often the hardest part of non-verbal communication to control, so can be another area where your nervousness can leak out. Smiling is good. It makes you feel better and puts your audience at ease.

Eye contact is also very important. It can be used to engage your audience and direct questions to individuals.

Think it over 9

The face is the most communicative area of your body. It contains over 44 muscles that can contort and twist into almost 5000 different expressions, which communicate hundreds of different messages.

It also uses more of these muscles to frown than it does to smile!

▲ Figure 1.27: A smiling face will convey a positive message to your audience.

Think it over 10

How would you feel if you were part of a small audience and the presenter never looked at you once? How would you feel if the presenter looked at you, and *just* you, all of the time?

As a general rule you should try to engage each member of your audience in eye contact if possible. This will make them feel at ease and communicate honesty and trustworthiness.

However, if you hold this eye contact for too long and end up staring at people this will have the opposite effect and make them feel uncomfortable. Two or three seconds should be long enough before you move on to another person.

Think carefully about all of these aspects of non-verbal communication and try to control and use them to your advantage. Get it right and you will communicate integrity and professionalism. But do not worry too much if you get it wrong at this stage – it is all part of the learning process and you will gain more confidence and skill with every presentation that you give.

Think it over 11

In the 1960s' US Presidential debate between the two main contenders, Richard Nixon was judged by most radio listeners to have been a clear winner over John F. Kennedy.

However, many of the 70 million who watched the debate on television were not impressed by Nixon's unshaven appearance and the image of him sweating under the television studio lights.

This became an enduring image of the campaign and is thought by many to have cost him the presidency.

Spoken communication

Although non-verbal communication is very important, you will also need to say something in your presentation! Speaking in front of a group can be a daunting task – even the most confident of people can become extremely nervous before making a speech.

Paralanguage

Paralanguage refers to the way in which you speak rather than the content of what you say. It is another aspect of your presentation that you will need to try to control and manipulate to your advantage.

People often have a tendency to speak too quickly when nervous, as if they were trying to get to the end as quickly as possible. You will need to slow down and set the pitch (not too high and shrill or too low and bassy), the tone (not too serious and not to jokey) and pace (not too slow and hesitant or too fast and manic) of your spoken language so that you are communicating effectively to your audience.

When people are nervous or are trying to think of what

to say next, they will often include fillers such as 'erm', 'y'know' and 'like', and will hesitate between words. You will sound more confident and come across in a more professional way if you are able to control and limit the use of such fillers and hesitations.

Theory into practice 18

Practise different ways of delivering your spoken language. It is a good idea to record the results and then listen back to hear what you sound like.

Be warned – your recorded voice will sound very different to the one that you are used to hearing!

p₃

Grading tips

To reach Merit level, make sure you communicate with clarity.

To reach Distinction level, make sure that your meaning is always clear and that the audience's attention is maintained throughout your presentation.

Register

Register refers to the choice of words that you use. You will have to select a register that takes account of the audience you are presenting to, the context and the level of formality.

You might feel a little embarrassed addressing your school or college friends in the audience with 'Good morning ladies and gentleman and welcome to this presentation', but the context of the pitch might demand such an introduction.

Figure 1.28: Using too many specialist terms ▶ may confuse your audience.

You should also be wary of using technical terms, jargon or abbreviations that some members of your audience might not understand.

Visual aids

When planning your presentation you also need to think carefully about the use of any visual aids you want to include.

Think it over 12

The effective use of OHT and PowerPoint slides is a skill that will need to be practised.

The slides should provide a concise summary of what you are saying rather than a running commentary. A common mistake that people make is to cram too much information on to each slide.

Postal questionnaires

- Pros: cost effective, can gather relatively detailed information and statistics from a large sample
- Cons: low response rates, less suitable for small sample, slow
- Approximate timings: (approx 8–10 weeks total)
  - write, design, print and mail = 4 weeks
  - allow time for responses = 2 weeks
  - data input and analysis = 2–3 weeks

▲ **Figure 1.29: Brief bullet points on a PowerPoint slide will get your message across more clearly than reams of text.**

You might want to use over-head transparency (OHT) slides or PowerPoint slides to help structure your talk and provide an alternative visual reference point to yourself.

If you are using PowerPoint in your presentation then you also need to be wary of having too many sound effects and transitions, as an audience can easily tire of such gimmicks. It can also make your presentation look rather superficial and can get in the way of the overall message that you are trying to communicate.

As an alternative to OHT and PowerPoint slides, you might want to consider using posters and flip charts to summarise your main points, or making handouts for your audience to read either in the meeting itself or after it has finished.

It is also a good idea to include an activity that involves your audience members. This is particularly important if the same people are listening to a whole series of presentations in a single day. You need to make your presentation stand out, so including some sort of interactive element, for example, that involves your audience looking at a sample or mock-up of your work then giving some feedback, can help you achieve this.

Theory into practice 19

To prepare effectively for your final presentation you will need to undertake a mock presentation on a topic of your choice.

1. Plan and deliver a short presentation on a topic of your choice.

2. Following feedback, assess how your presentation went.

3. Identify the skills that you need to develop to improve your presentation skills. Draw up a skill development action plan. **p**₃

Case study

Use of visual aids

Shilpa's presentation
When Shilpa was planning her presentation she decided to structure it with PowerPoint slides and include a sample recording of her work within the presentation. She used only brief bullet points in the slides, with each bullet point having a maximum of six words.

As part of her research and preparation for the presentation, Shilpa had experimented with different effects for the words appearing and special transitions between slides. However, after getting feedback from a sample of the target audience she decided that these effects and transitions were too obtrusive. She therefore chose instead to adopt a more conventional approach of simply cutting between slides and having each line appear at the click of the mouse.

John's presentation
John and his team also used PowerPoint slides, but they hadn't done as much research or planning as Shilpa had.

As a result, their slides were over ambitious in terms of the amount of information they had put on to each slide and the number of special visual and sound effects that accompanied the text. The audience were overwhelmed with information and found it difficult to focus on the actual product that was being proposed.

However, when the PowerPoint slides were over, John and his team ran a very effective question and answer session with the audience. They also showed them a sample of their video work on DVD, which was very well received.

- **What visual aids are you planning to use in your presentation?**

- **How will you make sure that you engage your audience?**

- **What skills will you need to develop to make sure your presentation is a success?**

Grading tips

To reach Merit level, you should present your ideas competently, expressing your ideas with clarity and with appropriate use of subject terminology.

To reach Distinction level, your presentation should be to near-professional standards and your ideas should be expressed fluently.

Written report

It is a good idea to also include a written report in your final portfolio of evidence. It is important that you present all of your written work in a logical and coherent manner.

Spelling, punctuation and grammar

In your presentation you had to take care to control your verbal and non-verbal communication so that you presented a professional and organised image. You now need to continue with this in your written report by ensuring that your spelling, punctuation and grammar do not let you down.

Think it over 13

However good your research has been, if you are hoping for a Distinction grade you will need to present the results of that research in an effective manner using fluent language and correct terminology.

There is no set way of writing up your final report. However, you do need to make sure that it is clearly and logically laid out, with the use of appropriate headings and sub-headings. You must also take care to check your spelling and grammar.

Structure

The structure of your report should be similar to that of your oral presentation, though of course there is the

opportunity for you to include more detailed information in a written report.

As a reminder, your report should include the following elements:

- an introduction in which you explain its purpose and aims
- an explanation of the research methods and techniques that you have used
- the research data itself, presented in a suitable form (such as tables, charts, graphs or diagrams)
- an explanation of what you found out from analysing the results of your research
- the conclusions that you can make from these results
- any proposals that you are making based on these conclusions.

Because this is a written report you should also include a bibliography in which you detail the books that you have used in your research project. You should also include details of any other sources of information, including websites, newspapers and magazines.

Additional research material such as copies of any questionnaires that you used, tally charts and respondents' answers should be included in an appendices section of the report.

Think it over 14

The sources that you have used should be referenced in your bibliography in a consistent way.

One of the most popular forms of citation is the style known as MLA, which stands for Modern Language Association. The Harvard method and APA (American Psychological Association) are two other styles that are often used.

The MLA style has the author's surname followed by his or her initial. This is then followed by the title of the book, which is sometimes written in *italics* or in **bold**. The final information is the place of publication, the name of the publisher and the year that the source was published. For example:

Hart, J. *Storyboarding for Film, TV and Animation*. London, Focal Press, 1999.

You should now be in a position to put your final portfolio together that will provide the evidence that you have met all of the required learning outcomes for this unit.

This will involve you collecting together and sorting through some of the work that you have already completed for this unit, as well as producing some additional pieces of work.

The End of Unit assessment activities on pages 43–44 will guide you through the evidence required to achieve each of the learning outcomes at Pass, Merit and Distinction level.

Knowledge check

1. Explain what key areas a presentation of your research should cover.

2. Explain fully what the following terms mean:
    a) intrapersonal communication
    b) interpersonal communication
    c) NVC
    d) paralanguage
    e) visual aids. **p**₃

3. What should you do to try to make your oral presentation as professional as possible? **d**₃

4. What should you do to make your written report as professional as possible? **d**₃

End of Unit assessment

Preparation for assessment

End of Unit assessment activity 1

This assessment activity will allow you to cover P1, M1 and D1 of the learning outcomes for this unit.

For this first assessment task you need to think carefully about the different purposes of research in the media industries. Then, in your own words:

– Describe the different purposes of research, making sure you cover both market research and product research. **p₁**

– Explain the different purposes you have described, showing not just what is done but why it is done, and illustrate the points that you make with appropriate examples. **m₁**

– To achieve a distinction grade you will need to make sure that you have fully explained the purposes of research in the media industries and have justified what you have said by using supporting arguments, evidence and examples. You should also make sure that you have used technical and specialist language correctly and expressed your ideas with fluency. **d₁**

Your work can be presented in both written and oral form and be accompanied by appropriate notes, logs and diaries as well as examples of research material that you have studied.

Whether producing a written or oral report you should ensure that you use appropriate subject terminology correctly and express your ideas clearly and fluently.

Look closely at the assessment evidence grid on page 45 to check what you need to do to gain a pass, merit or distinction for this part of the unit.

End of Unit assessment activity 2

To successfully cover learning outcomes P2, M2 and D2 you will need to submit evidence in your final potfolio that shows you have applied relevant research methods and techniques when undertaking both market and product research.

It was suggested in section 1.2 that it is a good idea if your research for this learning outcome is linked to some of the production work that you are undertaking in other units.

If you have followed this advice then your main task here is to gather together the research that you have already conducted and organise it so that it shows clear evidence that you have met all of the learning outcomes for a pass, merit or distinction grade.

If you haven't yet conducted both a market research task and a production research task then now is the time to reread the sub-section in 1.2 called *Undertaking your own research* (pages 27–33) and follow the guidance carefully in planning, developing and carrying out your own research projects.

– To achieve a pass grade you should ensure that you show clear evidence of applying a range of both primary and secondary research methods and techniques that generate both quantitative and qualitative data. At this level you can have had some assistance with your work. **p₂**

– To achieve a merit grade you will need to show that you can apply the relevant research methods and techniques competently with only occasional assistance. **m₂**

– To achieve a distinction grade you will need to apply relevant research methods and techniques to near-professional standards while working in an independent manner. **d₂**

End of Unit assessment activity 3

To meet the final set of learning outcomes you need to present your research project in the form of an oral presentation or a written report, or both. The content and quality of this presentation will mean that you are awarded either a pass, merit or distinction grade.

What you need to do to achieve these grades is explained below.

- To achieve a pass grade for this learning outcome you need to present the results of the research that you have carried out in the form of an oral presentation or a written report, or both. Whichever form you use you will need to make sure that you have used at least some appropriate subject terminology to be sure of a pass grade. **p**₃

- To achieve a merit grade you will need to ensure that the presentation of the results has been done competently and that your ideas are expressed with clarity. **m**₃

- To achieve a distinction grade you will need to also ensure that the correct terminology is used througout and that the language is fluent and used in the right context. Your meaning will need to be clear at all times and the attention of the reader or audience will need to be maintained throughout. **d**₃

If you decide to do an oral presentation then you will need to include a recording of it in your final portfolio of evidence as well as any additional supporting material.

Look carefully at the information covered in section 1.3. Make sure that your presentation covers all of the required aspects and that you present the results of your research in as professional a way as possible.

Grading Criteria			
To achieve a pass grade the evidence must show that the learner is able to:	To achieve a merit grade the evidence must show that the learner is able to:	To achieve a distinction grade the evidence must show that the learner is able to:	Activity
P1 describe purposes of research in the media industries, expressing ideas with sufficient clarity to communicate them and with some appropriate use of subject terminology	**M1** explain purposes of research in the media industries with well chosen examples expressing ideas with clarity and with generally appropriate use of subject terminology	**D1** fully explain purposes of research in the media industries with supporting arguments and elucidated examples expressing ideas fluently and using subject terminology correctly	End of Unit assessment activity 1
P2 apply research methods and techniques with some assistance	**M2** apply research methods and techniques competently with only occasional assistance	**D2** apply research methods and techniques to near-professional standards working independently to professional expectations	End of Unit assessment activity 2
P3 present results, expressing ideas with sufficient clarity to communicate them and with some appropriate use of subject terminology	**M3** present results competently, expressing ideas with clarity and with generally appropriate use of subject terminology	**D3** present results to near-professional standards, expressing ideas fluently and using subject terminology correctly	End of Unit assessment activity 3

Pre-production techniques for the media industries

Introduction

Pre-production is the vital ingredient in any successful media production. Pre-production involves careful research and planning. The research element might be finding resources, such as props, materials or crew, or sourcing suitable locations or talent (actors). All of this involves finding information, storing this information in an appropriate way and then using it to plan your production. Planning is essential if you want your production to go smoothly. You need to timetable when things will happen (production schedule), who will be responsible for making it happen (role allocation) and what you will do if things do not go according to plan (contingency).

Pre-production is the responsibility of a producer or a production team. Everyone has a part to play in this process, and you will have to undertake this work as part of Unit 2. No matter what your role, whether you are the location manager or the set designer, you will be an integral part of the pre-production process.

You will have to prepare a range of pre-production paperwork – examples of which can be found in this unit. You will follow case studies from a media production company of the pre-production work that it undertook for a media product. This will help you in your own production work.

This unit will provide you with the essential skills you will need to plan the production of media products. It will show you how vital it is that you plan carefully before you embark on the production phase.

After completing this unit you should be able to achieve the following outcomes:

- Understand requirements for production.
- Be able to obtain resources for production.
- Be able to apply production logistics.

Think it over

Pre-production is a vital part of any successful media product. Imagine arriving at a location to shoot material for your video or to take photographs for your newspaper. You find that no one knows you are coming, they do not want you on the premises and security is heading your way to eject you. You have with you a camera crew or a photographer, a number of models and the head of communications at your client's firm. Imagine the embarrassment, never mind the cost, of this problem.

It is essential that you plan your production to the last detail. You must ensure that the location is available, there are sufficient resources for you to use, all the crew know how to get there – and at what time – and you have all the materials you need.

Many media production companies will employ someone to ensure that pre-production is completed and everything is in place.

You will undertake pre-production a number of times on this course. You will be able to practise your pre-production techniques and apply them to productions in other units. You may be able to ask your teacher to take into consideration all of your pre-production work and ask them to mark you on the best pre-production work you have completed.

Production requirements

It is important that you understand the processes you will need to undertake when planning your production work. The diagram in Figure 2.01 will help you to understand the steps you should go through in producing your own media production project.

Case study

Recycle.com

In the next two units you will be following a group of four learners. They have been asked to prepare some ideas for media products by an environmental organisation, Recycle.com.

Recycle.com wants to make young people much more aware of environmental issues. It has decided to launch a campaign aimed at 12–16 year-olds to highlight the dangers of global warming and how they can help by recycling. Recycle.com has asked these learners to come up with some ideas for the campaign. It has suggested that it would like a range of media products to help get the message across to its audience.

The four learners are Joshua, Willomena, James and Rani. They are working together in a group to plan their media products. They have decided to meet on a regular basis in order to help each other with planning and production.

The first thing they discuss is what kind of media products they could produce for Recycle.com. They decide that each of them will make a different product. Joshua wants to make a website, Willomena has skills in using a video camera and decides to make a promotional video, James enjoyed his audio work and decides he will make a radio commercial, and Rani thinks that she would like to produce a four-colour newsletter.

They now need to think about how much it will cost to produce their media products.

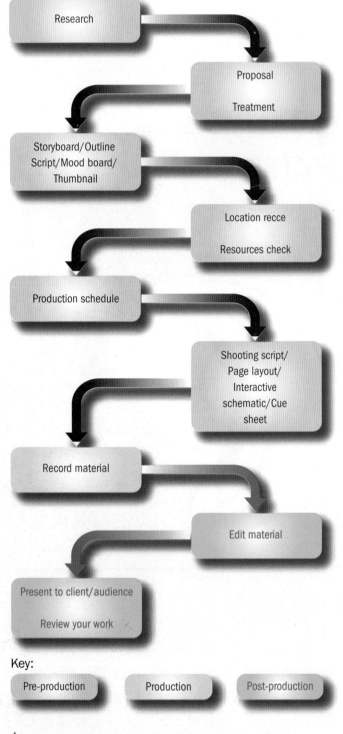

Figure 2.01: Major stages in the production process.

Research

As you can see from Figure 2.01, research is one of the first steps in the production planning process. Research can be required for a number of different aspects, for instance:

- the archives you can use to find particular information
- finding resources, such as crew members, actors, equipment suppliers, locations and studios
- where to find specialist advice on the material you are planning to use
- finding out what material is acceptable and whether it is copyright
- what issues there might be from regulatory bodies
- what issues might be encountered when employing crew and actors
- possible funding sources.

To find these resources you could use the Internet. Try using a search engine to find sources of crew, actors, equipment and studios. You will find lots of information that you can then download and store.

There are a number of sources for locations that you will find on the Internet. People often list their properties that they think might be of interest to producers on locations finding sites. Try to find some of these and keep the information you find.

Funding is not limitless, and it is important to keep in mind the costs of planning and production when undertaking pre-production. You must research costs carefully and ensure that you prepare a careful budget that takes into account all your expected expenditure. You must also be aware of **contingency** when developing your budget.

Key Term

Contingency is the part of the budget put aside to cover unexpected costs.

Case study

Recyle.com

Joshua, Willomena, James and Rani have had their first meeting and started their research phase. Each of them needs to consider what research they need to undertake and how to do it.

Joshua will need to consider how he will find information that will help him to develop his website.

Willomena needs to find resources for her video product.

James needs to identify resources for making his radio commercial.

Rani needs to find out what she needs to make her newsletter.

■ Background research

This is research to establish basic facts before moving on to more in-depth research activities. This might be researching archives to find old photographs, film footage or music. You may need specialist advice on a particular project, such as specialist techniques for filming time-lapse photography.

You should use a range of research techniques to find this preliminary information. Sources include:

- libraries or learning resource centres
- websites
- newspaper archives
- specialist bodies, such as the British Institute of Professional Photography (BIPP).

▲ Figure 2.02: BIPP is the foremost organisation for professional image makers in the UK.

The BIPP has over 3500 members covering every type of photography. The website has the world's largest search engine for qualified professional photographers.

Case study

Media Productions

Media Productions is a company that produces a wide range of media products for its clients. It was asked to develop a proposal for a client that makes pottery. The client wanted Media Productions to make a video programme showing how their products were made.

John Berry, the researcher at Media Productions, came up with an idea for filming the pottery being 'fired', or baked in the oven – known in the trade as a kiln. This shot would be key to getting the client to agree to the pitch for the job that Media Productions was planning to make.

After doing some research, John discovered that the kiln worked at over 1000°C. He also found out that there were no cameras that could withstand this level of heat. This meant that the key shot of the film could not be filmed. However, John then came up with another idea that involved filming from the inside of a teapot as it was being hand-moulded.

Through research on the Internet and in the library John discovered a company that made miniature cameras that could send a video signal back to a special recorder. This camera was small enough to fit inside a teapot and, after a trial shoot, proved to be a proposal-winning idea.

Before Media Productions could make a final decision on the use of the camera it had to ensure that it would be available for the project. It also had to ensure that the cost of the equipment was not so high that it would exceed the client's budget.

People research

People will be essential to your production, be they crew or talent, so finding the right personnel will also require research. You should thoroughly investigate the credentials of the people you are considering using.

Grading tips

To reach Distinction level, you should show that you have considered all your research requirements and stated what these are and how you intend to find them.

Resources research

There are many places you can go to find the resources you need. Your learning resource centre, for instance, should have books and magazines that will help you to locate the things required.

Case study

Media Productions

The team at Media Productions met to discuss how they might obtain the resources needed for their pottery programme.

They looked at productions they had made previously to see if any of the crew they had used were appropriate for this project. They also looked at the directors and producers they had used in the past.

The company had previously produced a video programme for another pottery and they looked at their archive to see if they had any footage that could be used in this project.

There are also many websites that will help you to find appropriate resources. Why not try using a search engine to find suppliers of materials, equipment, crew and talent. We will deal in more detail with resources in section 2.2.

Codes of practice and regulations

■ Legal

There are a number of legal issues you must consider when undertaking your pre-production work. The first is the issue of copyright.

Copyright

If you use any **copyright** archive material you must obtain permission, this is called clearing copyright. You will need to contact the copyright owner, which may involve further research to find out who that is. As well as getting permission, you might also have to pay a fee to the copyright holder.

Copyright gives the creators of certain kinds of material rights to control the ways their material can be used. These rights start as soon as the material is recorded in writing or in any other way. There is no official registration system. The rights cover:

* copying
* adapting
* distributing
* communicating to the public by electronic transmission (including by broadcasting and in an on-demand service)
* renting or lending copies to the public
* performing in public.

In many cases, the author will also have the right to be identified on their works and to object if their work is distorted or mutilated.

You will need to ensure that any material you plan to use in your production does not infringe copyright law. You must get permission to use material, and pay any required reproduction fee.

If you use something without the permission of the copyright holder, and they find out, they will certainly want payment and might even take you to court.

Key Terms

Copyright is the right of an author, composer or producer to ensure that no one uses their material without their permission.

MCPS-PRS Alliance is an organisation that deals with music copyright. It collects and pays royalties to its members when their music is recorded, performed, broadcast or otherwise made publicly available. It was created from a merger of two separate royalty collecting bodies, MCPS and PRS, in 1997.

Think it over 1

Imagine that you have written a book for young children. You have paid a lot of money to an illustrator for images to put in your book.

You open your newspaper to see that someone has taken your story and images and created a cartoon series for the newspaper.

* What would you think?
* What would you do?

In order to be sure that you do not breach any copyright law you should:

* produce your own material
* or get permission from the copyright holder to use copyright material
* pay the copyright holder a fee, if applicable, to use their material.

Copyright exists in all areas of the media. Do not be persuaded by a friend that it is alright to use just a small piece of chart music in your production. It is certainly not!

There are a number of organisations that can help you with copyright, for instance the **MCPS-PRS Alliance.**

Case study

Media Productions

Media Productions was working on a production for QuickCuts, a company that manufactured cloth-cutting machines. The production was a corporate video to be shown on their trade stand at a large event in Manchester.

The company had already decided on a company slogan that said:

'Feel Free with QuickCuts'

The client wanted to use a well-known piece of music as the sound track for the video and suggested that the Queen song 'I want to break free' would fit in well with their slogan. Although the production team advised that this song would be copyright protected the company insisted that it still wanted to use it.

The producer at Media Productions contacted the record company, EMI, and found out that the copyright belonged to John Deacon, Queen's bass player. A request was passed to the band for the use of this material and the producer was informed that a payment of £50,000 would be required.

The client was naturally shocked at this sum and quickly decided not to use the song after all!

The researcher at Media Productions then found a suitable track entitled 'Feel Free' on a CD of copyright music that could be purchased under an agreement with the MCPS-PRS Alliance. This music was used and a much smaller copyright fee paid to MCPS-PRS Alliance who distributed it to the composer.

Remember!

You can get into serious difficulties if you use someone else's material in your media product. Always check that any material you use is not copyright, or if it is, find out how you can get this material 'cleared' for your own use.

Theory into practice 2

What other organisations can you find that deal with copyright?

How would you ensure that you are not using copyright material? **P1**

Grading tips

To reach Merit level, you should use well-chosen examples of organisations and explain clearly how you would ensure you were not using copyright materials.

To reach Distinction level, you should explain why you chose these organisations, giving reasons for your choice, and clearly explain how you would ensure that you are not using copyright material.

Case study

Recycle.com

Joshua, Willomena, James and Rani have to consider their use of copyright material.

Joshua wants to use some images of factory chimneys belching smoke that he has seen in a magazine. He contacts the publisher and asks for permission to use them on his website.

Willomena would like to use some footage she has found in a news item from ITN. She has contacted them to ask for permission and an estimate of the cost of using this library footage.

James would like to use some classical music for the music soundtrack on his commercial. He contacts the MCPS-PRS Alliance to ask for the cost of using this music. He has to give them the titles of the pieces he wants to use, details of the recording, the running time of the music, and the how long the total programme will be.

Rani has found some images of people dumping rubbish on the roadside. These were taken by a local photographer, so she contacts him for permission to use them in her newsletter.

Insurance

It is a legal requirement that all companies have some form of insurance to cover their employees and members of the public. This is vital when working in a location where members of the public might be injured or otherwise affected by your activities or equipment.

Health and safety

There is a wide range of health and safety issues you need to consider when planning your production. Later in this unit you will be looking in more detail at health and safety considerations.

Regulatory bodies

Regulatory bodies are independent organisations, usually established by government, that regulate the activities of companies in a particular industry. There are a number of regulators that operate in the media industry, and when you are planning your work you will need to take them into account.

Suppose you are planning to make a commercial for a client to sell a new range of snack food to children. You need to be aware of the regulations about what you can and cannot say in an advertisement. Both the ASA and Ofcom have guidelines on this and you would have to follow these if you wanted your advertisement to be shown on television.

You would also have to be aware of the regulations regarding child protection if you wanted to use children in your commercial.

The following are regulatory bodies that deal specifically with the media industry.

The Advertising Standards Authority (ASA)

The ASA makes sure that all advertising, wherever it appears, meets the high standards laid down in its advertising codes. The ASA website (asa.org.uk) will tell you more about the rules for advertising, and explain how the ASA aims to keep UK advertising standards as high as possible. It is also possible to complain about an advertisement via the ASA website.

Figure 2.03: ASA logo.

The British Board of Film Classification (BBFC)

The BBFC is an independent, non-government body that has classified films since it was set up in 1912, and videos since the passing of the Video Recordings Act in 1984. This also includes DVD releases. You can find out more about the BBFC on its website, www.bbfc.co.uk.

Figure 2.04: BBFC logo.

Independent Committee for the Supervision of Standards of the Telephone Information Services (icstis)

The Independent Committee for the Supervision of Standards of the Telephone Information Services is the industry-funded regulatory body for all premium-rate charged telecommunications services. It is non-profit making and regulates the content and promotion of services through its Code of Practice. It investigates complaints and has the power to fine companies and bar access to services. It also offers free advice and guidance to both existing and new service providers. For more about icstis, visit its website at www.icstis.org.uk

Figure 2.05: icstis logo.

Office of Communications (Ofcom)

Ofcom is the regulator for the UK communications industries, with responsibilities across television, radio, telecommunications and wireless communications services. It ensures that broadcasting technology is used effectively, that communications services are available throughout the UK, and that TV and radio services are of a high quality and wide appeal. It prevents **monopolies** in broadcasting and makes sure programmes are not unduly offensive, harmful or unfair, and do not infringe personal privacy. You can find more information at www. Ofcom.org.uk.

Figure 2.06: Ofcom logo.

Key Term

Monopoly is when a single body or group gains sole control of a particular market, pushing out all other competitors.

Press Complaints Commission (PCC)

PRESS COMPLAINTS COMMISSION

▲ Figure 2.07: PCC logo.

The PCC is an independent body that deals with complaints from members of the public about the editorial content of newspapers and magazines. The service is quick and free, with most complaints being dealt with in just 25 working days. You can find out more on the PCC website, www.pcc.org.uk.

Theory into practice 3

See how many regulatory bodies you can find and make a note of the main areas that they cover. **P1**

Will you have to consider any regulatory issues when undertaking pre-production of your media product? **M1**

Grading tips

To reach Merit level, you should use well-chosen examples of regulatory bodies and make careful notes of the main areas that they cover, using examples.

To reach Distinction level, you should explain clearly any regulatory issues you might have to consider, using a wide range of examples, and say how this might affect your work.

Case study

Media Productions

Media Productions was filming a sequence for a programme for young children. The scene required footage of children playing in the sand on the beach.

The producer initially planned to simply go to the south coast and find a location. She would then ask parents' permission to film their children playing on the sand and jumping through the waves.

After careful consideration it was decided to hire several child models and take them to the beach. This solved a number of problems, such as getting to the location only to be denied permission to film the children. Parents approached out of the blue might have demanded a large sum of money or could have simply telephoned the police if they suspected the crew were not genuine.

Using child models meant that the budget could be controlled and permissions easily obtained.

Media Productions still had to get permission to use the beach for filming and avoid filming other bathers.

Knowledge check 2.1

1. Identify three organisations that deal with copyright. **P1**

2. Identify how you would make sure you did not breach copyright. **P1**

Careful planning is essential for a successful media production project. This includes finding resources, such as equipment, personnel and materials. You will then have to gather these resources together, and in the case of equipment and materials, store them appropriately and be able to find them when needed.

It is important that you learn to undertake this work independently and work effectively as a producer or as part of a production team.

Equipment

You must think carefully about the equipment you will need. This will depend on the media project you are producing. A video product, for instance, might require:

- video cameras
- microphones
- lighting
- support equipment
- hardware
- software.

You might need similar resources for a website if you are putting video images on it, as well as text and graphics.

It is a very good idea to do an **audit** of the equipment you will need. To do this you should complete an equipment audit form. This will give you a clear picture of just what equipment will be required to complete work on the project and will form part of your production schedule.

Key Term

Audit is a review of the availability of skills, equipment, personnel, etc. involved in a project.

Case study

Media Productions

Media Productions received a commission from a client to produce a video programme to support parents of a group of disabled children.

The Media Productions team met to discuss the implications of working on this programme. They identified immediately that they would be filming in some challenging situations. Many of the children would be in wheelchairs, be mobility impaired and, in some instances, sight or hearing impaired.

The team had to make decisions on the equipment needed to film these children. They had to ask themselves a number of questions:

Would they be able to use conventional camera support systems?

Would they have to work in confined spaces and how would this impact on conventional choice of cameras?

Would working with this client group affect the number of film crew?

How would the client group react to the presence of the crew, bright lights, etc.?

How would the crew communicate with the client group?

Case study

Recycle.com

Joshua, Willomena, James and Rani have different equipment requirements.

Rani and Joshua will need computers and appropriate software to produce and edit their projects.

Willomena will require a video camera, camera support, lights and microphones to produce her video footage. She will also need a computer and software to edit her video.

James will require a microphone and minidisk to record his sound material. He will also need a computer and software to edit his sound material.

They all undertake an equipment audit to ensure that the resources they need are available. If they are not available they will have to identify where they can be found.

Personnel

Some of the issues in the case study on page 55 affected who Media Productions chose as crew to make the programme. Similarly, you will have to consider who you want working on your projects. You will need to have a team of people with the skills to produce the material you require.

You will need to produce a list of all the personnel you need for your production. This list should clearly indicate their role in the production and their contact details.

You must ensure before you start that you have all the right people with the right skills in the team. Once you have assigned people's jobs and the production has started, you cannot expect people to change role to suit you just because you have not properly thought through your exact personnel requirements.

Before you compile this list, you must have a clear idea of the structure of your project, the personnel and equipment you will be using and the timescale for production. The timescale will be important as many media personnel work on a freelance basis. They take on a number of projects and have to schedule their work

carefully. You will have to be sure that the timescale you have produced fits in with the crew you require.

Case study

Media Productions

Once the team at Media Productions had identified the equipment they needed for their programme they had to think about their crew. They wanted to keep the team small because of the confined spaces and the disruption and stress a large crew might have caused the clients.

They had to consider who would be suitable for a sensitive programme such as this.

Who had a track record of working on similar projects?

Were they cleared through the **CRB** to work with children?

Were they available at the time of the planned location shoot?

They also considered hiring multi-skilled people to reduce the total crew number. This had to be decided with practical factors in mind. It would not, for instance, be appropriate to hire a camera operator and expect them to hold a boom microphone or record sound at the same time.

Once they had cleared up all of these issues they could start to put the team together.

Media Productions has a file of potential crew members that includes their CV, show reels, names of previous work and references. They use this to identify potential crew members and then contact them to see if they are available.

Key Term

CRB is the Criminal Records Bureau, a government agency set up to help organisations make safer recruitment decisions. They check names against records of known offenders.

Remember!

You will need a crew for your project. Ask your colleagues to fill in a form that highlights their particular skills.

You could ask them for a copy of their CV and details of projects they have produced.

Grading tip

To reach Distinction level, you should show that you can undertake this type of work to near-professional standards, that is, that you can work without constantly having to ask your teacher for help. Your work should show you have a real ability to plan effectively.

Case study

Recycle.com

Joshua, Willomena, James and Rani have sourced their equipment and now need to finalise their crew.

At the start of the project they all agreed to help each other with production and post-production.

They each complete a skills audit that lists their particular skills. From these they can choose who will undertake what job in their crews.

The work they do for other members of their team can be used as extra evidence of their skills when they are assessed by their teacher.

Figure 2.08 is an example of a crew list that Media Productions produced for their programme about children with a disability.

Media Productions MP
Video and New Media Production

Crew List

Programme Title: The Mary Hirst Trust
Client: MHT Support Group
Writer: James Subrami
Date: 18 January 2007

Title	Contact Details
Director: Scott Mundy	mobile 0700 140290
Producer: Sally Ferguson	mobile 0704 030711
Cameraperson/Photographer: Bill Smith	mobile 0797 770431
Writer: John Grundy	mobile 0700 031844
Editor: Sani Samara	mobile 0761 104862
Production Assistant: Josh Zebrundra	mobile 0799 844112
Soundperson: Mandy Abrahams	mobile 0779268103
Multimedia Designer: Philip Jones	mobile 0704 047215
Graphic Designer: Mary Routh	mobile 0797 884862
Music Composer: Gary Hargreaves	mobile 0799 924141

▲ Figure 2.08 Crew list.

Theory into practice 4

Make a list of all the crew and talent you will need for your production. **P2**

Ask them to provide you with a CV. **M2**

Record their contact details in order to keep in communication with them. **M2**

Begin to allocate roles to people. **M2**

Materials

Once you have identified the equipment and the personnel required for your project you will need to consider the materials you require. These might be:

- archive footage
- archive photographs
- commissioned graphics
- commissioned music
- costumes
- properties
- scripts.

You will need to ensure that any materials you need have been commissioned in good time in order to ensure the smooth running of your project.

There are a number of sources you should try for archive images. If you are looking for old film or newsreel footage you could contact the British Film Institute or British Pathé. For contemporary news footage try ITN or the BBC. For contemporary or historical stills there are many photo agencies such as Getty Images, Alamy and Mary Evans Picture Library.

You must remember that all of these resources require a payment before you can use them. Copyright exists on many media products. Even for classical music, where the composer has been dead for over seventy years, there will be copyright on the performance and this will require you to pay a fee to use the material.

You must find out how to use copyright material in your own work. It may be simpler and cheaper to take your own photographs or compose your own soundtrack.

Think it over 2

Here are some sources of still and moving images. Look at their websites and find out more about how they charge for use of their images. Can you think of anywhere else to look for images?

British Film Institute – www.bfi.org.uk

British Pathé – www.britishpathe.com

ITN – www.itn.co.uk

Getty Images – www.gettyimages.com

Alamy – www.alamy.com

Mary Evans Picture Library – www.maryevans.com

Theory into practice 5

Think about the material you might want to use for your production.

Will you need images – where can you find them? **P2**

Will you need music – how can you find the right music or can you compose your own? **M2**

If the material you need is copyright, how will you go about gaining permission to use it in your product? **M2**

Start to compile a list of the materials you might need for your production. **M2**

Grading tip

To reach Distinction level, you must show that you can complete this work to a standard that is near to professional practice. Your list of materials required should be comprehensive and accurate. You should demonstrate that you have worked independently using skills that a professional might use when gathering resources.

Gathering and collating

Once you have sourced your equipment and materials you will need to ensure that they are available when you need them. You could use a form that allows you to identify what you need and where the resources are to be found. You can also identify where materials can be sourced should you run out.

Why not use a form such as the audit sheet shown in Figure 2.09 to do this. This example is for a video programme and indicates where equipment might be stored and material obtained.

Media Productions MP
Video and New Media Production

VIDEO EQUIPMENT AUDIT SHEET

Equipment needed	Available Y	N	If not available where to find it
DV camera	✓		
Tripod	✓		
Microphone	✓		
Lighting kit			available from the Drama Department
DV tapes	✓		4 available, can buy more from Currys
Computer with editing facilities	✓		
Editing software Premier Pro	✓		only two machines have this software installed

▲ Figure 2.09: Video equipment audit sheet.

Knowledge check 2.2

1. Make a list of all the people you would use in your crew or as talent. **P2**

2. Ask for, and store, a CV for each member of the crew and talent. **M2**

3. Decide who would be best for each role. **M2**

4. Make a list of all the materials you will need and identify how you will obtain them. **D2**

Planning

When you have established your resources you will need to plan carefully for their use. This will involve producing a range of planning documents. This documentation will enable you to demonstrate that you have made careful plans. It will also provide valuable evidence for assessment of your work.

Schedules

Schedules are planning documents that provide not only dates for various production activities but also details of resources and materials requirements.

The production schedule helps to clarify all of the details of the production in one document. It should include details of when the production started and when various activities are planned to take place. This information, although not necessarily industry standard, is vital for your records. The production schedule will form a major part of the evidence required for the pre-production and the production stages of this unit, therefore you must store it carefully and have it available for the assessment of your work. The production schedule should contain:

- details of proposal/treatment start finish dates and when these were circulated to the client
- agreed dates for activities, such as location shooting, editing and review by the client
- details of production equipment required and its location
- transport required
- crew required, with names
- talent (actors) required, with names
- properties required, with the name of the person whose responsibility this is
- post-production equipment required.

Your production schedule should be monitored and any changes recorded on it.

Theory into practice 6

Start to think about your planning. You need to consider:

- time
- personnel
- costs
- resources
- weather
- the client.

Produce an initial schedule. How does this fit with the time you have available for production? Make sure you will have enough time to produce your product. **P3**

Grading tip

To reach Distinction level, you should show that you have worked independently when making your schedule. You will have considered all the elements for production at a level that reflects professional practice.

Figure 2.10 is an example of the first part of a production schedule for Media Productions' programme on disabled children. The schedule provides a clear picture of the way that project is progressing.

Part two of the production schedule enables you to have a clear picture of the various requirements needed for the production (see Figure 2.11).

The production schedule can be supplemented by a daily schedule (see Figure 2.12) that shows the resources required for just one day. This is known as a call sheet and gives details for the crew and actors of where to be and at what time. It can also contain details of transport arrangements, props needed, materials required for the day's work and location catering arrangements.

Media Productions MP
Video and New Media Production

Production Schedule Part 1

Programme Title: The Mary Hirst Trust
Client: MHT Support Group
Writer: James Subrami
Date: 21 October 2006

	Date	Date
Programme started:	12/11/06	Completed:
Proposal started:	24/11/06	Completed: 26/11/06
Treatment started:	11/12/06	Completed: 14/12/06
Agreement from client:	23/12/06	
Shooting script started:	27/01/07	Completed: 09/02/07
Storyboard started:	11/02/07	Completed: 15/02/07
Production started:	12/03/07	Completed: 13/04/07
Post-production started:	16/05/07	Completed: 25/05/07
Rough-cut supplied to client:	27/05/07	Agreed with client: 29/5/07
Final version completed:	01/06/07	

Figure 2.10: Production schedule part 1.

Media Productions MP
Video and New Media Production

Production Schedule Part 2

Programme Title: The Mary Hirst Trust
Client: MHT Support Group
Writer: James Subrami
Date: 23 January 2007

Production equipment required
cameras
lights
microphones
tripod

Crewing requirements
cameraperson
sound recordist
production assistant
lighting technician
props technician

Actors
1 male actor
1 female actor
3 extras

Transport requirements
Transport to 3 locations required for approximately 20 people

Props/scenery
None needed

Post-production requirements (format,effects,music, voice-over)
Editing on FCP by mac platform
Graphics for titles and credits
Music throughout programme
Sound effects where necessary

Media Productions MP
Video and New Media Production

Production Schedule Call Sheet

Programme Title: The Mary Hirst Trust
Client: MHT Support Group
Writer: James Subrami
Date: 21 November 2006

Crew
Camera: Robin Williams
Sound: Rory Smith
Lighting: William Sparks
Production assistant: Kate Azhami
Technicians: John Brown/Bill Bailley
Transport: John Smith – Just Cars
Props: Gary Musazawksi

ARRANGEMENTS
Meeting at: W H Headquarters, 36 Main Road, Spoforth WH9 4ZX
Location venue: Office and interview
CALL DATE: **29 January 2007**
CALL TIME: **6.30am**
Transport: arranged from Media Productions HQ – leaving at 6am prompt otherwise use own transport

INSTRUCTIONS: Crew to be smartly dressed

Actors:	Bill Foreman: Parent	Jane Smith: Parent
Make-up:	Bill: 7.30am	Jane: 8am

Wardrobe: Bill: 7am   Jane: 7.30am
Location catering: Breakfast required for 30 people from 7am
Lunch required for 30 people from 12.30pm
Evening meal for 10 people from 6pm
Coffe/tea on at all times
Chuck Wagon caterers on site at all times
Properties: None required

Figure 2.12: Daily schedule or call sheet.

When you do your planning remember to keep everyone informed about the schedule. If someone does not attend when expected there is no excuse if they have been given a call sheet.

Budget

Once you have worked out all the requirements for the media product you can begin to formalise a realistic budget. So far your ideas have been built on the practicalities of scripting and scheduling but now you need to take into account all the costs involved in producing your media product.

Figure 2.11: Production schedule part 2.

Try to make your budget as realistic as possible. In order to do this you should research the prices charged for equipment hire, the cost of materials (including reproduction fees) and the cost of hiring your crew. You will need to take into account:

- equipment
- materials
- talent (actors, walk on)
- team or crew members
- transport
- catering (meals etc.)
- location
- clearances (model release, location release, copyright)
- post-production
- contingency.

A good place to start researching equipment costs is to contact a local media equipment hire company. This will give you a good idea of the standard rental costs of anything from a video camera to a computer on which you design and build a website.

For the going rates for personnel, try contacting BECTU, the union for moving image, radio and information design industries. They will have a rate card for various roles within the industry.

Theory into practice 7

What do you need to put in your budget? Your list might include:

- hire of equipment
- cost of materials
- crew payments
- actors' fees
- location charges
- travel
- subsistence, e.g. meals, accommodation
- contingency, e.g. equipment breakdowns, bad weather delays.

Think about the things you need to include and start to compile your budget. **P3**

Make sure that everything you will need has been taken into consideration in your budget. **M3**

Grading tip

To reach Distinction level, you should show that you have worked independently when producing your budget. You must have considered all the elements of a budget in a way that reflects professional practice.

Figure 2.13 is the outline budget for Media Productions' programme on disabled children.

Media Productions MP
Video and New Media Production

Production Schedule Outline Budget

Programme Title: The Mary Hirst Trust
Client: MHT Support Group
Writer: James Subrami
Producer: Amanda Philips
Director: Barry Norman
Date: 21 October 2006

Materials	Cost	Total
DVCAM tapes	£20 each	
Equipment		
Hire of Sony DVCAM camera	£150 per day x 3 days	
Hire of 1 tripod	£20 per day x 3 days	
Hire of lighting kit	£50 per day x 3 days	
Hire of microphone kit	£75 per day x 3 days	
Actors		
I male actor	rehaersal day £50 x 3 days	
	shooting day £150 x 3 days	
I female actor	rehearsal day £50 x 3 days	
	shooting day £150 x 3 days	
Props/scenery		
1 map	purchased for £30	
Post-production		
Editing suite	£150 per day x 3 days	
Editor	£100 per day x 3 days	
Graphic designer	£100 per day x 1 day	
	Total	**£3,175**
Contingency @10% of budget		£318
	Total budget	**£3,493**

Figure 2.13: Outline budget.

Bookings

It is important that you ensure that all the equipment you need for your production is booked well in advance.

Imagine arranging an interview with a well-known celebrity. You arrive at your office to collect the equipment you need only to find that someone else has booked it out.

You should keep careful records of all your equipment bookings and double-check to make sure that the booking is still in place.

Contingency

It is advisable to make a contingency plan in case things do not go as expected. You will have seen on the initial budget that Media Productions had allowed 10 per cent of the budget for contingency.

Contingency planning can be about equipment, locations or personnel. Sometimes equipment can fail and you need to have a back-up plan if your camera does not work or your microphone dies.

The weather might be bad and you cannot film on location; the light might be poor so you cannot film or take photographs or the wind be so strong you cannot record your radio interview.

It may be the case that a key member of your crew is taken ill, leaving you with a problem. How can you replace them at the last minute? If you have some spare budget, that will be invaluable to cover costs, but hopefully if you have done your pre-production research well, you will have records of other suitable people you could approach to fill the gap.

You may need to build in some contingency planning for the post-production phase as well. The editing might take longer than you thought so you should build some flexibility into your post-production schedule to meet your delivery deadline for the final product.

Case study

Media Productions

Media Productions always include a contingency amount in their budget to cover reasonable extra costs in the event of unforeseen circumstances. This allows for things such as alternative locations if there is a problem with the planned shoot. If the client decides that a location must include their office in another country, for instance, the contingency fund could be used.

Recently a client bought another company in Ireland. It was essential that this new acquisition was included in the filming. The team at Media Productions had allowed for contingency in their budget and were able to pay for the extra expenses without going back to the client to ask for a change in the budget.

However, the client then decided they wanted to shoot some scenes in the USA. This would have gone over the amount of contingency planned in the budget, and was an unreasonable extra cost. In this case the client had to agree to an increase in the budget if they wanted to include these scenes.

Case study

Recycle.com

Joshua, Willomena, James and Rani have met together to discuss their contingency planning. As a team they have agreed to fill in any gaps that might occur if anyone is ill.

They have identified what to do if equipment is faulty or the materials they need do not arrive on time.

They have all undertaken a risk assessment and location recce for the locations they intend to use. This includes contact details for the locations so that they can confirm everything with the location the day before.

They have agreed to make a few days available in case the weather is not suitable for their location work, or their post-production falls behind schedule.

Theory into practice 8

Think about the things that could potentially cause problems in your production. **P3**

Make a list of these and try to identify how you would overcome them. **M3**

Grading tip

To reach Distinction level, you should show that you have worked independently when producing your contingency plan. You will have considered all the problems that you might encounter and have clearly identified how these might be overcome in a way that reflects professional practice.

Communication

It is vital that you keep in communication with your team and your teacher. Everyone needs to know what is going on and what they have to do next.

Think it over 3

Imagine you have made plans to film a scene in a local cinema. You have secured permission from the manager and she has allowed you just thirty minutes to film when the cinema is closed.

You arrive at the cinema with your camera, but your crew and your actors do not turn up.

How should you have ensured everyone arrived as scheduled?

What do you say to the manager?

How would you go about organising a second opportunity to film this vital scene?

You should have regular meetings with your team so that decisions about pre-production can be made. These meetings will carry on right through the pre-production process to production and post-production.

Figure 2.14 is an example of a meeting record sheet that you might use to record all your team meetings. The meeting record sheet should be circulated to all your crew so that they know what is happening in your production planning.

Meeting Record Sheet

Date: Time: Place:

Present:

Apologies for absence:

Minutes:

▲ Figure 2.14: Meeting record sheet.

You should ensure that all your contributions are recorded on the meeting record sheet. This might prove valuable evidence for your teacher when assessing your contribution to a project.

If someone other than you has taken the minutes, check them carefully, and if anything was not recorded correctly, ask for them to be amended at the next meeting.

Theory into practice 9

Start to compile records of meetings, notes you have taken, conversations with the crew and the client and any decisions you have made.

These could be in note form, in an audio file, a video diary or a written report. **P1**

Grading tips

To reach Merit level, make sure that your records are comprehensive and well-organised. Be able to refer to discussions you have made and be able to find records of them easily.

To reach Distinction level, you should show that you have worked independently when producing your records of meetings. Keep records in a way that reflects professional practice.

▲ Figure 2.15: Appoint someone to keep the minutes of all important production meetings.

Health and safety

It is very important to consider health and safety when planning for location, studio and post-production work. You need to understand the requirements of the Health and Safety At Work Act.

The following are examples of health and safety issues you need to be aware of when undertaking your pre-production work:

- handling recording and editing equipment safely
- awareness of trailing cables
- handling hot lights
- organising teams to work together in a safe environment
- recognising the dangers of prolonged use of VDU screens
- working in a sensible way and responding to directions.

You need to be aware of electrical safety at all times, for instance not using electrical equipment in the rain. Consideration of health and safety issues should form part of your **location recce** (see below).

In order to understand what risks there might be on a location you should undertake a **risk assessment**. Figure 2.16 is an example of the risk assessment undertaken by Media Productions for their programme on disability.

Key Terms

Location reconnaissance (recce) is a visit to a location to ascertain if it suitable for use. This might involve checking the security of the location, if there are appropriate power supplies and access for vehicles.

Risk assessment is where you identify potential risks to staff, the public and equipment and show how these risks might be minimised.

Media Productions MP
Video and New Media Production

Risk Assessment Sheet

Programme Title: The Mary Hirst Trust
Client: MHT Support Group
Writer: James Subrami
Producer: Amanda Philips
Director: Barry Norman
Date: 21 October 2006

Major issues/risks	Solutions
Filming at WH Headquarters	
1. General public visiting building	Ensure someone checks that area is clear for filming
2. Slippery wooden floors	Take floor covering to ensure safety of equipment
3. Visibility of crew when on site	Crew to wear high visibility vests at all times when on site
4. Desks arranged in close proximity in open plan office	Client to arrange for the interview to be in an office with space for filming
5. Lack of electricity supply for equipment	Portable generator to be available, if required

Contacts
- Site Safety Manager   Bill Brown 0320 719618

Emergency Services
- On Site Services: 0320 719543
- Local police: 0320 254873
- Local fire: 0320 453991
- Local hospital: 0320 8843

▲ Figure 2.16: Risk assessment sheet.

Case study

Media Productions

The team at Media Productions has a clear policy on Health and Safety. Every production they undertake has to have a risk assessment before the production can start. This involves producing a document that identifies all the risks involved. This might include:

- staff working late at night
- staff working on a location on their own
- transport for staff working on locations and in the studio
- use of hazardous materials in a studio or on location
- ensuring the safety of the public when filming in a public area.

All staff contribute to the development of the risk assessment according to their part in the production process.

Location reconnaissance

Location reconnaissance is the first step towards planning the production. This is where you can visit any locations or studios you are planning to use and check out the lighting, power supply and accessibility for your crew and cast. You may have to organise a contact person to let you in early to set up your equipment. You should assess if there are any health and safety hazards to overcome.

All of this information should be recorded in a location visit sheet that must be attached to your production schedule. It is no good turning up at a location only to find that permission has not been granted for filming or the location is closed.

It is also not good practice to film at a location where innocent bystanders could become unwittingly involved in your operations. There have been cases of students staging mock hold-ups outside bank premises, for instance, without gaining permission or notifying the local police. In just such a case students were put at risk when teams of armed police arrived at the scene as they thought a real robbery was taking place.

▲ Figure 2.17: Be careful with your locations and ensure all authorities know what you are doing.

Case study

Recycle.com

Joshua, Willomena, James and Rani have found their locations and undertaken risk assessments at each.

Joshua has found a location where he can take some photographs of waste material being processed into usable compost. He has asked permission and been to the location to see what risks might be involved.

Willomena has found a landfill site location and she has approached the local council for permission to film there. She has identified the risks in filming and has completed a risk assessment form. She realises that she needs to take extra crew members as she will be filming near to moving machinery and needs someone to ensure she is safe.

James wants to interview the manager of the local refuse disposal site and has sought permission to record there. As he will be recording his interview in an office he has little to add to his risk assessment. He does have to ensure that someone knows where he will be and at what time he will be returning to college.

Rani is mostly using found material and photographs purchased from the Internet for her magazine. She does include in her risk assessment the dangers of prolonged exposure to a digital display and the risk of repetitive strain injury.

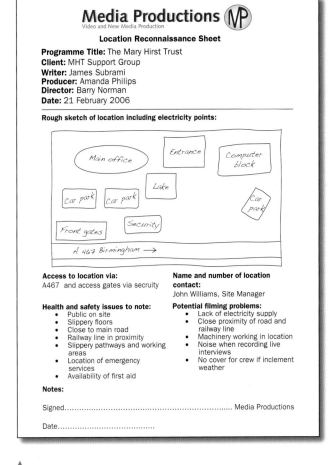

Figure 2.18: Location reconnaissance sheet.

Theory into practice 10

Undertake a location recce for your planned location or studio work. **P3**

Produce a risk assessment for your location work. **P3**

Grading tip

To reach Distinction level, you should show that you have worked independently when undertaking your location recce and risk assessment. Show that you are able to undertake these activities and record them in a professional way.

■ Safe working practice

No one wants to work in a dangerous situation if this can be avoided. Your location reconnaissance should identify potential hazards so you can begin to compile a risk assessment document. This document is a vital piece of evidence for your pre-production work.

Think it over 4

There is a wide range of health and safety issues you need to think about when planning your production. You need to refer to several pieces of legislation. The main ones are:

- Health and Safety at Work Act 1974
- The Management of Health and Safety at Work Regulations 1999
- Manual Handling Regulations
- Display Screen Equipment Regulations
- COSHH

What sort of issues do they cover?

Documentation

It is important that you keep careful records of your pre-production work. This includes all the documentation you produce when planning for production. These may include:

- production schedules
- location plans
- scripts
- storyboards
- thumbnails.
- call sheets
- studio plans
- shooting scripts
- mood boards

You should consider keeping your documentation in a folder that is indexed for each section of the pre-production process.

On the following pages you will find examples of some of the paperwork that Media Productions used in the pre-production planning for their programme about disabled children.

You may not need to use all of these in your media product as they are related specifically to a video product.

Key Term

Script is a blueprint for the making of a programme, whether for film, television or radio. It sets out all dialogue, locations and action. The programme starts with an initial script that is then fine-tuned to produce a final script. In many television series the scriptwriters are working on redrafts of the script as the programme is being made.

Key Terms

Storyboard is a graphic, step-by-step description of the story. Many film producers storyboard the whole production to ensure coverage of all the scenes and to aid special effects generation.

Mood board is a way of showing your visual ideas for a page layout or design. Could be used for a web home page or a theme for a magazine.

Thumbnails are reduced-sized versions of pictures or images that give an idea of what will appear in the finished product.

Non-verbal communication (NVC) – This term refers to all of the features of body language that occur during interpersonal communication. It includes such features as the clothes that you wear, your posture, facial expression and hand and arm movements.

Media Productions MP
Video and New Media Production

SCRIPT

Programme Title: The Mary Hirst Trust
Client: MHT Support Group
Writer: James Subrami
Producer: Amanda Philips
Director: Barry Norman
Date: 21 February 2006

Scene 6: Interior of Mary Hirst Head Office / interview with Doctor Jakes

Presenter: Can you tell me about Mary Hirst Syndrome?

Scene 7: Interior of Mary Hirst Head Office

Presenter: We are now going to see something of the work that the Mary Hirst Trust does with the children and parents.

Scene 7a: Interior of atmosphere room

Presenter: This room is where children can experience the sounds and colours from a range of sources. You can see that the children are reacting to the stimulae.

Scene 8: Interior of atmosphere room

Presenter: I am talking to one of the parents of a child that is here today...What do you think the Mary Hirst Trust does for parents like you and your wife / husband / partner?

Scene 9: Exterior of atmosphere room

Presenter: I am talking to Ms Bindley, the chief executive of the Mary Hirst Trust.

Ms Bindley, what does the Mary Hirst Trust offer to parents/carers of the kind of children we have just seen?

▲ Figure 2.19: Part of a script.

Media Productions (MP)
Video and New Media Production

SHOOTING SCRIPT

Programme Title: The Mary Hirst Trust
Client: MHT Support Group
Writer: James Subrami
Producer: Amanda Philips
Director: Barry Norman
Date: 21 February 2006

Shot	Camera	Scene/Action/Sound

Scene 6 Interior of Mary Hirst Head Office

17	presenter to camera	'Can you tell me about Mary Hirst Syndrome?'
18	2 shots over the presenter's shoulder	'Can you tell me about Mary Hirst Syndrome?'
19	mid shot of doctor	Doctor's response/radio mic
20	zoom to close up of doctor	Doctor's response/radio mic
21	noddies from presenter	no sound/some atmos
22	2 shots over the shoulder with noddies	no sound/some atmos
23	presenter to camera for sign off	presenter / radio mic

Scene 7 Interior of Mary Hirst Head Office

24	presenter to camera	'This room is where …reacting to these stimulae.'

Scene 7a Interior of atmosphere room

25	long shot of room interior	atmos
26	C/U of child listening and watching colours	atmos

▲ **Figure 2.20: Part of a shooting script.**

Media Productions (MP)
Video and New Media Production

STORYBOARD

Programme Title: The Mary Hirst Trust
Client: MHT Support Group
Writer: James Subrami
Producer: Amanda Philips
Director: Barry Norman
Date: 21 February 2006

No.	Time		Description	Audio
17	0.20-0.22		presenter to camera	Presenter: 'Can you tell me about Mary Hirst Syndrome?'
18	0.22-0.25		2 shots over the presenter's shoulder	
19	0.25-0.27		mid-shot of doctor	Doctor's response/ radio mic
20	0.27-0.30		zoom to close up of doctor	Doctor's response/ radio mic

▲ **Figure 2.21: Storyboard.**

▲ **Figure 2.22: Mood board.**

▲ **Figure 2.23: Thumbnails.**

Planning logistics for production

It is important to plan your production effectively and keep careful records of your actions and planning processes. You will need these to demonstrate your understanding of pre-production and you own pre-production planning skills.

One way to plan is to produce a personal pre-production diary. This will be a useful document when you want to demonstrate what you did and how well your pre-production was planned.

There is an example of a pre-production diary in Figure 2.28. Figure 2.27 is an example of a pre-production planning sheet that you could use to ensure you have everything under control.

You need to ensure that everything required for production is in place. This includes:

- your crew or team
- talent (actors)
- materials
- locations
- transport, where appropriate
- catering, where appropriate
- accommodation, where needed.

You must also remember to make sure that you have agreement from the locations you are planning to use. You could use the example location permission form shown in Figure 2.24 as a template.

Do not forget to obtain permission from *everyone* that might appear in your media product. This includes people who might only appear in the background, whose voice might be heard in a radio broadcast or whose image might be included in a photograph for your newspaper or website. You must get them (or their parent or guardian if they are under 18) to sign a 'release and consent agreement form' similar to the example shown in Figure 2.25. Failure to do this could result in legal action being taken by a person featured in your programme.

Remember!

A recent advertising campaign for a telephone directory company included two figures dressed up as 1970s-style athletes. A famous athlete from this period, who they closely resembled, tried to sue the production company and the client as he had not been consulted or paid for the use of his image.

So be aware of copyright and permissions issues, not just regarding the people you use but also the images that you portray.

Planning resources for post-production

It is easy to get bogged down with the organisation for the actual shoot, recording or creation of other original material, and forget to plan for post-production. You must plan ahead for your *whole* project during pre-production, and this includes the post-production phase too. Imagine that you have produced all of your original material and you now have to edit it into a final product. You have forgotten to book a computer for your editing and the only machine available is an old, slow machine that that does not have the right software installed.

Do you:

- sit in the corner and cry?
- wait for three weeks until the right equipment is available and miss your deadline?
- find an alternative piece of equipment and pay over the odds for its use?

None of these are satisfactory solutions. If only you had planned in advance you would have had a trouble-free edit!

You must remember to:

- book facilities
- ensure hardware and software are available
- book appropriate crew (e.g. editor, graphic designer, sound engineer, interactive designer, layout artist and support staff)
- check again to make sure your bookings are in place once your production phase has started.

On the following pages you will find examples of planning documents that you could use to plan your own production and post-production.

Theory into practice 12

Using the post-production planning form shown in Figure 2.30 on page 74, start to plan how you will undertake your post-production.

You will need to consider the following:

- equipment
- software and hardware
- personnel
- material
- time.

Use the post-production form to plan how and when you will start and finish your post-production. Add this to your pre-production folder. **P3**

Demonstrate that you have considered all the elements you need for post-production. **M3**

Grading tip

To reach Distinction level, your documentation should be produced independently and show that you understand professional practice.

Theory into practice 13

Before you start the production cycle of your media product you should consider the following points:

- Have I completed all of my pre-production paperwork?
- Do I have enough information to allow me to start producing my media material?
- Is there enough evidence in my folder to demonstrate that I have done my pre-production thoroughly?
- Have I done a risk assessment?
- Do all my crew understand what I am doing?
- Is my client happy with my planning?
- Do I have enough resources to undertake my production work?
- Do I have sufficient time to complete my work? **P3**

Grading tips

To reach Merit level, make sure your review is comprehensive and covers all the main issues.

To reach Distinction level, your documentation should be produced independently and show that you have an understanding of professional practice.

Case study

Recycle.com

Joshua, Willomena, James and Rani are confident that they have done all the necessary planning for production and post-production.

They have checked that the resources they need are available.

They have produced all the pre-production documentation they require.

They have identified their team members and have all their contact details

They can now move on to the production and post-production phase of their Recycle.com project.

Key Terms

Pre-production is preparing of all the elements needed for successful production.

Production is the actual process of making a product, such as recording or filming material.

Media Productions (MP)
Video and New Media Production

Location Permission Form

Media Productions request permission to use any footage filmed at the following location –

....

in any programme defined as broadcast or non-broadcast or for commercial exploitation by a client.

Media Productions undertakes to abide by any directions from the management of the above location with regard to filming positions/ health and safety/audience safety.

Media Productions undertake to ensure that all filming will be undertaken in a professional manner taking account of changes during the shooting period as defined below.

Date of location shoot...Sunday 10th July 2007

Programme...Revelator Band - promo and pilot programme

Signed on behalf of Media Productions..

Date...

Signed on behalf of the above location..

Designation..

Date...

Figure 2.24: Location permission form. ▶

Key Terms

Post-production is shaping and manipulating the material to form a finished product.

Logistics is managing and controlling the resources needed for production and post-production.

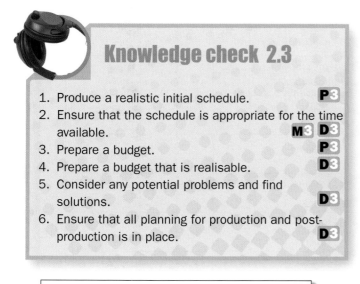

Knowledge check 2.3

1. Produce a realistic initial schedule. **P3**
2. Ensure that the schedule is appropriate for the time available. **M3 D3**
3. Prepare a budget. **P3**
4. Prepare a budget that is realisable. **D3**
5. Consider any potential problems and find solutions. **D3**
6. Ensure that all planning for production and post-production is in place. **D3**

Media Productions MP
LOCATION PLANNING SHEET

	Day 1	Day 2	Day 3	Day 4	Day 5	Day 6
Studio						
Location						
Equipment						
Crew						
Actors						
Props						
Transport						
Post-production						

▲ **Figure 2.26: Location planning sheet.**

Media Productions MP
Video and New Media Production

RELEASE AND CONSENT AGREEMENT

Name.. (

Date...   )

Producers name and address
herein called The Producers

Production title / event
....

Location..

Thank you for your assistance with the above production/event, Our agreement is as follows:

a) You hereby grant the Producers the sole and exclusive rights to record, edit and distribute your participation in (   ) on the (   ) at (   ) you consent to the use of your name, likeness, voice and biographical material in connection with the publicity and exploitation of such sequences forever.

b) All rights in the (   ) shall vest with the Producers and they shall be entitled to assign, licensed and/or exploit the same by means and in all media as they may at their discretion elect.

c) In full consideration for all rights and benefits hereby granted by you to the Producers they shall pay the following fees or provide the following considerations:

d) This agreement shall be freely assignable by the Producers and shall be interpreted in accordance with the laws of England and Wales and Scotland and especially the Copyright Designs and patents Act 1988.

Kindly indicate your acceptance of the above by signing and returning to the Producers the enclosed duplicate agreement.

Yours faithfully

Read, understood and agreed by

.... Dated
....

▲ **Figure 2.25: Release and consent agreement.**

Media Productions MP
Video and New Media Production

Pre-production planner

	Week 1	Week 2	Week 3	Week 4	Week 5	Week 6
Ideas Development						
Research						
Proposal						
Treatment						
Script						
Storyboard						
Review (with client)						
Book equipment						

▲ **Figure 2.27: Pre-production planner.**

Media Productions MP
Video and New Media Production

PRE-PRODUCTION DIARY

Project: Mary Hirst Trust

Pre-production tasks	Date started	Date completed
Write to head office for permission to film in the offices.	Monday 13th May	Monday 14th May
Contact Gearhouse for quote on hiring HD Camera.	Tuesday 14th May	Tuesday 14th May Email received with quote

▲ Figure 2.28: Pre-production diary.

Media Productions MP
Video and New Media Production

Production Planner

	Week 1	Week 2	Week 3	Week 4	Week 5	Week 6
Studio						
Location						
Equipment						
Crew						
Actors						
Props						
Transport						
Edit suite						

▲ Figure 2.29: Production planner.

Media Productions MP
Video and New Media Production

Post-production Planner

	Week 1	Week 2	Week 3	Week 4	Week 5	Week 6
Logging material						
Finding resources						
Preparing master/s						
Editing material						
Reviewing edit						
Producing initial version						
Review (with client)						
Produce master						

▲ Figure 2.30: Post-production planner.

End of Unit assessment

Preparation for assessment

Your local council has invited you to produce a television commercial to publicise a major arts festival in your area. The commercial will be shown on regional television at prime time. The council has already decided on the style and content of the commercial and you have been commissioned to produce the finished product. The arts festival will be taking place in four months' time and the council will need to be reassured that the commercial will be ready on time.

In Unit 3: Production management project, you are asked to produce a proposal or pitch and undertake the management of this project. You must now undertake pre-production work for this commission.

End of Unit assessment activity 1

You must produce a report or presentation that clearly demonstrates your understanding of the requirements for this production. Provide relevant examples of the resources you require with justification as to why this will be necessary for this project. You will have some constraints on your budget so you must be really clear about why these are required

- To achieve a pass grade you must demonstrate your understanding of the requirements for this production. **P1**

- To achieve a merit grade you must demonstrate understanding of the requirements for production with reference to well-chosen examples. **M1**

- To achieve a distinction grade you must provide examples of materials, resources and personnel that you have considered and then rejected. You could give reasons for your rejection of these and indicate what you have chosen instead **D1**

Arts Fest

Date as postmarked

Dear Sir/Madam,

Arts Fest is a major arts festival that will bring together many art forms from across the whole community. We intend this festival to be representative of the whole spectrum of art, performance and music.

Arts Fest will take place in May and last for six days. We need to attract a wide audience for this event in order to make it a financial success. There will be performances of both popular and classical music, exhibitions of art across a wide range of styles and the staging of several plays in various venues. We intend to make this festival a real community event with exhibitions from a range of community organisations, a 'real ale' festival and a street parade. We have already secured sponsorship from a local brewery and a major clothing retailer.

The council has asked me to commission you to produce a television commercial that we intend to show on regional television prior to the festival. The commercial will emphasise the community nature of the event while generating interest across a wide audience. We need the commercial to be thirty (30) seconds in length and it must include information about the wide range of events on offer.

I would be grateful if you could proceed with planning the production of the commercial. I would like to meet with you once you have completed your pre-production work to ensure that we have everything in place.

Yours faithfully

Bilal Mudawi

Arts Fest

▲ Figure 2.31: Commissioning letter from the Arts Fest organiser.

End of Unit assessment activity 2

You must gather together all the resources required for production. This will include making bookings for equipment, sourcing materials, researching the availability of specialist materials or techniques, identifying and contracting crew and talent and storing this information accurately. Store all this information in a folder so that you can find it easily.

- To achieve a pass grade you may gather resources for production with help from your teacher **P2**
- To achieve a merit grade you must gather your resources for production competently. You should demonstrate that you understand how to do this task and ask your teacher for help occasionally. **M2**
- To achieve a distinction grade you should compare what you have produced to a professionally produced pre-production folder. You could provide evidence of your independent working through a pre-production diary. This diary could list all the activities you have undertaken, comments on how you found information yourself and even comments from your teacher on how you have worked independently. The emphasis should be on how you obtained resources, equipment, researched for talent and crew and stored this information. **D2**

End of Unit assessment activity 3

You must be able to apply all of your work to the production process. To do this you must produce all the relevant documentation you require for production.

Produce your pre-production file that contains:

- the proposal and treatment
- a production schedule
- all your bookings, planning, location recces and contingency plans
- all your health and safety investigations and risk assessments
- your planning for post-production resources.

  - To achieve a pass grade you must apply your production logistics to the production and may have some help from your teacher. **P2**

- To achieve a merit grade you must apply your production logistics competently and only ask your teacher to help you when it is really necessary. **M3**
- To achieve a distinction grade you should reflect on the way in which media professionals apply production llogistics. You must demonstrate that you can do this independently and in a way that reflects how a professional would work. The emphasis will be on the quality and accuracy of your budget and planning for production together with the quality of your documentation. **D3**

You should review your pre-production work as part of Unit 4: Working to a brief in the media industries. You will be able to comment on the effectiveness of your pre-production work as part of this unit.

Grading Criteria						
To achieve a pass grade the evidence must show that the learner is able to:	TiP	To achieve a merit grade the evidence must show that the learner is able to:	TiP	To achieve a distinction grade the evidence must show that the learner is able to:	TiP	Activity
P1 demonstrate understanding of requirements for production	1 2 3	**M1** competently demonstrate understanding of requirements for production with reference to well-chosen examples	1 2 3 4	**D1** thoroughly demonstrate understanding of requirements for production with supporting justification and elucidated examples	1 2 3	End of Unit assessment activity 1
P2 apply gathering of resources for production with some assistance	4 5	**M2** apply gathering of resources for production competently with only occasional assistance	4 5	**D2** apply gathering of resources for production to near-professional standards, working independently to professional expectations	4 5	End of Unit assessment activity 2
P3 apply production logistics with some assistance	8 10 11	**M3** apply production logistics competently with only occasional assistance	6 7 8 9 10 11	**D3** apply production logistics to near-professional standards, working independently to professional expectations	6 7 8 9 10 11 12 13	End of Unit assessment activity 3

Production management project

Introduction

To work successfully on a media product you need to understand the role that production management plays. Whatever the media product is, a promotional video or DVD, a print product, a radio programme, a website or a computer game, you will have to ensure that production goes smoothly. This will involve managing the pre-production, production and post-production phases of the project.

In this unit you will learn how to originate and research suitable ideas for a media product. You will develop these ideas into a proposal that you will 'pitch' to a client or your tutor. Finally, you will learn how to manage the production process to ensure the project runs smoothly.

You could use this unit to demonstrate both your management of a media product and your skills in production. For instance, you could use your work on this unit to manage a corporate and promotional programme you are making in Unit 27. The production management project skills you demonstrate when producing this product could provide evidence for your work on this unit. This unit contains a variety of activities, exercises and case studies that will help you to understand and put into practice production management project techniques.

After completing this unit you should be able to achieve the following outcomes:

- Be able to originate and research ideas for a media product.
- Be able to pitch a proposal for a media product.
- Be able to manage the production process to create a media product.

Think it over

Working in the media industries may require you to take control of the production of a media product. Many media products are made by a team of people, with one person leading the team. The skills needed to lead a team are essential life skills and are transferable into whatever career you choose to follow.

The teams you work in will contain people with a range of skills and creativity. Allocating people appropriate roles and developing their skills and talents is an essential element of production management. Your media project will come to life with the correct composition, management and enthusiasm of the team.

You will gain experience in production management from the initial development of ideas right through to the planning and production of the media product. This will mean managing a team of your friends and classmates. Think about how you will ensure that they do what you want them to do. Of course, you can offer to work for them in return.

Managing a project can be really exciting. To see a project through from your initial idea to the finished product can be very rewarding.

Production processes

You need to understand the processes that you go through when producing your media product. Look again at the diagram on page 48 at the beginning of Unit 2 to remind yourself of what these are.

This unit requires you to control the whole process of pre-production, production and post-production. As you can see from the diagram (Figure 2.01) there are a number of stages you will have to go through when managing your media product.

It is important to remember that whatever product you choose to make, these stages and the management skills needed for them will be similar.

The first stage you will need to address is the origination of appropriate **ideas** for your media product. This will involve a number of different tasks.

Ideas

First of all you must think about the medium you intend to use for your media product. For instance, will you produce a video programme, an audio recording, a website, a computer game, a magazine or a poster?

Whatever medium you choose you will need to come up with appropriate ideas. One way of deciding on which ideas to use is to undertake a mind mapping exercise. This involves thinking of a number of ideas and then assessing each one on the grounds of suitability, availability of resources and size of the project, and rejecting any that are not going to be appropriate.

Case study

Recycle.com

In this unit you will be following a group of four learners. They have been asked by their client, an environmental organisation called Recycle.com, to prepare some ideas for media products. They will then manage the production of their products from concept to delivery.

Recycle.com wants to make young people much more aware of environmental issues. It has decided to launch a campaign aimed at 12–16 year-olds to highlight the dangers of global warming and show how young people can help by recycling.

Recycle.com has asked the learners to come up with some ideas for the campaign. It has suggested that it would like a range of media products to help get the message across to its audience.

Joshua is producing a website, Willomena is producing a video programme, James is producing a radio programme and Rani is producing a newsletter.

The learners have decided to work as a team to help each other with the production of their media products. They will individually manage their own media product using the other team members as crew and talent.

Case study

Media Productions

Media Productions is a production company that makes a range of media products. It has been commissioned by a local manufacturer of pottery to produce a video programme about a line of kitchenware. This particular line, called Yorkshire Blue, has been produced by the company on the same site for over 100 years.

The team at Media Productions has an in-house producer whose job it is to oversee the development and production of all their video projects. The producer has arranged a meeting with the client, Yorkshire Pottery, to discuss their requirements.

At the meeting the Media Productions team is told that the client needs a programme that shows the public how their range of kitchenware is produced. They want to show this video at the 'point-of-sale' in the kitchenware departments of large stores.

The team and client arrange to meet again in five days once Media Productions has had time to come up with a concept for discussion.

Back in the office the team put all their ideas on to a mind map. They then discuss each idea fully before rejecting some and finally coming to decision to develop one particular idea. See Figure 3.01.

You can see from their mind map that the Media Productions team thought of a wide range of ideas. They decided against some of the ideas on grounds of cost and others on the grounds of feasibility.

Ideas have to be feasible in the timeframe that the client has given them. In this case they have to produce the programme in time for a launch of the new range of products in three months' time. In order to complete the work on time the team has to dismiss the idea of a location shoot in the USA – a key market for the product.

They also have to reject the idea of simply providing lots of still images, edited together to make a slide show. The producer has suggested to the client that the programme should focus on the age of the range and its 'retro' look. This would not come across in a simple slide show.

After consideration, the team decides that the programme should be based on the traditional values represented by the kitchenware. The programme researcher has found that this range of kitchenware has been used in a number of UK television programmes and films as it reflects a very traditional British image.

The team wants to build on this and so suggests that the programme focuses on the fact that the product is produced in a traditional way.

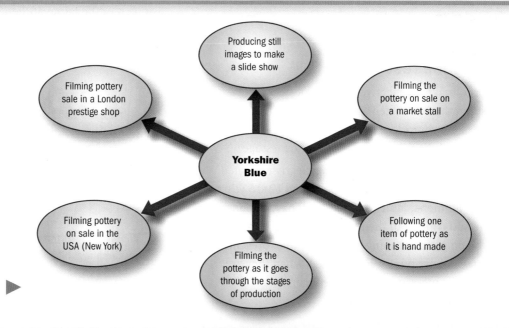

Figure 3.01: Media Productions' mind map considered a number of ideas.

■ Audience research

In order to make an effective media product you must understand the **audience** you are intending to reach. Consider how your ideas might reflect the age of the audience and how they would receive the message.

In the case of Recycle.com, they have clearly indicated that they want to reach young people aged 12–16 years. Joshua, Willomena, James and Rani will have to consider the style and content of their media products carefully. It would be no good planning a media product presented by a cartoon fluffy bunny, for instance, when they are trying to get a message across to teenagers.

▲ Figure 3.02: Know your target audience. There is little point including the latest chart music in a programme aimed at retired people.

You will have to take into consideration the number and type of viewers you can expect to watch your product. This is particularly important when you are planning to make a broadcast programme. Your client will want to be sure that for the money they are spending they will reach as much of the target audience as possible.

There are a variety of organisations that can provide figures for audience reach.

▲ Figure 3.03: RAJAR, BARB and ELSPA are all audience research organisations.

Just as you have to think about the age of the audience, you will have to think about their gender. There are some elements that may not be suitable for a male audience or equally for a female audience.

There may be socio-economic issues relevant to the group being targeted that you need to take into account.

Think it over 1

Knowing your audience is key to success. A television broadcaster has decided to produce a quiz programme based on a format of a darts match in a pub. The contestants have to hit a certain score with a dart in order to answer general knowledge questions.

Would the producer decide to ask questions about Greek tragedy or celebrity gossip?

■ Content research

In order to identify the style and **content** of your media product you will need to undertake research.

Primary research:

- interviews with the intended audience
- preparing a questionnaire to find out the audience's views
- using your own observations of the intended audience.

Secondary research:

- looking at existing media products to see how they have been produced
- using the Internet or looking at magazines to see how other people have made their products.

You may also be able to research your competitors in the market place for your media products.

You may be able to gather together a **focus group** of people from your target audience. If so, you could ask them questions, show them some examples of your ideas and ask for their feedback.

Once you have carefully undertaken your research you will need to collate the information you have gathered and use it to inform the production team of your media product.

Case study

Media Productions

The researcher for the production team at Media Productions had been given the task of looking at the content and style of the proposed product.

He used a variety of research methods to identify what the target audience might want to see, for instance:

- **asking current purchasers of Yorkshire Blue what would attract them in a point-of-sale programme**
- **asking shoppers in several high-street stores about the Yorkshire Blue range, and if they knew how it was made**
- **watching existing 'point-of-sale' material used in stores.**

The researcher presented his findings to the rest of the team.

Key Term

Focus group is a group of people drawn from the audience the production company wants to target. They are invited to offer ideas and give opinions about proposed products.

Figure 3.04: Focus groups and questionnaires are excellent methods of collecting primary research data.

Constraints

You will find that there will be **constraints** on the way that you plan to produce your product. As a production manager you will have to take these into account when planning your production.

These constraints could be:

- Time – will you have sufficient time to complete all the work on the media product?
- Costs – will you have sufficient budget to make the product?
- Personnel – will you be able to find the right crew to make your product, and can you get permission from people appearing in your production?
- Legal and ethical considerations – will you get permission to use locations; will you be making statements that might offend people?
- Codes of practice – will you be following the codes of practice as laid down for some areas of the media e.g. doorstepping interviews, filming covertly?
- Copyright – will you able to ensure that any material you use in your production is copyright free or that you have obtained clearance to use it?

As a production manager it is your responsibility to ensure that any constraints have been identified and cleared before you begin the production process.

Figure 3.05: Detailed planning is essential if you want to avoid disasters like this.

Case study

Recycle.com

Joshua, Willomena, James and Rani have all undertaken some initial research with their target audience and meet up to discuss their progress.

Joshua produced a questionnaire that gave him information on what young people want to see on a website.

Willomena looked at other video programmes on recycling and then asked a small focus group of young people what would encourage them to recycle.

James listened to some radio programmes and commercials and then asked young people what they would like to hear in a radio commercial.

Rani drew up a simple front page for her newsletter and asked a sample of young people what they thought about its style and content.

They all presented the results for their research to the rest of the group. The group then discussed the research findings and gave some feedback.

Each member of the group found this useful as it gave them extra information that they could use in their planning.

Contingency

You will need to make **contingency** plans to ensure that your production goes smoothly. This might involve:

- keeping part of the budget to one side in case costs rise
- planning extra days for producing and editing your material in case of equipment failure
- having extra equipment available in case of faults or damage
- having extra talent and crew on stand-by in case of sickness
- allowing time for unforeseen circumstances.

Refer back to the case study in Unit 2 page 63 to see an example of how Media Productions used their contingency budget.

Key Terms

Audience research is research undertaken to determine audience needs.

Content research is research to discover what style and content an audience would prefer.

Constraints are the potential problems you might encounter when planning and producing a product.

Contingency is planning for unforeseen circumstances. It requires an amount of vision to see where issues might arise, e.g. if a camera does not work or if the weather is too bad to film. A contingency plan will make allowances for this.

Keeping records

To help you keep track of decisions and why you made them you should keep careful records of meetings, conversations and decisions.

Remember!

It is important to keep careful records of all the decisions you make. You should record all of your ideas, stating why they were or were not suitable, and why some ideas were chosen and others rejected.

You must also keep your own records of management decisions you take, including contingency plans.

Your research work should be carefully collated and stored with easy access to the information.

It is important to find appropriate research that is not simply downloaded material from the Internet.

All of this material will help you to produce evidence of your individual production management work.

Case study

Recycle.com

Joshua, Willomena, James and Rani have kept detailed records of all their meetings. This allows them to demonstrate where, when and why they have made decisions and what these decisions were.

This is an example of one of the meeting record sheets produced by Joshua, Willomena, James and Rani.

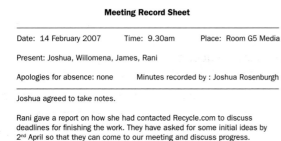

Meeting Record Sheet

Date: 14 February 2007   Time: 9.30am   Place: Room G5 Media

Present: Joshua, Willomena, James, Rani

Apologies for absence: none   Minutes recorded by : Joshua Rosenburgh

Joshua agreed to take notes.

Rani gave a report on how she had contacted Recycle.com to discuss deadlines for finishing the work. They have asked for some initial ideas by 2nd April so that they can come to our meeting and discuss progress.

Willomena has done some research into recycling companies and presented to the group some videos she has found. The group looked at the images and decided that they needed to make sure that all the products they produced were as good as these.

James said that he had listened to a number of radio commercials but could not find any about recycling. Joshua suggested that he contacted Radio Zero and ask them if they had ever produced any commercials of this type, and if so have they got any examples.

Rani had found some really useful websites on recycling and showed the group what she had found.

We all agreed to help each other to find research materials.

Willomena asked if we could help her with her production as she needed a sound person, a production assistant and someone to look after the lighting. We all agreed to help in whatever way we could.

The meeting finished at 10.30am.

Date of next meeting – 28 February 2007

▲ **Figure 3.06: Meeting record sheet.**

Theory into practice 1

Think of ideas for a media product that you can produce.

To do this you should:

Task 1 Identify the media product you would like to produce. **P1**

Task 2 Decide what the format of the media product will be. **P1**

Task 3 Produce at least five ideas for the content and style of your media product. **M1**

Task 4 Undertake a mind mapping exercise for all the ideas you have for content and style. **M1**

Task 5 Finalise your ideas for content and style by undertaking research with the target audience. **D1**

Task 6 Identify the constraints on production and make plans to cover this. **P1**

Task 7 Prepare a contingency plan. **M1**

Grading tip

To reach Distinction level, you should show that you can use professional techniques for developing your ideas. You should show creativity and flair in the development of your ideas.

Knowledge check 3.1

1. Think of ideas for a media product. **P1**

2. Research your ideas as much as possible using the Internet, libraries and market research. **M1**

3. Map out your ideas using a mind map, and reject any unworkable ideas. **M1** **D1**

4. Once you have come up with your final idea develop a contingency plan for it. **D1**

Proposal, pitch and treatment

You have identified your media product, conducted research into content and style and made your contingency plans.

The next stage is to present your ideas to the client. This is undertaken in a number of ways in the media industries. It may be that you send a **proposal** to the client that 'sells' your idea for the product. This is generally the norm in many of the media industries. There are many formats for a proposal but for the purposes of this unit you will be following the proposal that was produced by Media Productions for their point-of-sale programme for Yorkshire Blue. You will be able to adapt their proposal format for whatever media product you are proposing to produce.

Whatever proposal format you use you must remember to 'sell' your idea in an appropriate way to the client. They need to understand exactly what you are proposing so that they can then ask you for more detail.

This further detail would be in the form of a **treatment** The treatment develops your ideas further and provides the client with sufficient information for them to make a decision on whether or not to commission you to produce the work.

The proposal

The proposal is a document in which you set out your ideas to sell to a client. The proposal should include sufficient information for the reader to understand what you intend to do. The proposal has been described as a sales tool – in other words, it is used to whet the appetite of a potential client.

Figure 3.07 has been prepared by Media Productions for their kitchenware client.

Case study

Media productions

Media Productions has a staff of specialists. The company has identified that they want to employ staff who are multi-skilled. This is becoming the norm in many media production companies.

The team comprises John – a researcher, Katie – a producer, Bill – a director, Mary – an editor, Thomas – a website designer who also designs DVD menus, and Sally – an assistant producer.

This team meets on a regular basis to discuss on-going projects. Each team member has an equal voice in the discussion. They are able to offer each other advice and where needed practical support. In this way they are all developing new skills. They are also developing a team culture of mutual support.

Their production manager is Sharon who co-ordinates the development of the various productions. This might involve managing five or six programmes at any one time.

All of these people need to understand what each other does and at some stage have an opportunity to try these roles for themselves. The management at Media Productions wants the team to be trained in all areas of media production as this means productions can run smoothly should someone be missing when a programme is being produced.

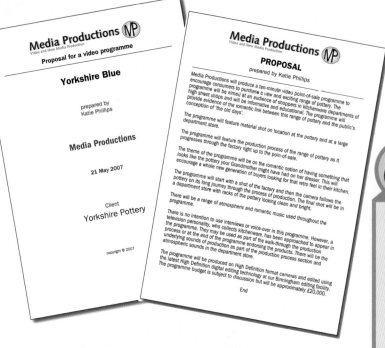

Figure 3.07: Media Productions' proposal for their kitchenware client. Note that this has been copyrighted.

Key Terms

Proposal is a document that sells your idea to a client or commissioner.

Pitch is a verbal presentation that allows for the expansion of the key points of a proposal. Generally a pitch is made to a client or commissioner.

As you can see the proposal is used to 'sell' the preferred idea to the client. In this instance the main concept is a romantic approach. It also gives the client an idea about detail options, such as featuring a celebrity and the use of sounds and music.

Your proposal should be a based on an idea that is feasible and something you really feel you could make. It can be in whatever media format you want to use.

The example proposal you have seen is short and to the point. It is generally accepted that a proposal should be no more than two sides of A4 paper (not including a front cover with your contact details).

Figure 3.08: Inappropriate selling techniques will adversely affect both the sales and the reputation of the product.

■ Audience factors

When Media Productions were writing their proposal they had to consider just who would look at the programme and where they would look at it. They had to consider the language level and style, the music to use for the appropriate audience and the kind of images they might want to see.

It would be inappropriate, for instance, to produce a programme aimed at kitchenware buyers in a department store and then use drum and bass music as the soundtrack. Equally, if you were producing a project for very young children you would not include images of violence and swearing.

Legal and ethical factors

Media Productions also had to consider legal and ethical issues when preparing the proposal. It would be no good preparing a proposal if there was a problem with the use of copyright material proposed for the project. There might also be issues of representation where the client does not want women to be stereotyped as working in a kitchen, or where there might be images that would alienate some parts of society.

Once you have produced your proposal you should pitch it to the client. In your case this might be your teacher.

The pitch

The process of selling your proposal to your client is called a **pitch**. This is a method used extensively in the media industries.

Whatever your product is, be it a video, poster, radio programme or publication, the pitch is your chance to demonstrate to your client the feasibility of the product. In the pitch you can also show your client how you intend to be creative and enthuse them with your skills and flair.

Presentation

There is a variety of ways you can choose to make your pitch, but you should try to be as creative as possible to demonstrate to your client that you are capable of undertaking this work. A common way of pitching your proposal is to produce a presentation. This might be:

- using a software programme that generates slides
- a sample of your product handed out to the client plus a verbal presentation
- a video that demonstrates how the product could appear.

Whichever way you choose to do your presentation you must provide the following materials for the assessment of your work:

- notes of your presentation for the client
- samples of your ideas, where appropriate
- a copy of the presentation, software and hard copy, as appropriate.

Your teacher will be observing you in the pitching process and will probably be making notes about you. You should prepare for the pitch by practising your delivery, ensuring that the slides work and that other visual/audio material is cued up and ready to roll.

Case study

Recycle.com

Joshua, Willomena, James and Rani have each prepared a pitch for their client. They have created extra material for their pitch based on the comments they gave each other on their proposals.

Joshua has found some samples of websites that provide an illustration of what he is proposing. He intends to include some screen grabs in his presentation. He has also produced a handout with copies of his slides and a space for comments.

Willomena has found some interesting video footage and intends to take some small samples of each and include them in her presentation. She has found that the video clips can be imported into her presentation software. She has cleared copyright with the video creator. She will also be presenting the client with an illustrated handout.

James has researched carefully all the radio items he could find on recycling. He has taken the transcript of some of these and intends to include them in his presentation. This will show the client that he has thought carefully about the way that radio can be used to put over a message. After talking to the other members of the group he has decided to have a music track playing as he makes his presentation. This will be the same music he thinks he will use in his radio programme.

Rani has found some interesting images in her research. She is going to incorporate these into her presentation. She will also use these as examples of the type of images she intends to use in her newsletter. She has already had some initial thoughts about a layout and intends to include these in her presentation and in her handout.

It is important to make your presentation as professional as possible. Think about including:

- images
- video
- sound
- page layouts.

Make presenter's notes so that you do not stumble over your words. Keep eye contact with your client or audience.

You should be prepared to answer any questions the client has about your presentation. Think before you respond and ensure that what you say is what you mean.

Figure 3.09 shows the first two slides of the presentation produced by Media Productions for their kitchenware client. You will see that they have started with a clear identification of who they are and who they have worked for on previous projects.

Note that Media Productions have taken time to theme their presentation. They have thought about selling themselves as a production company.

The rest of the pitch consisted of a number of slides detailing:

- research they have undertaken
- results of that research
- ideas for their media product
- skills that they will bring to this project
- timeframe for completion
- the care that they will take to produce the right media product
- methods they will use ensure complete customer satisfaction
- sample thumbnails/sketches/storyboards/scripts
- an outline budget for the project.

This is only an initial development of their ideas. Media Productions always make it very clear to the client that should they be successful in their pitch they will produce a detailed treatment for the client. This treatment will go into more depth and detail and will provide the client with a final budget.

The treatment will also provide more evidence of the research undertaken and a justification for the intended delivery format of the product.

Case study

Recycle.com

Joshua, Willomena, James and Rani have decided to pitch their proposals using PowerPoint presentations and a data projector on a large screen.

Joshua has included some samples of web pages he has produced for another client. He has also prepared some initial ideas of how the site might look. Although these are only simple ideas at this stage, it does demonstrate his creativity and flair.

Willomena has produced some ideas for the video and a page of a storyboard. She has also added some video clips to her presentation to show what she has produced in a previous project.

James has added some sample sound clips to his presentation.

Rani has produced a basic page layout for the front cover of her newsletter. She has also included in her presentation some simple sketches of suggested artwork.

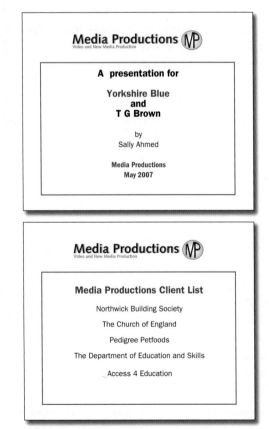

Figure 3.09: First two slides of a pitch presentation.

The creative director at Media Productions pitched the proposal to the managing director at Yorkshire Pottery in a meeting at the client's head office. This is how they recorded the results of the meeting.

Media Productions MP

Video and New Media Production

CLIENT MEETING RECORD SHEET

Date: 1 March 2007   Time: 10.45   Place: Yorkshire Pottery HQ

Present: Graham Meade (Media Productions)
Susan Spencer (MD Yorkshire Pottery)
James Sibrucarmy (Marketing Director Yorkshire Pottery)

Apologies for absence: None

1 GM introduced the concept of the idea for the point of sale project.

2 GM presented the proposal on a PP presentation and talked about the ideas as they arose.

3 GM asked for comments.

4 SS liked the idea but was a little concerned about the logistics of filming in the factory.

5 JS suggested that this would not be a problem and that he could arrange for department store location.

6 JS thought that the romantic idea was fine but really needed more detail of what the final programme would look like.

7 GM suggested that Media Productions could develop the idea further if they were happy with the concept.

8 JS and SS thought that this would be a sensible idea and agreed to Media Productions developing the idea further.

9 GM suggested that the team at Media Productions produce a treatment that explored the idea further and expanded on the content.

10 This was agreed and date for a further meeting was agreed.

Date of next meeting: 23 March 2007.

▲ **Figure 3.10: Client meeting record sheet. The record is made in a succinct form, using short sentences, numbered points and initials.**

Grading tip

To reach Distinction level, you should use subject terminology correctly and express your ideas fluently. For example:

'The programme will feature material shot on location at a large school, a waste recycling plant and a large landfill site. The programme will be fronted by a well-known environmental spokesperson and will be accompanied by music from a chart band. We have approached Coldplay to provide an appropriate track and their response has been positive.'

'The spokesperson will appear on screen when interviewing the young people about the choices they are about to make. Graphics will be used to reinforce the facts and figures about the effects of pollution on the planet.'

'The programme will be produced on digital format cameras and edited using the latest digital editing technology at our Birmingham editing facility.'

'The programme budget is subjected to discussion but will be approximately £20,000.'

The treatment

The **treatment** is the development of your idea from the proposal. It should include:

- an indication of the size and content of the product
- an initial script/storyline (where applicable)
- an indication of the proposed production schedule
- an estimated cost for production
- an idea of the personnel involved in the project
- a contingency plan
- a storyboard/mood board/thumbnails/layouts/ schematics
- any research carried out for the production.

A treatment should be produced in DTP and look professional.

Here is an example of a treatment form produced by Media Productions for their client.

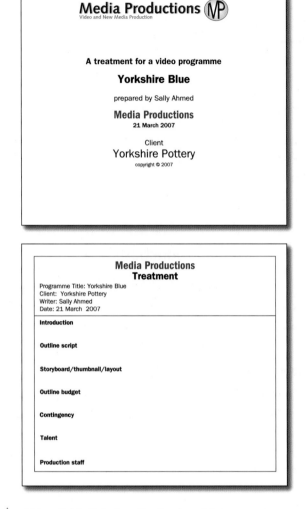

Figure 3.11: Note how the treatment is organised and how headings are used.

Case study

Recycle.com

Joshua, Willomena, James and Rani have successfully pitched their proposal and have been given the go-ahead to prepare treatments.

Their treatments indicate to Recycle.com the estimated budget, a schedule for production and a more detailed description of their final products.

They send their treatments to the client and wait for approval before starting the production process.

■ Treatment structure

It is important that the treatment provides as much detail as possible for the client. The headings on the second page of the treatment allow the writer to organise the extra detail needed.

Introduction

This is a short opening section that summarises the original proposal and the approach that you will take to develop the idea. This is an opportunity for you to really sell both yourself and the idea.

Outline script

In order to understand what actual resources you may need, and the timing of your work, you will need to produce an outline script. This brings together your ideas into a format that clearly demonstrates how the product will progress, and what it will look like when it is finished.

In order to complete the outline script you must have a clear picture of your media product.

Storyboard/thumbnail/layout

The storyboard is a paper visualisation of the product. It helps to form ideas about the way that the visual and sound elements work together.

Feature films and television productions will have developed a comprehensive storyboard before a single frame is shot. This is done to ensure that all of the scenes are feasible before expensive equipment is hired and staff employed.

Thumbnails are smaller versions of pictures being used in a printed or interactive media project. They give the client an idea of the style of images you will be using in the product.

Layouts can give clients a good idea of how the product will look.

Outline budget

It is essential that you understand the budgetary requirements of your planned project. You will have to produce a realistic budget for the product that you are producing. You must use real examples of equipment hire and other costs when developing your budget.

Contingency

It is not always possible to plan a production down to the last detail, especially if things change as the production progresses. There may be a number of reasons for changes to happen, such as:

- the client changes their mind about the content of the product after agreement has been reached
- the price of materials or equipment changes once production has started
- an actor is ill or suddenly unavailable
- equipment breaks down during a production
- severe weather conditions mean you cannot work on location and have to hire a studio.

Contingency planning allows for unexpected events both in the schedule and the budget.

Talent

This is where the ideas for appropriate performers, presenters and voice-over artists can be added. It will give the client a real feel for who might be in their project.

Production staff

This is an opportunity to tell the client which staff, or hired-in personnel, will be working on the project.

Case study

Media productions

Media Productions included a contingency plan in their treatment. They then produced a budget with a 10 per cent figure to pay for any unforeseen circumstances – something they have been very glad of in the past.

In a recent production the actor chosen to appear was taken ill at the last moment. This meant that a new actor had to be found, auditioned and a new date agreed with them for when they were available. The original actor's illness and no-show also meant that the equipment booked for the original shoot was no longer required on that day and had to be rebooked. This incurred a cost with the hire company, which was also covered by the contingency budget.

Theory into practice 3

You must now produce a treatment. This should be word-processed and presented in an appropriate format. **P2**

You must include all the key elements of the production to ensure that your client has all the information they need to make a final decision on your proposed product. **M2**

You must use appropriate media language when preparing your treatment. **P2**

This might be:

'The team will be managed throughout the process.'
'Accurate records will be kept.'
'I will constantly monitor the progress of the project to ensure completion on time.'
'I will ensure that the material produced will be of the highest quality.'
'I have a contingency plan in place in case of unforeseen situations.'
'The budget will be closely monitored.'
'Any proposed changes to the project will be discussed with the client.'
'Only appropriate crew and talent will be used in this project.'

Grading tip

To reach Distinction level, you should use subject terminology correctly and express your ideas fluently.

Your teacher will tell you what is required from you in the way of a proposal and treatment. This is an essential element of managing a production and the skills you will learn from undertaking this process will be invaluable when producing work for other units in this qualification.

Knowledge check 3.2

1. Produce a proposal and pitch this to your client. **P2**

2. Produce a proposal and pitch this confidently using appropriate language. **M2** **D2**

3. Produce a treatment that includes all the correct elements. **D2**

In this section you will be planning and managing the production of your media product. It is vitally important that you understand the management process. If you do not get this right there is every possibility that your media product will not be fit for purpose, or ready on time.

The production manager should keep accurate records of all of the activities undertaken. A good way to do this is to keep a production diary.

This is an example of part of the production diary the production manager kept when working on the Yorkshire Blue production.

Case study

Media Productions

Media Productions' production manager always keeps a comprehensive production diary. This can help when reviewing the finished product with the client, particularly if there is a dispute. In one instance, for example, a client decided at the last minute that they did not like one particular sequence, and suggested that they had not given approval to this scene.

From records in her production diary, the production manager was able to point to the date and time of a discussion with the client when the content of this scene was discussed and agreed.

Media Productions MP
Video and New Media Production

Production Manager Diary

Name: Sharon Whitehouse

Production: Yorkshire Blue

Date	Action taken
1 August	Met with client to discuss the location at Yorkshire Pottery. Client agreed to contact YP to clear the location shoot.
3 August	Met with cameraperson to discuss issues with camera safety when working on factory sites. Agreed that the camera must be protected against clay material and that this was the responsibility of the camera crew.
7 August	Met with the director to discuss the location shoots. There was agreement on the length of time required for each location shoot – this was set at one day for each location.
15 August	Met with camera crew to brief them on the locations we would be using. Discussed the Health and Safety hazards when working on a factory site. Each member of the crew took a Risk Assessment document and agreed to read and follow the instructions on the form.
16 August	Location day at ABS – weather good. Camera crew arrived thirty minutes late at the location. The management at ABS were expecting us but confirmed with ABS the nature of location shoot and what the footage would be used for. This was completed and confirmed by ABS senior management.

▲ **Figure 3.12: The production manager's diary can be a vital record of events.**

Case study

Recycle.com

Joshua, Willomena, James and Rani have each decided to keep a diary of their production management.

Joshua is going to keep his as a web log (or blog).

Willomena has decided to keep a video diary of all her production management work.

James has devised a simple audio programme where he can record all his work on a daily basis and then copy it onto a CD.

Rani is going to keep a personal diary, but in the style of a newsletter. She feels this will help her to improve her layout skills.

Even though each member of the team has a different method of recording their production management work, they are all aware that they need to keep accurate documentation as well.

They have decided to meet every week to discuss progress and to compare notes on their production management work.

Planning

As stated earlier in this unit, it is vital to the successful completion of your media product that you plan carefully.

Case study

Media Productions

The production manager at Media Productions always chooses her team carefully. She knows the strengths of all the staff and allocates roles on this basis.

On a recent project there was a requirement to film an underwater scene. The production manager knew that one of the camera crew was a qualified diver and so was able to allocate this role to him.

The first thing you must do is identify the production roles that members of your team will be undertaking in this project. You should meet with your team and ensure that everyone understands the role they are to play in the production process.

Case study

Recycle.com

Joshua, Willomena, James and Rani have agreed to help each other with the production of their media products. They have also identified that they may not have the skills for some of the roles required.

Joshua needs someone with photographic skills to produce images for the website. He also needs a graphic artist to design some of the site graphics.

Willomena needs a cameraperson, a sound recordist and an editor for her project.

James needs a sound recordist and an editor for his radio commercial.

Rani needs a journalist, a photographer and a layout artist for her newsletter.

They have agreed to undertake the roles that they have skills in and will look for other colleagues to fill in where necessary.

▲ Figure 3.13: Regular, well-organised production meetings are vital to keep the project on schedule and on budget.

Production meetings

Once you have established your team you will need to hold regular production meetings. These are meetings that you might chair and use to get a progress review of the project. It is essential to minute these meetings in order to provide evidence of your production management skills.

Use the meeting record sheet on page 91 as a basis for your own meeting records. This can be customised with your own name or a company name.

You should appoint a minutes secretary to keep notes, write them up as official minutes and circulate them to all your team members. This will ensure that everyone is kept informed of progress.

These minutes will also help you to monitor the work in progress, see who is not turning up and identify anyone not working as a team member.

Production schedules

The production schedule helps to clarify all of the details of production in one document. It should include details of when the production started and when various activities are planned to take place. This information, although not necessarily industry standard, is vital for your records. The production schedule is a vital piece of evidence for your planning and production work, therefore you must store this carefully and have it available for the assessment of your work.

See section 2.3 starting on page 60 for further information.

Part two of the production schedule gives you a clear picture of the various requirements needed for the production.

Case study

Recycle.com

Joshua, Willomena, James and Rani have each produced a production schedule. They have talked to each other to ensure that their schedules do not overlap.

They will be helping one another, but each one of them is keeping a management file to show how they have managed their resources and personnel.

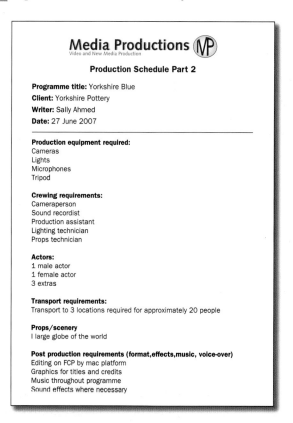

Media Productions Ⓜ️Ⓟ
Video and New Media Production

Production Schedule Part 1

Programme title: Yorkshire Blue
Client: Yorkshire Pottery
Writer: Sally Ahmed
Date: 27 June 2007

	Date		Date
Programme started:	12/4/07	Completed:	
Proposal started:	24/4/07	Completed:	26/4/07
Treatment started:	11/5/07	Completed:	14/5/07
Agreement from Client:	23/5/07		
Shooting script started:	27/6/07	Completed:	9/7/07
Storyboard started:	11/7/07	Completed:	15/7/07
Production started:	12/8/07	Completed:	13/8/07
Post-production started:	16/9/07	Completed:	19/9/07
Rough-cut supplied to client:	21/10/07	Agreed with client: 23/10/07	
Final version completed:	01/11/07		

▲ Figure 3.14: Production schedule part 1.

Media Productions Ⓜ️Ⓟ
Video and New Media Production

Production Schedule Part 2

Programme title: Yorkshire Blue
Client: Yorkshire Pottery
Writer: Sally Ahmed
Date: 27 June 2007

Production equipment required:
Cameras
Lights
Microphones
Tripod

Crewing requirements:
Cameraperson
Sound recordist
Production assistant
Lighting technician
Props technician

Actors:
1 male actor
1 female actor
3 extras

Transport requirements:
Transport to 3 locations required for approximately 20 people

Props/scenery
I large globe of the world

Post production requirements (format,effects,music, voice-over)
Editing on FCP by mac platform
Graphics for titles and credits
Music throughout programme
Sound effects where necessary

▲ Figure 3.15: Production schedule part 2.

Media Productions
Video and New Media Production MP

Media Productions
VIDEO EQUIPMENT AUDIT SHEET

Equipment needed	Available Y	N	If not available where to find it
DV camera	✓		
Tripod	✓		
Microphone	✓		
Lighting kit	✓		available from the Drama Department
DV tapes	✓		4 available, can buy more from Currys
Computer with editing facilities	✓		
Editing software Premier Pro	✓		only two machines have this software installed

Media Productions
PRINT EQUIPMENT AUDIT SHEET

Equipment needed	Available Y	N	If not available where to find it
Digital stills camera	✓		
Tripod	✓		
Memory card	✓		245 available but could borrow 512
Computer with USB/memory	✓		
Colour printer		✓	can use reprographics dept. machine with permission

Media Productions
Video and New Media Production MP

Media Productions
WEB SITE EQUIPMENT AUDIT SHEET

Equipment needed	Available Y	N	If not available where to find it
Digital camera	✓		
Tripod	✓		
Computer with web design software	✓		
Scanner	✓		
Digital sound recorder	✓		available from the Drama Department

Media Productions
SOUND RECORDING EQUIPMENT AUDIT SHEET

Equipment needed	Available Y	N	If not available where to find it
Minidisk recorder	✓		
Microphone	✓		
Computer with sound edit facility	✓		
Minidisks	✓		4 available, can buy from supplier

▲ Figure 3.16: Equipment audit.

As production manager you will use the production schedule to ensure that you keep to deadlines and that you have identified all the resources you will need. You must also ensure that equipment is available and secured for your production or that you can obtain it from elsewhere, if necessary. Record this information on an equipment audit.

Above are examples of equipment audit documents from Media Productions.

Risk assessment

It is important that you take into consideration the possible risks to yourself, your crew and the general public involved in producing your media product. You must consider all the hazards you might encounter in a studio, on location or even in the edit suite.

You may have allocated some of your budget to ensure that there are no problems with health and safety. This might be for security on-site if you are working with famous actors. It may be that you are required to have a safety officer on-site if you are working in a hazardous area. If you do not consider these safety issues then you may find yourself in breach of health and safety legislation.

Think it over 2

There is a wide range of health and safety issues you need to think about when planning your production. You need to refer to several pieces of legislation. The main ones are:

- Health and Safety at Work Act 1974
- The Management of Health and Safety at Work Regulations 1999
- Manual Handling Regulations
- Display Screen Equipment Regulations
- COSHH

What sort of issues do they cover?

You should consider using a risk assessment form, such as the one that Media Productions used in their Yorkshire Blue shoot, for all your locations.

Media Productions (MP)
Video and New Media Production

Risk Assessment Form

Programme title: Yorkshire Blue
Client: Yorkshire Pottery
Writer: John Williams
Producer: Katie Phillips
Director: Bill Smith
Date: 25 July 2007

Major issues/risks

Filming at pottery

1. Waste on factory floor making it dangerous for crew and equipment
2. Machinery operating in the area
3. Visability of crew when on site
4. Contamination of equipment by clay materials and clay dust
5. Lack of electricity supply for equipment

Solutions
Ensure someone checks that area is clear for filming.
Have a look-out person to ensure that crew are aware of operating machinery.
Crew to wear high visibility vests at all times when on site.
All equipment to be covered, where possible, by protective covers.
All equipment to be cleaned before being returned to base.
Portable generator to be available, if required.

Contacts
- Site Safety Manager Bill Brown 0186 314516

Emergency services
- On site services 0186 318817
- Local police 0186 750448
- Local fire 0186 569910
- Local hospital 0186 827765

Figure 3.17: Risk assessment form.

Key Terms

Production schedule is a document or set of documents that detail production activities, provide dates and times, list crew and talent and requirements for resources.

Equipment audit is an essential record of all the equipment available and where it can be found, plus where alternatives can be found.

Risk assessment is where you identify potential risks to staff, the public and equipment and show how these risks might be minimised.

Production management
Monitoring progress

An essential part of the management of your project is keeping it to time and budget. In order to do this, you must monitor progress and keep careful records.

These records might be paper-based or electronic, using a project management software package. Whatever system you use you must monitor:

- the use of resources
- the use of crew
- time spent in production and post-production.

Managing people and resources

Everyone has their own management style, but there are some approaches to be avoided!

Figure 3.18: This is a less than ideal management approach!

Costume drama shoot

Imagine this scenario:

You have to film a mini drama series that will take three weeks of location work and two weeks of studio work. The film is based on an opera libretto and takes place in the year 1699. The leading actors have no spoken lines but have to lip-sync to the music score that has been recorded in a studio.

You have:

- six actors and fifty supporting artists
- a crew of fifteen
- a large range of props
- fifty period costumes
- several items of period transport.

The locations range from the interior of a country church to the exterior of a large manor house.

The exterior filming must take place in January to avoid tourists.

Without careful planning the whole thing could be a shambles. The production manager needs to have a clear plan of when things are needed and why.

It would be silly to have an expensive resource, such as a horse-drawn carriage and driver booked for a day when there is no chance of this being used.

Which of the following two systems would you use to plan for this production?

1. **A calendar with each day mapped out and the requirements for each day.**

2. **A large sheet of paper on the wall with coloured pins representing all the resources you will need and the days you will need them.**

Think about the logistics of ensuring the smooth running of a project such as this and then see how your production needs to be planned.

You must ensure that you have a clear idea of what you need and when you need it for your production. You also need to keep in communication with all your team.

This can be achieved by producing a daily plan that outlines what will be happening the following day. This is generally referred to as a call sheet and it lists the requirements for the next day's work.

You must also keep in communication with your client. It is important to know, for instance, if they have any last minute changes of plan, or any other requirements that need outlining on the call sheet.

Media Productions

Media Productions were well into the production of their programme on Yorkshire Blue when the client asked for a meeting.

The client had decided to launch another variety of kitchenware and wanted to include this in the point-of-sale programme.

The creative director at Media Productions had to inform the client that as the work was now so far advanced they would not be able to add anything into the programme.

However, to ensure that the client was not disappointed, the creative director agreed to put an additional scene at the end that showed the new range.

Think it over 3

Imagine that you are nearly at the end of your project and the client changes their mind. What would you do?

The templates at the end of Unit 2 (pages 72–74) will help you to plan your programme effectively. You could customise them with your company name and the title of your project.

Production planner/Pre-production planner/ Location planning sheet

These documents will help you to ensure that everything is in place for your project.

Location permission form

You will need permission to use their land or premises of your locations. This form must be signed by an authorised person, either at the location on the day, or preferably prior to your location shoot.

Release and consent agreement

This form is vital when filming on location. Imagine you are filming in the street and in the background is a busker. He is one of your shots and will appear in your film. You will have to get his permission before you can show the film. His signing a release and consent form will show that he has agreed to this.

Examples of the following are on page 102:

Staff list

This is where you can identify your crew and their contact details.

Call sheet

The daily document you should use to ensure that everyone knows where to be and at what time.

Theory into practice 4

You should now complete the production management cycle by drawing up a production schedule. You may need help from your teacher to do this. **P3**

This should demonstrate how you plan to produce your media product. You will need to demonstrate your own work rather than relying on your teacher or colleagues. **M3**

You must ensure that it covers:

- planning for resources and materials
- risk assessment
- details of crew and talent
- clear evidence of timescales for completion
- a production diary
- evidence of monitoring and reviewing production work.

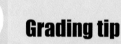

Grading tip

To reach Distinction level, you should demonstrate near-professional skills in managing the project and be able to show that you have worked with little help from your teacher or colleagues. You should use subject terminology correctly and express your ideas fluently.

Case study

Recycle.com

Joshua, Willomena, James and Rani have carefully compiled their production management files containing copies of all the documents they have used.

They have all produced a staff list with their contact details. This might seem a little strange as they are working together, but this will provide evidence of their management skills.

Willomena shot some material on location so she has a location permission form and a release and consent form signed and dated.

Rani wanted to use some copyright photographs so her file has an agreement with the copyright holder to use these photographs.

James found some copyright-free music so he has a record of where this came from, including the CD name and number and the publisher.

Joshua needed to use some logos in his website so there is a copy of the agreement to use these in his file.

All of them have completed pre-production and production planning forms.

Here are two examples of component parts of the production documentation that Media Productions uses. You may find them helpful models to follow when preparing your own production schedule.

Media Productions (MP)
Video and New Media Production

Staff List

Programme title: Yorkshire Blue
Client: Yorkshire Pottery
Writer: Jane Worth
Date: 14 July 2007

Title	Contact details
Director: Bill Smith	0797 103680
Producer: Katie Worth	0779 831413
Cameraperson/Photographer: Julie Brown	0796 426682
Production assistant: Sally Ahmed	0779 462338
Soundperson: Rob O'Brien	0798 577911
DVD designer: Thomas Mahmud	0796 998721
Graphic designer: Sara Mugabe	0798 442698
Music composer: James Jones	0797 088455
Editor : Mary Roberts	0779 233876

▲ Figure 3.19: Staff list.

Theory into practice 5

You must now produce your media product. Follow the plans you have drawn up to make the product. You should use subject terminology correctly and express your ideas fluently. **P4**

Follow closely your production schedule. **P4**

Monitor the production process carefully and keep notes as this progresses. **M4**

Produce a finished media product with accompanying documents. **M4**

Consider the client and audience and ask for their feedback on the quality of the product and its fitness for purpose. **M4**

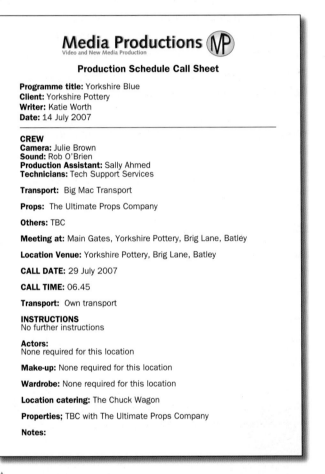

Media Productions (MP)
Video and New Media Production

Production Schedule Call Sheet

Programme title: Yorkshire Blue
Client: Yorkshire Pottery
Writer: Katie Worth
Date: 14 July 2007

CREW
Camera: Julie Brown
Sound: Rob O'Brien
Production Assistant: Sally Ahmed
Technicians: Tech Support Services

Transport: Big Mac Transport

Props: The Ultimate Props Company

Others: TBC

Meeting at: Main Gates, Yorkshire Pottery, Brig Lane, Batley

Location Venue: Yorkshire Pottery, Brig Lane, Batley

CALL DATE: 29 July 2007

CALL TIME: 06.45

Transport: Own transport

INSTRUCTIONS
No further instructions

Actors:
None required for this location

Make-up: None required for this location

Wardrobe: None required for this location

Location catering: The Chuck Wagon

Properties; TBC with The Ultimate Props Company

Notes:

▲ Figure 3.20: Call sheet.

Product

Once you have completed your work on the media product you will need to review it with your client and, if appropriate, the target audience.

It is important that any necessary changes that have not been identified through the production and post-production phases are now identified and any amendments made.

Case study

Media Productions

The team at Media Productions takes great care to ensure that the production and post-production processes are carefully monitored.

It is expensive to go back at the end of the project and make changes. However, if the client is not happy with the product, or it does not meet the approval of the target audience, the product will have to be modified.

To ensure that the client is happy at all stages the team communicate on a regular basis with the client.

If they feel that something is not correct they will ask the client for their views.

Once they have finished the editing process the team will supply a version of the product to the client for their thoughts. This is sometimes referred to as a 'rough cut' or 'trial layout'.

Once the client has agreed that this is acceptable the final version can be produced.

▲ Figure 3.21: Focus groups are useful for gauging a product's likely reception.

You will have to produce a rough cut or trial layout for your client and ask them for their views.

You may be able to form a focus group and ask the audience for their views on your product before it is finally released. Take into account what your client or audience has to say about your finished product. You may have to make changes and, if you do, keep clear records of how and why these changes were made.

Remember!

Always keep careful records of your meetings. This will allow you to demonstrate to your client that you have produced the product requested in the initial brief.

Always keep copies of the various versions of your work so that you can go back and see where changes have been made.

Always keep the documents you have produced in your management role – this will be vital evidence for your assessment in this unit.

Knowledge check 3.3

1. Produce an appropriate production schedule. **P3**

2. Produce a production schedule that has all the elements for production. **M3 D3**

3. Create a media product following your plans **P4**

4. Create a media product using some imagination with only some help from your teacher. **M4**

5. Create a media product with little help using your creativity and flair. **D4**

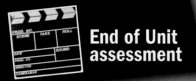

End of Unit assessment

Preparation for assessment

Your local council has invited you to produce a television commercial to publicise a major arts festival in your area. The commercial will be shown on regional television at prime time. The council has some ideas about the style and content of the commercial and has asked you to think of some ideas and then prepare a proposal to pitch to a committee of councillors. If the pitch is successful the council would like you to produce the commercial. See the letter on page 75.

The arts festival will be taking place in four months' time and the council will need to be reassured that the commercial will be ready on time.

You have been asked to consider some approaches to this commission. In order to do this you should think of a number of ideas, mind map these ideas, review the viability of each idea and produce a proposal for the chosen idea.

In Unit 2: Pre-production techniques for the media industries, you are asked to undertake the pre-production work for this project.

End of Unit assessment activity 1

Think of five ideas for this commission. Undertake research into these ideas for feasibility and relevance to the commission. Choose one idea for further development.

- To achieve a pass grade you must originate and research your ideas working within appropriate conventions. **P1**

- To achieve a merit grade you must originate ideas for your media product competently, showing some imagination. Your ideas must be viable and you should be able to take these ideas through to production. Your ideas will show that you have used your imagination to engage an audience. Your research will show that you have undertaken effective and appropriate research. **M1**

- To achieve a distinction grade you must originate and research ideas to a quality that reflects near-professional standards, showing creativity and flair. You should use a wide range of research techniques and technology. It will not be sufficient to produce a questionnaire and hand it to 10 people. Your mind mapping must be effective and you should justify which ideas have been deleted and why the final idea has been chosen. **D1**

End of Unit assessment activity 2

Prepare a proposal based on your chosen idea.

- To achieve a pass grade you must use appropriate research techniques to demonstrate the relevance of the style and content you have chosen for the commission. **P2**

- To achieve a merit grade you must effectively pitch a proposal for a media product and express your ideas with clarity. You must generally use appropriate subject terminology. Your pitch must be effective and you need to use appropriate techniques to engage the audience. Your language should demonstrate that you have understood the need for clarity when pitching your ideas. Your use of subject terminology should demonstrate to the client/audience that you have a good understanding of media techniques and technology. **M2**

- To achieve a distinction grade you must produce a proposal that reflects professional practice. **D2**

End of Unit assessment activity 3

Pitch your proposal to your client using appropriate presentation techniques and technology. Use whatever technology and materials you think would be persuasive in order to sell your idea to the client. Prepare a handout with examples of your idea where appropriate. Be prepared to answer questions from the client.

–   To achieve a pass grade your pitch must express your ideas clearly and use some subject terminology. **P2**

–   To achieve a merit grade you must carry out a management role in the production of a media product. You must show that you can do this competently and only ask your teacher to help you when it is really necessary. **M2**

–   To achieve a distinction grade your pitch must be highly effective and use a range of presentation techniques such as a PowerPoint presentation with accompanying handout and presenter's notes. You may be able to show examples of the style of commercial you intend to produce. You must undertake the pitch in a professional way using eye contact, addressing the audience directly and answering any questions they may ask. You must use correct terminology in your pitch. **D2**

End of Unit assessment activity 4

Your pitch has been successful. You must now produce a treatment for the commercial. The treatment must contain all the relevant documentation to demonstrate your management of the production process.

–   To achieve a pass grade you must undertake your management role competently but with some assistance in order to ensure the successful completion of this production. **P3**

–   To achieve a merit grade must undertake your management role competently and with little assistance in order to ensure the successful completion of this production. **M3**

–   To achieve a distinction grade you must clearly demonstrate how you managed the production with little or no assistance, using effective documentation, your personal production diary and comments from the client, your crew and your teacher. **D3**

End of Unit assessment activity 5

You must demonstrate that you can successfully produce a media product. You must undertake the production and post-production process demonstrating your management skills through controlling your team with creativity and flair.

–   To achieve a pass grade you must see through the production of the commercial. **P4**

–   To achieve a merit grade you must create your media product to a good technical standard showing some imagination. You will be able to show that you have used a range of techniques and technology to make a product that looks and/or sounds good. You will have asked your teacher for help only when it was really necessary. **M4**

–   To achieve a distinction grade your final product must reflect professional standards in commercial production. You must demonstrate your creativity and flair when suggesting ideas, changes and final amendments to the commercial. **D4**

Grading Criteria						
To achieve a pass grade the evidence must show that the learner is able to:	TiP	To achieve a merit grade the evidence must show that the learner is able to:	TiP	To achieve a distinction grade the evidence must show that the learner is able to:	TiP	Activity
P1 originate and research ideas for a media product, working within appropriate conventions	1	**M1** originate and research ideas for a media product competently, showing some imagination	1 2	**D1** originate and research ideas for a media product to a quality that reflects near-professional standards, showing creativity and flair	1	End of Unit assessment activity 1
P2 pitch a proposal for a media product, expressing ideas with sufficient clarity to communicate them and with some appropriate use of subject terminology	2 3	**M2** pitch a proposal for a media product effectively, expressing ideas with clarity and with generally appropriate use of subject terminology	2 3	**D2** pitch a proposal for a media product to a near-professional standard, expressing ideas fluently and using subject terminology correctly	2 3	End of Unit assessment activity 2 End of Unit assessment activity 3

Grading Criteria						
To achieve a pass grade the evidence must show that the learner is able to:	TiP	To achieve a merit grade the evidence must show that the learner is able to:	TiP	To achieve a distinction grade the evidence must show that the learner is able to:	TiP	Activity
P3 carry out a management role in the production of a media product with some assistance	4	**M3** carry out a management role in the production of a media product competently with only occasional assistance	4	**D3** carry out a management role in the production of a media product to near-professional standards, working independently to professional expectations	4	End of Unit assessment activity 4
P4 create a media product working within appropriate conventions and with some assistance	5	**M4** create a media product to a good technical standard, showing some imagination and with only occasional assistance	5	**D4** create a media product to near-professional standards, showing creativity and flair and working independently to professional expectations	5	End of Unit assessment activity 5

Working to a brief in the media industries

Introduction

Most of the work undertaken by media companies, be they large, small or individuals working freelance, is produced for a client. There is little opportunity to develop a product that is independently produced with no client or target audience.

Media professionals generally have to work to a client brief. This might be rigid or negotiable. It might be for a large broadcast television programme with a budget of £750,000, or a corporate programme with a budget of under £10,000. The client may be a large multinational corporation or a local company that wants a flyer to hand out in the street. Or it might be a competition brief where specific instructions have to be followed to meet the competition requirements.

In this unit you will learn about briefs, including how to negotiate a brief and how to work with a client. You will learn how to develop your ideas to meet a brief, produce a media product to a specific brief and, most importantly, how to review your work.

This unit contains a variety of activities, exercises and case studies that will help you to understand, and put into practice, working to a brief. Throughout the unit you will be following a project undertaken by a media production company. This demonstrates the processes from initial contact with the client to reviewing the finished product.

After completing this unit you should be able to achieve the following outcomes:

- Understand the requirements of working to a brief.
- Be able to develop a planned response to a brief.
- Be able to apply a response to a brief.
- Be able to review work on completion of a brief.

Think it over

Working to a brief is the way that many media professionals work. At some point you might be asked to work on a brief for a product you have no knowledge of. Many media professionals will take on such a brief because it allows them to develop new skills in an area of the media that they are unfamiliar with. It is always possible to find the expert help you need to understand the requirements of a brief.

There will be times when you can negotiate the work you undertake. Maybe you have a different idea or a different approach to the client's original idea. Maybe you have just discovered a new technique or style that you think would work well in this brief. Introducing these ideas is all part of the negotiation process. However, sometimes the client has very fixed ideas that you will have to work with to produce the product they want.

You may be able to link the work you do in this unit with a work experience opportunity. However, you should be aware that when you are undertaking your work experience that you may not be able to produce your own response to a brief. You may not be able to respond to a client if your work experience provider does not allow you to liaise directly with their client.

It is often better to find a client that wants you to produce a media product for them and is willing to allow you to use this work as evidence for this unit.

You may be able to find an opportunity in your school or college to undertake work on a brief provided by your head teacher or marketing manager.

Structure of briefs

There are many types of briefs in the media industry. The most common types of brief are:

Contractual – this is where a contract exists between the commissioner and the producer.

Negotiated – these are briefs that are negotiated between the commissioner and the producer. The negotiation might be on the content or the cost of the production.

Formal – these are briefs that are carefully written using precise language. They are often written to strict legal guidelines.

Informal – these are briefs that are written with the intention to provoke a response from a client. They may be written in colloquial (informal, day-to-day) language. In the folklore of film it is often said that the best briefs are written 'on the back of a cigarette packet'. This means that they have been discussed and developed in a social setting with little formality.

Commission – this is where a client asks the contractor to submit ideas for a project to a specified cost.

Tender – this is where several prospective contractors provide an estimated cost and description of how the product might be produced. The proposals are discussed by the commissioner and one of the tenders chosen.

Co-operative – this is a brief that is shared with other producers. Each may be in charge of one section of the project.

Competition – this is a brief that provides details of what you have to do and by when. There will generally be a prize awarded for the best product.

Reading a brief

It is important that you are able to read through a brief and understand just what is required. It may help to note down key words or points as you work through it. This will help to identify any issues that you need to clarify. You should be particularly aware of any legal or ethical points in the brief. You may have to ask someone else, such as a solicitor, for their advice on these.

There is no point undertaking a brief without being sure that it will be a feasible undertaking for you.

Case study

Media Productions

Throughout this unit you will be following a project that started with a brief from a client. A researcher at Media Productions saw an advertised commission in the trade press for a government agency (GDA). This commission was to produce an interactive DVD to use in a training package for teaching assistants. You will see the process that Media Productions went through from their initial research right through to a review of the finished product.

The senior team responded to the advertisement and received a pack of information from a government procurement department. This laid down the requirements for the production and gave an indication of the budget available. It was clear from the pack that this was a remake of out-of-date material.

In order to understand just what the client wanted the researcher at Media Productions read the pack carefully and looked at the material previously produced. These made it clear that the government agency was recruiting a writer to produce the content of the DVD, and the production company would be providing the technical expertise to create the finished interactive DVD.

The following are important questions that need to be asked and answered at preliminary meetings with the client.

- What particular elements do you want to highlight?
- What is the timescale of the production, and does this give you sufficient time? If not, is the client prepared to make compromises regarding quality?
- Is the medium proposed appropriate/cost effective?
- What is the budget and are there any restrictions regarding what it can be spent on?
- Is the budget realistic? If not, what compromises is the client prepared to make?

Case study

Media Productions

Before Media Productions responded to the client, their creative director, Sally James, carefully read through the information pack provided. She made notes of all the points in the pack, and discussed the brief with her company's legal adviser and the producer who would be assigned to the project, should they be given the job.

Sally used the notes prepared by the researcher, John Charles, to assess whether or not the scenario for the interactive DVD prepared by the client was feasible. She and the Media Productions team then worked out a response.

The team meeting was held at Media Productions' offices.

Sally's assistant took notes of all the issues discussed at the meeting. This allowed Sally time to concentrate on the discussion. These notes would prove very useful when Sally produced a response to the client.

Theory into practice 1

You have been approached by your head teacher or principal to produce a promotional video programme for your school or college highlighting its excellent resources. They intend to give this programme to parents on a DVD.

They have identified the key areas that they think will show the main resources and want the video finished in two weeks' time, ready for the next parents' evening.

They have indicated that a small budget will be available, but have not stated what this will be.

You have read through the information from your head teacher or principal, made some notes and arranged a meeting with them.

- What questions would you ask at this meeting? **P1**
- Do you foresee any problems with the proposed format? **M1**
- What recommendations would you make to the head or principal? **M1**
- Is the timeline feasible? If not, why not? **M1**
- How would you propose allocating the budget?
- How would you access the budget? **M1**

Grading tip

To reach Distinction level, you should use well-chosen and appropriate examples when discussing this with the principal or head.

Remember!

It is essential that you read the brief carefully before the meeting. You will have to ask the right questions in order to fully understand the client's requirements.

It is no good leaving the meeting with important questions not asked or answered.

Negotiating the brief

Once you have ascertained just what the client wants in their production you can begin to negotiate your position. The client may not have fully understood the constraints that you might have in production. It is your job to ensure they understand the implications of issues such as copyright, post-production time, insufficient budget, over-ambitious expectations and any other practical considerations that you as a professional are aware of, but which they might not know about. This insider knowledge is the expertise they are paying for. There is no point agreeing to their terms if it is not going to be possible to deliver.

The proposal

A proposal should outline the main ideas and help to sell the concept to the client.

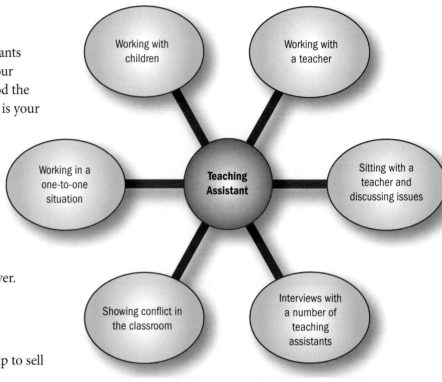

▲ Figure 4.01: Media Productions' mind map for the GDA commission explored a number of areas.

Case study

Media Productions

The team at Media Productions decided to undertake a mind mapping exercise to see what ideas they could come up with for their proposal.

The team looked at the suggested ideas and made decisions on their feasibility. Any ideas that were not feasible because of cost, time or resources were crossed out.

The team finally came up with an idea that they thought would be suitable for the training DVD. The next step was to prepare a **proposal** for the client.

The client had already indicated that they had asked other companies to send a proposal for this project. Media Productions had to ensure that their proposal was effective.

One member of the team was assigned to write the proposal. But first he needed to be sure of his facts.

John, the researcher, found examples of the materials previously commissioned by GDA. He found that the previous product was outdated and lacked any real interactivity. This was something the proposal writer could pick up on.

Sally, the creative director, asked Paul, one of the DVD specialists in the company, if he could prepare a short explanation of the features now available in the latest version of DVD software. This, again, would be used by the proposal writer to demonstrate to GDA what could now be achieved in an interactive DVD.

The proposal writer met with John and Paul to get a clear idea of what he should write in the proposal.

The finished proposal was reviewed by Sally, and the content agreed, before it was sent to GDA. It contained all the information the client would need in order to make a judgement on their idea. Media Productions hoped it would convince the client that they could produce an excellent interactive DVD.

Key Terms

Reading the brief is studying the brief and understanding what is required, and by when.

Negotiating is discussing ideas and proposals with a client and coming to a mutual agreement.

Mind map is a method of gathering together ideas and then, one by one, discarding those that are not feasible.

Proposal is a document that sets out the producer's idea for the proposed media product in order to 'sell' it to a client.

Pitch is the process of selling the idea to a client using an appropriate format, e.g. a PowerPoint presentation.

Theory into practice 2

How would you undertake research for the promotional material on your school or college? **P1**

Can you suggest alternative ideas for the programme that has been suggested? **M1**

What would you need to do before writing a proposal for this project? **M1**

Grading tip

To reach Distinction level, you should use a wide range of examples of the research and alternative ideas you would use in your work. You must explain why and how you would use them.

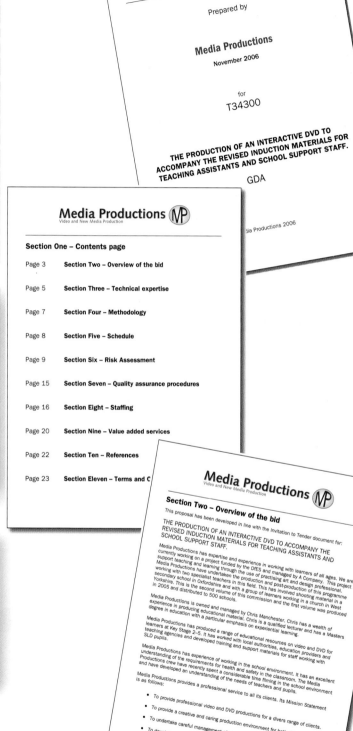

Figure 4.02: The proposal that Media Productions sent to GDA. ▶

Media Productions MP
Video and New Media Production
Proposal

Prepared by

Media Productions
November 2006

for
T34300

THE PRODUCTION OF AN INTERACTIVE DVD TO
ACCOMPANY THE REVISED INDUCTION MATERIALS FOR
TEACHING ASSISTANTS AND SCHOOL SUPPORT STAFF.
GDA

...dia Productions 2006

Media Productions MP
Video and New Media Production

Section One – Contents page

Page 3	Section Two – Overview of the bid
Page 5	Section Three – Technical expertise
Page 7	Section Four – Methodology
Page 8	Section Five – Schedule
Page 9	Section Six – Risk Assessment
Page 15	Section Seven – Quality assurance procedures
Page 16	Section Eight – Staffing
Page 20	Section Nine – Value added services
Page 22	Section Ten – References
Page 23	Section Eleven – Terms and C...

Media Productions MP
Video and New Media Production

Section Two – Overview of the bid

This proposal has been developed in line with the Invitation to Tender document for:
THE PRODUCTION OF AN INTERACTIVE DVD TO ACCOMPANY THE REVISED INDUCTION MATERIALS FOR TEACHING ASSISTANTS AND SCHOOL SUPPORT STAFF.

Media Productions has expertise and experience in working with learners of all ages. We are currently working on a project funded by the DfES and managed by A Company. This project is to support teaching and learning through the use of practising art and design professional. Media Productions have undertaken the production and post-production of this programme working with two specialist teachers in this field. This has involved shooting material in a secondary school in Oxfordshire and with a group of learners working in a church in West Yorkshire. This is the second volume of this commission and the first volume was produced in 2005 and distributed to 500 schools.

Media Productions is owned and managed by Chris Manchester. Chris has a wealth of experience in producing educational material. Chris is a qualified lecturer and has a Masters degree in education with a particular emphasis on experiential learning.

Media Productions has produced a range of educational resources on video and DVD for learners at Key Stage 2–5. It has worked with local authorities, education providers and teaching agencies and developed training and support materials for staff working with SLD pupils.

Media Productions has experience of working in the school environment. It has an excellent understanding of the requirements for health and safety in the classroom. The Media Productions crew have recently spent a considerable time filming in the school environment and have developed an understanding of the needs of teachers and pupils.

Media Productions provides a professional service to all its clients. Its Mission Statement is as follows:

• To provide professional video and DVD productions for a diverse range of clients.

• To provide a creative and caring production environment for both clients and staff.

• To undertake careful management of resources.

• To develop professional production techniques in a wide range of individuals.

• To empower individuals and organisations to use new technology for communication.

• To provide an opportunity for new entrants to the media profession to gain relevant experience.

You may be able to use another project for which you received a brief to write a proposal, rather than the one in this Theory into practice exercise. If you do, still consider the points in Theory into practice 3.

Theory into practice 3

Remember the brief from your head teacher or principal?

You must now:

- Undertake a mind map exercise for all the ideas you can think of for this programme. **P1**
- Discuss the ideas from your mind map and take out any unsuitable ideas. **P1**
- Refer to your research on any new technology you could use. **M1**
- Prepare a proposal based on your idea. **M1**

Grading tip

To reach Distinction level, you should use well-chosen and appropriate ideas in your mind map and use relevant media terminology in your research and proposal. You must explain why and how you would make the product in your proposal.

The pitch

It is common in the media industries to **pitch** your proposal to a commissioning editor or a client. You will have seen in Unit 3 how this might be done.

As you can see from the case study, Sally had prepared well for this pitch. She knew all about the proposal, the resources available at Media Productions, the size of the budget needed and the key personnel who would be involved in the production.

She had practised the pitch with some colleagues and was confident in the meeting, giving a good professional impression to the client.

Imagine going into a meeting like this without being so well prepared.

Case study

Media Productions

The Creative Director, Sally James, at Media Productions pitched the proposal to the GDA at a meeting in the GDA office in London.

Sally introduced the pitch with a few facts and figures about Media Productions. This included details of previous clients and the products they had produced for these clients.

The presentation used PowerPoint and a data projector. The slides were colourful and included some images of previous work and some video footage of a similar project. There were examples of interactive DVD projects already completed by Media Productions.

The pitch was accompanied by a handout of the presentation with room for notes next to each slide image.

At the end of the presentation Sally asked if the client had any questions.

Sally had prepared well for the pitch and was able to use her notes to answer the questions raised by the client. She did tell the client that if she could not answer any of the questions she would be able to respond to them by email the next day.

Theory into practice 4

Prepare a pitch to your client based on your proposal. **P1**

Use an appropriate presentation technique and provide relevant handouts. **M1**

Where appropriate, provide examples of your previous work and examples of how the finished product might look. **M1**

Grading tip

To reach Distinction level, you should use well-chosen and appropriate ideas in your pitch and use relevant media terminology. You must explain why and how you would make the product in your proposal with examples of the style and content of the proposed product.

At the end of the meeting with GDA Sally produced a written record of the meeting to distribute to the rest of the Media Productions team. This could also have been produced as a sound recording or presented to the staff using presentation software and distributed on the company intranet.

Here is an example of the meeting record sheet that Sally produced.

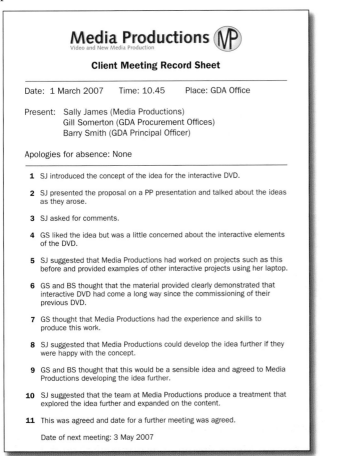

Figure 4.03: Client meeting record sheet.

As you can see from the meeting record there was discussion on the style and content of the proposed DVD product. The final outcome of the meeting was that the team at Media Productions was asked to produce a treatment.

After the pitch, if you are commissioned to take the project further, you will need to discuss the style and content of your proposed media product. This might involve making amendments:

- to the final product
- to the budget as a result of any changes
- to any conditions set down by the client.

Any changes you decide to make to your proposal must be carefully recorded. This will be useful later when you review your work in this unit.

Opportunities

You will need to be clear about the opportunities for your own personal development when negotiating and fulfilling a brief. This is a life skill that you can transfer to many other situations.

You will find a section at the end of this unit on reviewing your work. You should use this an opportunity to demonstrate just what you have learned from undertaking the negotiation of a brief.

You should ask yourself:

- What new skills have I developed?
- Am I now multi-skilled?
- What are my contributions to the development of the project brief?

You should keep a diary of the skills you are developing, the decisions you have made and the changes you suggested. All of these will be valuable evidence for your review of your work.

Theory into practice 5

You must now pitch your own ideas to your client (teacher). **P1**

Use appropriate presentation techniques in your pitch. **M1**

The following are useful guidelines.

- Keep eye contact with your audience.
- Speak slowly and use appropriate language.
- Refer to your handout and examples if you want to emphasise a point.

Answer any questions thoughtfully.

Knowledge check 4.1

1. List and describe eight different types of brief. **P1**

2. Use examples to illustrate your competent and thorough understanding of briefs. **M1 D1**

3. List all the elements to look for when reading a brief. **P1 M1**

4. Provided an analysis of a brief you have read showing your reasoning and examples of issues raised. **D1**

Grading tip

To reach Distinction level, in your pitch you should address all the elements of your proposed product. You should be able to make your client (teacher) want to ask for further development of your proposed idea. You should provide clear examples of what you intend to do and say why you have chosen this idea and how it will work.

4.2 Be able to develop a planned response to a brief

Planning stages of a media product

In this section you will be undertaking the planning of a media product in response to the work you have already undertaken.

Planning

It is essential that you plan carefully for production. A successful production relies on forward planning to ensure that everything is in place and on time.

The team at Media Productions undertakes careful planning to ensure that they have every contingency covered. As you saw earlier in this unit the Media Productions team produced a proposal and pitched this to the client. The result was that the client wanted to see a **treatment**.

Key Term

Treatment is the development of your idea from the proposal.

■ Treatment

It is important that the treatment provides as much detail as possible for the client. Refer back to Unit 3 pages 92–94 for how to construct a treatment, but here is a quick reminder of what it can include:

- an introduction
- an indication of the size and content of the video product
- an outline script
- a storyboard
- an indication of the proposed production schedule
- an approximate budget for production
- an idea of the personnel involved in the project, both talent and crew

- a contingency plan
- any research carried out for the production.

A treatment should be produced in DTP and look professional. Figure 4.04 was produced by Media Productions for their client. They also attached a risk assessment and an outline budget (Figures 4.05 and 4.06).

Media Productions (MP)
Video and New Media Production

RISK ASSESSMENT FOR FILMING IN SCHOOLS AND COLLEGES

ACTIVITY: Location recce and location recording (page 1 of 2)				DATE OF ASSESSMENT	
SCHOOL/COLLEGE			TEAM		
WHO MIGHT BE HARMED?					HOW MANY ARE AFFECTED?
HAZARDS (including inadequate/lack of arrangements)	EXISTING CONTROL MEASURES	✓ if in place ✗ if not	IF 'x' STATE THE ACTION TO BE TAKEN WITH TIMESCALES OR INDICATE ANY ADDITIONAL CONTROL MEASURES	RESIDUAL RISK RATING High, Medium, Low	
Adequate planning/ preparation	• Are staff 'competent' (e.g. trained) to carry out the recce?				

▲ **Figure 4.05: Risk assessment.**

Case study

Media Productions

Media Productions always include a contingency plan in their treatment. This allows them to produce a budget with a 10 per cent allowance to pay for any unforeseen circumstances.

In a recent production the team had planned to use a helicopter to film views over the Yorkshire Dales. This was vital shot to set the scene for the programme. The crew had hired a local company to provide the helicopter, together with a steadicam support and a specialist camera operator. This was an expensive

process but the client thought that this would make a big difference to the quality of the programme.

On the day of the shoot a storm was forecast and the helicopter company could not get the planned aircraft from its base in London. Another day for the shoot had to be scheduled. Media Productions still had to pay the specialist camera operator and for the hire of the steadicam kit. This cost was covered by the contingency in the budget and the extra day required for filming was included in the production schedule.

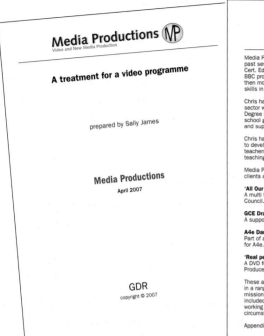

Page 1 (title page):

Media Productions MP
Video and New Media Production

A treatment for a video programme

prepared by Sally James

Media Productions
April 2007

GDR
copyright © 2007

Page 2:

Media Productions MP
Video and New Media Production

Treatment

Media Productions has been producing educational and training videos for the past seven years. The company is owned and managed by Chris Manchester Cert. Ed, M.Ed. Chris started his career as a second cameraman on numerous BBC productions working for a freelance film crew based in Nottingham. He then moved to in-house productions at Rolls Royce in Derby where he honed his skills in the move from film to video production.

Chris has been involved in education as a lecturer in the Further Education sector where he gained his Certificate in Education and then his Masters Degree in Education. He has spent considerable time in the primary sector as a school governor and also chair of governors. This involved liaison with teaching and support staff in the primary sector.

Chris has continued his links with the education sector and is working to develop vocational qualifications in the media. He provides training for teachers and support staff. This allows him to keep up with changes in teaching and teaching support.

Media Productions has produced educational video and DVD productions for clients across the education sectors. This includes programmes such as:

'All Our Worlds'
A multi faith educational programme for Key Stage 2 produced for Derby City Council.

GCE Drama and Theatre Studies 'Approaches to Unit 6'
A support DVD for Key Stage 5 produced for Dramaperks.

A4e Dance Academy Choreography Series – 'Street Dance'
Part of a series of dance DVDs aimed at Key Stage 4 students produced for A4e.

'Real people, Real Art, Real Design Volume 1'
A DVD for teachers on bringing vocational learning into GCSE Art and Design Produced with support from the DfES.

These are just a few of the programmes produced with teachers and students in a range of schools and colleges. Media Productions has also, as part of its mission statement, worked with charities to produce support material. This has included a programme for the Wolf Herschhorn Support Group. This involved working with a range of severely disabled children and adults under difficult circumstances.

Appendix One has images from some of these programmes.

Page 3:

Media Productions MP
Video and New Media Production

Media Productions is aware of the potential problems when filming in the school environment. When filming in a school or college Media Productions ensures that all potential contributors have been made aware of the nature of the filming and the programme being produced. Release forms have been circulated to parents and guardians of all children likely to be filmed and permissions obtained.

There have been occasions where permission has not been granted for children to be filmed. Media Productions is sensitive to this.

Chris Manchester will be working as Executive Producer. He has been CRB checked although this is in the process of being updated. At this time the crew members have not been determined. But once this is known all the crew will automatically be CRB checked.

Media Productions has a clear understanding of the role of the Teaching Assistant in supporting learning and interaction with children. Teaching Assistants:

* support classroom management and assist with general administration
* help manage pupil behaviour
* support pupils' health, safety and emotional / social development
* establish relationships with learners
* help pupils to access the curriculum
* support the development and effectiveness of work teams
* work with other professionals
* liaise effectively with parents.
Source : National Training Standards for Teaching Assistants

In order to inform understanding of these roles Media Productions has a small team of creative consultants. These consultants currently work in the teaching profession at Key Stages 2–5. The team consists of:

Patricia Smythe – ex primary head and now learning mentor
Sally Brown – support staff and student counsellor in secondary school
Janet Collins – head of year in primary school
Susan Holmes – ex nursery and primary teacher
Ken Houseman – lecturer in media (Higher Education)
Paul Charles – head of department (Further Education)

These consultants advise Media Productions on issues from each of the relevant sectors. Chris Manchester is actively involved in education matters through his role as an education consultant and monitors developments in the education sector. Chris has worked with government bodies including:

Qualifications and Curriculum Authority:
* Developing vocational qualifications such as GNVQ Media/GCE Media
* Developing the 2005 Compatibility Study for vocational qualifications
This work provided an opportunity to work closely with teachers and learners in the secondary sector.

Page 4:

Media Productions MP
Video and New Media Production

Media Productions has an understanding and knowledge of the pressures in the schools sector.

We would undertake to ensure that all of the schools and individuals participating in these productions are treated with respect.

Media Productions will endeavour to ensure that all participants are kept informed at all times of the requirements for filming.

Media Productions are aware of the need for careful management of this project. To this end Media Productions will:

* produce sufficient material to ensure coverage of all the requirements of the Primary TA, Secondary TA and Support TA modules.
* liaise with the writers of these modules to ensure coverage of all elements of the modules
* maintain contact with the writers and project manager
* maintain a dialogue with the writers to ensure the quality and accuracy of recorded material
* liaise with schools and personnel to ensure that location shoots are problem free and not obtrusive for schools, teachers and pupils
* discuss implications of filming that might be at odds with the writer's concept for the module
* provide a feedback scenario for writers to be fully involved in the initial stages of post-production
* enable writers to be engaged in the on-line or final edit of the material
* maintain regular contact with the project manager to ensure the smooth running of the project
* ensure that sustainable materials are used wherever possible in the filming, editing and authoring of this project

Staffing
Executive Producer: Chris Manchester

Personal details
Address: 181 Hollow Way, Thame, RG1 6BX

chris@blablainternet.com

Page 5:

Media Productions MP
Video and New Media Production

Camera crew will be appointed on a freelance basis once the contract awarding has taken place.

Media Productions uses personnel with appropriate qualifications and experience. These are sourced wherever possible from previous work undertaken for Media Productions.

Media Productions has a policy of employing recent graduates with appropriate qualifications as part of their mission statement to support developing talent.

Value added services

Media Productions has an understanding and knowledge of the pressures in the schools sector. We would undertake to ensure that all of the schools and individuals participating in these productions are treated with respect.

The experience of the Executive Producer will ensure that all participants in this project can relate in a positive way to the production team. Participants can feel confident that the production team understand the pressures that teachers can feel and the production team will consider this when filming material.

Media Productions are aware of the changing needs for the master material. To this end Media Productions could:

* Film the video material on High Definition format to allow for future proofing
* Use the latest versions of DVD authoring software
* Test the finished DVD with the latest playback technology to ensure compatibility
* Hold the shot footage in our library in the High Definition format
* Provide samples of the High Definition to the client for viewing

---

Page 6:

Media Productions MP
Video and New Media Production

Media Productions intends to undertake this work by:

* ensuring that there is a line of communication between the project manager, writers, schools and the production team at Media Productions
* providing quality pre-production processes to ensure the production and post production phases run smoothly
* using broadcast quality equipment and techniques to record, edit and author the DVD
* undertaking this work in a professional manner
* keeping to deadlines
* providing on-going feedback to the project manager on progress
* working closely with teachers and pupils to support them when filming the video material
* providing the writers with unedited material for them to make decisions on the shot footage and the text material required for the finished DVD
* producing the finished masters on an appropriate format
* adhering to all guidelines and legislation when working for the GDA.

▲ **Figure 4.04: Treatment.**

▼ Figure 4.06: Outline budget.

Media Productions MP
Video and New Media Production

Outline Budget

Programme Title: T34300
Client: GDA
Executive Producer: Chris Manchester
Date: April 2007

Pre-production

Meeting days @ £400 per day x 10 days	£4,000
Liaison with schools @ £500 per day x 2 days	£1,000
Schedule planning @£500 per day x 2 days	£1,000
Research @ £500 per day x 2 days	£1,000
Travel @ 37p per mile x 2,000 miles	£ 740
Subsistence @ £120 per visit x 5 visits	£ 600
Pre-production total	**£7,340**

Production

Executive Producer @ £700 per day x 8 days	£5,600
Camera crew per day @ £950	
incl. materials and kit x 8 days	£7,600
Travel @ 37p per mile x 2000 miles	£ 740
Subsistence @ £120 x 4 crew x 8 days	£3,840
Sub total	**£17,780**
Contingency @ 10%	£ 1,770
Production total	**£19,550**

Post-production

Editing off line	
incl materials and off-line editor @ £600 per day x 8 days	£4,800
Editing on line	
incl materials and on-line editor @ £600 per day x 6 days	£3,600
Executive Producer @ £700 per day x 14 days	£9,800
Graphics/Music @ costs (approx)	£2,000
Preparation of Masters	£1,000
Sub Total	**£21,200**
Contingency @ 10%	£ 2,120
Post-production Total	**£23,320**

Pre-production	£ 7,340
Production	£19,550
Post Production	£23,320
Total	**£50,210 excluding VAT**
Cost per edited minute	£ 233.50p (approx)

■ Health and safety issues

When you plan the production of your media product you must take health and safety into consideration.

The production team at Media Productions takes health and safely very seriously. They are often filming in quite difficult and hazardous situations and always do a risk assessment before a project is started.

Their risk assessment might include:

- assessing when and where team members might be at risk
- how these risks could be minimised
- what precautions should be considered prior to production and post-production
- who will be responsible for heath and safety.

■ Personnel

It is important that you know exactly who will be working on the production of your media product. An individual working alone might find it difficult to produce a quality media product so at an early stage you need to ask:

- What team members will I need in my team?
- Who will be working on the project?

You should investigate the different roles involved in producing the media product you have chosen. For example, in the programme for GDA the following personnel are involved:

The *director* is responsible for turning the script into the visual medium of video or film.

The *camera operator* works with the camera getting the best possible shots under the guidance of the director.

A *sound recordist* is primarily concerned with recording the best possible sound and working in a team with the camera operator.

An *editor* works with camera original material and links together the shots required for the finished video or film, working closely with the director in the editing suite.

A *production assistant* is the vital link between the director and the crew, keeping notes of the requirements of the production and ensuring that everything runs smoothly.

A *graphic designer* prepares the images to be used in the interactive DVD. This could be the images and text used in the DVD menu or material used throughout the product.

A *DVD author* brings together the video material, the images and text and the interactive elements. They will have control of how the DVD looks and works.

The *producer* is in charge of the logistics of the production; they hire the staff and manage the locations, materials and resources needed for a successful production.

Think it over 1

Who will you be working with to produce your media product?

How will you ensure that all the team members are working safely?

What planning can you do to ensure the safe production of your media product?

Theory into practice 6

You have seen a sample of a risk assessment sheet that Media Productions used in their production. You should produce one for your own production. **P2**

- Consider all the risks involved.
- Plan for the safe production of your work.
- Produce a clear risk assessment strategy. **M2**

Grading tip

To reach Distinction level, you should show that you have worked independently when undertaking your risk assessment work. This should show that you are able to undertake this activity with little help from your teacher or colleagues, and show that you have a professional approach to this work.

Once you have completed work on your treatment this should be presented to the client. They can then have a clear picture of the proposed media product, including what it will cost, when it will be delivered, the format for delivery and the style and content of the finished product.

There must be sufficient information to allow the client to sign a contract that is binding for both parties.

Timescales

You will need to plan carefully if you are to meet the deadline for delivery. You will also have to make plans to ensure that everything you need is in the right place at the right time.

Production schedules

A **production schedule** is a way of ensuring that deadlines are recorded and adhered to. It is a vital document when it comes to careful management of your time and resources. It includes details of all the requirements for production and post-production.

▲ Figure 4.07: Meeting deadlines can mean a few late nights.

There is no hard and fast rule about the style of a production schedule as producers and production managers all have their own way of recording their planning. However, you will need to produce a production schedule that works and that you can demonstrate has helped you to plan and manage your production effectively.

The production schedule is made up of a number of key elements that will make up your planning for the production. These are:

- key dates for the production and post production
- identification of key personnel
- details of locations required and location recce documents
- identification of technological resources needed
- identification of materials needed
- a budget
- outline scripts and storyboards
- daily schedules.

Figure 4.08 is an example of the production schedule prepared by Media Productions for their GDA production.

Media Productions MP
Video and New Media Production
Production Schedule
Programme Title: T34300
Client: GDA
Date: May 2007

Activity	Date
Tender awarded	28th March 2007
Preparation period	18th April– 12th May 2007
Initial start-up meeting	12th May 2007
Visits to potential locations for risk assessment Potentially 5/6 schools Details of school to be finalised Dates in agreement with schools/writers	13th May– 23rd May 2007
Filming in identified schools Details to be finalised Contingency in place for a selection of available dates to suit schools and writers	4th June– 31st June 2007
Logging of footage and initial paper edit of material	1st July– 6th July
Consultation with writers on initial paper edit – all rushes supplied on time coded VHS or DVD	7th July– 10th July
First rough edit in agreement with writers' comments	12th July– 17th July
On-line version to be compiled in consultation with writers – writers to attend edit for agreement on final DVD masters Dates to be confirmed with writers/project manager	19th July– 23rd July
DVD to be compiled	26th July
DVD masters to be delivered	27th July

▲ **Figure 4.08: Production schedule.**

Key Term

Production schedule is a document or set of documents that detail production activities, provide dates and times, list crew and talent and map requirements for resources.

You can look back at Units 2 and 3 to see more about production schedules. But here is a reminder of some of the elements they should include.

■ Call sheet

A daily schedule that shows the resources required for just one day is known as a call sheet and gives details for the crew and actors of where to be and at what time.

Remember!

You will need to keep careful records of your planning and production.

A production schedule should be updated on a regular basis.

The changes to your production schedule should be recorded in an appropriate way.

It can also contain details of transport arrangements, props needed, materials required for the day's work and location catering arrangements. When you do your planning remember to keep everyone informed about the schedule. If someone does not attend when expected there is no excuse if he/she has been given a call sheet.

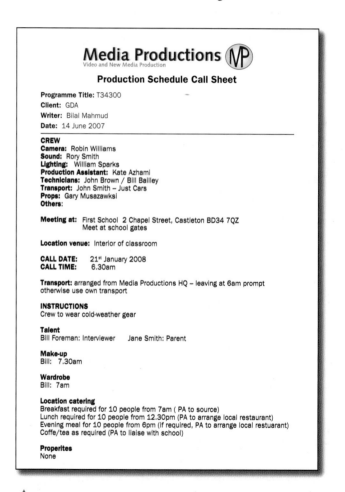

▲ **Figure 4.09: Call sheet.**

■ Outline script

The outline script will help you to understand what resources you may need and the timing of your work. It brings together your ideas into a format that clearly demonstrates how the product will progress and is an essential tool for planning the timescale of your work.

■ Storyboard

The storyboard sets down on paper how the visual and sound elements will work together. Depending on your product, you may develop a very detailed storyboard to help your timescale planning and to ensure that all of the scenes are feasible before expensive equipment is hired and staff employed.

■ Budget

It is essential that you understand the budgetary requirements of your planned project. You may find the following websites useful to find out the going rates for a number of different elements involved in a media production.

■ Location reconnaissance

This is one of the first steps towards planning the production where you visit any locations or studios you are planning to use and check out the lighting, power supply and accessibility for your crew and cast. You may have to organise a contact person to let you in early to set up your equipment. You will be able to see if there are any health and safety hazards to overcome. There is more about location recces in Unit 2 (pages 65–66).

Case study

Media Productions

The team at Media Productions is well aware of the dangers of working on location. The location used for the GDA project was a primary school. This posed particular problems as the producer had to compile a comprehensive risk assessment document to ensure the safety of the crew and the teachers and their pupils.

Knowledge check

You will need to find out the costs involved in production and post production. You may find the following links helpful:

www.bectu.org.uk – rates for freelance personnel

www.broadcast-services.co.uk – hire rates for equipment

www.gearhousebroadcast.com – hire rates for equipment

www.audiohire.co.uk – hire rates for audio equipment

www.4rfv.co.uk – directory for hire companies

www.itrentals.com – hire rates for computers

www.hireacamera.com – hire of stills and video cameras

www.comparestoreprices.co.uk – directory for hiring and buying software

For music and sound effects you could try these links:

www.bl.uk/collections/sound-archive/soundeffects.html

www.sound-effects-library.com/ – sound effects

www.kpm.co.uk – copyright music library

www.audiolicense.net – production music library

www.slicktracks.com – royalty-free music site

www.samplenet.co.uk – music sample library

For the cost of using actors or voice-over artists you could use these links:

www.equity.org.uk – actors union for finding fees

www.mbagency.co.uk – a typical actors agent site

www.at2global.co.uk – directory of actors agencies

Alternatively, you could a search engine such as www.google.co.uk or www.yahoo.co.uk

You must be careful when using Internet links to find information as some sites you may be directed to could contain offensive material.

This an example of the location recce carried out by Media Productions for one of their school location shoots.

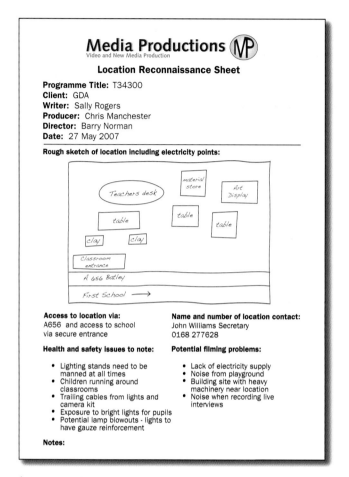

Media Productions MP
Video and New Media Production

Location Reconnaissance Sheet

Programme Title: T34300
Client: GDA
Writer: Sally Rogers
Producer: Chris Manchester
Director: Barry Norman
Date: 27 May 2007

Rough sketch of location including electricity points:

Teachers desk | material store | Art Display | table | table | table | clay | clay | Classroom entrance | A 656 Batley | First School →

Access to location via:
A656 and access to school via secure entrance

Name and number of location contact:
John Williams Secretary
0168 277628

Health and safety issues to note:

- Lighting stands need to be manned at all times
- Children running around classrooms
- Trailing cables from lights and camera kit
- Exposure to bright lights for pupils
- Potential lamp blowouts - lights to have gauze reinforcement

Potential filming problems:

- Lack of electricity supply
- Noise from playground
- Building site with heavy machinery near location
- Noise when recording live interviews

Notes:

▲ **Figure 4.10: Location reconnaissance sheet.**

Once you have undertaken all the tasks necessary to ensure that this project will be successful you can begin the production phase.

Theory into practice 7

Your proposal and pitch have been successful. Your client has asked for a treatment to be prepared. You must:

- undertake any further research needed **P2**

- prepare the necessary components for your treatment **P2**

- keep a careful check on the progress of your treatment **M2**

- record any changes you make to your treatment as you write it **M2**

- present your treatment to your client for their approval. **P2**

Grading tip

To reach Distinction level, you should show that you have worked independently when preparing your treatment This should show that you are able to undertake this activity with little help from your teacher or colleagues and show you have creativity and flair and that you have a professional approach to this work.

Knowledge check 4.2

1. Plan a response to a brief that meets the requirements of the brief. **P2**

2. Plan a response to a brief that meets the requirements of the brief that shows you have used imagination in your planning. **M2**

3. Produce your planning in a way that reflects professional practice. **D2**

Production stages

In order to apply your response to the brief you will have to implement:

- pre-production
- production
- post-production.

You will have to put into place all the planning you have done in order to make the production and post-production phases successful.

You must remember to communicate with your client throughout the production process. They need to be kept informed of progress and any potential problems that you encounter.

Pre-production

In Unit 2 you will have learnt about the pre-production process. You now have to put this into practice.

In the previous section you looked at the documentation that Media Productions used for their planning for the Yorkshire Blue production. You will now have to use similar material in your own pre-production. In order to ensure the success of your production you will need to:

- produce a treatment
- produce a production schedule
- undertake a risk assessment
- undertake a location or studio recce.

Production

It is essential that you undertake careful project planning to ensure you to obtain the right production material, which you will then shape in the post-production process.

Time management is important if you are to complete your work on time. Your production schedule will remind you of the deadlines you have set.

Thinking ahead is the secret to pre-production, you must make sure you have prepared and sourced everything you need in good time. If you do not think ahead all your planning could be worthless.

■ Booking and using equipment

You should ensure that you are going to use the correct technology for the recording of your material. This might be a digital stills camera or a full video location kit.

Once you have established the right equipment for the job you will need to ensure that it will be available when you need it. You will need to book all of the equipment you will need as early as possible. Try to book dates that you know you will keep rather than block-booking equipment over a longer period. Someone else might want to use the equipment and if you have booked it and not used it they will be annoyed.

It is no good going to all the trouble of booking equipment and making sure it all works if you do not know how to use it. You need to be sure that you have the skills to get the best out of the equipment. This might involve asking your teacher to refresh your memory on:

- how to set the correct aperture
- how to use a microphone without getting handling noise
- how to use depth of field to get a creative shot
- how to set white levels
- how to store your images on the memory stick or memory card.

Do not feel that you cannot ask for extra help. It is better to ask now than to have to do the work again.

You may already know how to use the equipment but some of your team might not be so familiar with it. Why not arrange to go through the equipment with them before you go on location?

There is nothing more embarrassing than arriving at a location with equipment that does not work. If you do not have fully functioning equipment you will not be able to produce quality material. On the day before you are due to pick up the equipment make sure that the batteries are charged and the equipment is in working order. To double-check, you should test the equipment before you leave your school or college premises.

Media Productions (MP)
Video and New Media Production

Qty	Item of Kit/Description	Out	In
	First Camera:		
	Sony DSR 300 & Carry Case		
	Battery Belt & Charger / Mains Adapter		
	(CHARGE)		
	Quickset Tripod & Plate		
	JVC Playback Monitor & Appropriate Wires (in Toolkit 1)		
	Second Camera:		
	Sony DCR-TRV25E & Carry Case		
	2 Batteries & Charger		
	(CHARGE)		
	Small Tripod & Carry Case		
	Media:		
	Blank DVCAM Tape: 64 min		
	94 min		
	124 min		
	184 min		
	Mini DV Tape: 60min		
	Lighting:		
	Lighting Bag: 2 Redheads & Tripods (Barn Doors, Gels & Pegs)		
	Sound:		
	Radio Microphone: Transmitter & Ariel / Receiver & Ariel		
	Mains Power, Cable & 2 12v Batteries		
	Neck-Tie Microphone & Cable (In Toolkit 1, Green)		
	Rifle Microphone & Pistol Grip & Boom		
	Softy		
	Microphone Stand & Head		
	Extras:		
	Toolkit 1 (Green)		
	Toolkit 2 (Grey)		
	Extension Lead (Red Reel)		
	Spare Second Tripod		

Media Productions (MP)
Video and New Media Production

Notes:	
e.g. Equipment problems, faults	
Project	
Date:	
PA Signature:	
Director Sign:	
Returned in Good Condition & on Time	Signed............................. Date..............................

Figure 4.11: Checklist.

It is good practice to have a list of all the equipment you are taking with you. You could use this as a checklist before you leave for your location.

It is good practice to regularly inspect the material you have recorded to ensure that you have something on tape or on your minidisk. It does not look good if you have to return to a location because you did not record any sound or the picture is out of focus.

■ Effective communication

This is your media product and you will need to keep control of the production and post-production process. Sometimes, you may have to make decisions with which not all of your crew will agree. It is a test of your leadership skills to stand by your decisions and ensure that everyone follows your instructions.

However, there are benefits in taking advice from your team members. They need to feel valued and may come up with some good ideas. You can make a note of the advice and act on it if appropriate. Remember that you may well be a part of their team later.

You will need to keep your team members up to speed with the production and post-production process. This might be through word of mouth or you could keep in touch with them by email. You have already developed your call sheets but you might want to give them further information as the production progresses.

■ Production diary and other production records

In order to work effectively you will need to monitor your work on a regular basis. You will need to complete paperwork that demonstrates your monitoring process.

Figure 4.12: Keep your production diary up to date – it is a vital record of your work and will help you to plan and review your media project.

During the production process you should use your production diary to record the work you do. You need to record your production processes in your production diary. This will be really useful when you review your work in section 4.4.

You may want to add to your diary a 'To do' list that demonstrates you have thought about the tasks you still have to complete.

Your monitoring will allow you to make changes as and when they are needed. This might be on a location when you discover that you have not recorded sufficient sound or images. Imagine sitting at your computer ready to put together your page layout for a magazine. You have specified in your treatment that you will have six photographs that demonstrate a particular theme. When you open your photo file you have only five photographs that are usable. What do you do?

Keeping careful records at the time the work is recorded can help to ensure that you do have sufficient material for post-production.

Case study

Media Productions

A well-known producer came to work on a short-term contract for Media Productions. The company was developing a programme for broadcast on terrestrial television.

The producer related a scenario that he had encountered in a previous production. This was a ninety-minute programme based on a musical work about the famine of Easter 1699. The film had to match the words and music. The programme had a budget of nearly one million pounds and the producer had to balance this budget.

He employed one of his friends, a well-known director, to film all of the material for this programme. One of the scenes involved a very expensive location shoot in central London. The scene was shot at night with an elaborate set that had cost £35,000 to design and build. They had only one night in which to film.

When the post-production started the producer found that the director had not shot enough material on this very expensive location, to cover the music from the libretto. This was very important as the music was the main focus of the programme. To fill the gap, the producer used one shot twice.

During the rough-cut showing, the client noticed the repeated shot in this sequence and on being told who was responsible, instructed the producer to sue the director for breach of contract.

You will probably not have this kind of problem, but you can see that it is vitally important to monitor your work. If the director in question had recorded what had been shot, and how much time was needed for coverage, he would not have made the mistake.

You should use appropriate paperwork such as a field footage log sheet to record what you are doing on a location.

◄ Figure 4.13: You must keep detailed records, using the right paperwork to record what is happening on a shoot.

This is an example of one page of the field footage log that Alan, the production assistant at Media Productions, produced when recording the material for the interactive DVD project.

Media Productions MP
Video and New Media Production
Field Footage Log Sheet

Programme title: T34300
Client: GDA
Production Assistant: Alan Smithers
Producer: Chris Manchester
Director: Barry Norman
Date: 14 June 2007

Tape No.	Take No.	Time Code In	Time Code Out	Description	Comments
2	1	00.01	00.09	L/S of school	good shot – clear sounds
2	1	00.10	00.25	M/S of school	slightly out of focus
2	2	00.26	00.35	M/S of school	good shot / good sound
2	1	00.37	00.55	children in playground	good shot
2	1	00.57	01.10	C/U children playing	good shot – poor sound
2	2	01.16	01.25	C/U children playing	good shot – sound better
2	1	01.26	01.59	M/S children playing	good – teaching asst in background
2	1	01.60	02.45	interview with teacher	OK – poor background
2	1	02.46	03.59	interview with teacher	better background
2	1	04.00	04.50	L/S teacher and children	good
2	1	04.51	05.48	M/S teacher with children	good – teaching asst in background
2	1	05.49	07.35	interview with Head	good – sound good

■ Logging of source material

It is important to log all of the original material you have available for editing. Imagine having twenty different camera tapes with footage you need for a commercial. There is footage required at some point on all of the tapes. If you have not effectively logged what is on each tape, you could spend many hours going backwards and forwards through them to find the footage you need.

If you have taken photographs on a number of memory cards and need to use them in a random way you will need to log the location of each one and number each memory card.

The same can be done for all the recorded material you produce, whether for an audio recording or material for an interactive media product.

It is advisable to use a consistent style of logging whatever the product you have chosen to make. The log should include:

- scene/take/image number
- brief description
- comments
- time code, where appropriate.

It is always interesting to go back and look at material you shot some days or weeks earlier. With good logging records, you can quickly find what you need. They also help to jog your memory of the shoot.

◄ Figure 4.14: Field footage log sheet.

Post-production is the shaping of source material. We shall look at post-production of video, sound, photographs, text and interactive media.

■ Video

There are various elements that may need to be shaped during the editing process. You may want to change the order of the visual material from the camera original footage. This may be to make the sequence logical or it could be to remove poor footage.

The sound you record on location or in the studio may need to be edited. This could be done to take out unwanted passages or instructions from the director.

You may wish to add a title at the front of the product and/or credits at the end.

There may be a need to add graphics, such as animations or pictures. The editing process will allow you to make room in your product for these to be added.

You may also be able to correct the colour of your images or the level of your sound recording during editing.

The initial editing process is called the **off-line edit**. This process involves editing together the sequences and making a version that can be viewed and changes suggested.

The final editing process is called the **on-line edit** and this is where the final effects and finishing details are included.

Key Terms

Off-line edit is the first editing process for film or video.

On-line edit is the final edit where all the final effects are placed.

■ Sound

There may be a number of reasons for editing sound material. Sometimes you record more than you need and unwanted material will have to be removed.

The required material may have to be recorded out of sequence. The editing process will allow the sequence to be re-arranged.

Original sound quality may be poor and you have to enhance it or re-record certain parts, such as voice-overs.

There may be a need to add sound effects, voice-overs or music in order to complete the product. These will all be added at the editing stage.

■ Photographs

Photographic images may need to be cropped, cut out or stretched to fit into a layout. They may need enhancing, such as by changing the colour contrast. You may wish to add visual effects such as making an image sepia, or adding digital effects. This can all be achieved in the editing process.

■ Text

The editing process for text can be used to change the type style or to make layout amendments such as changing columns or spacing on a page. The text needs to be edited carefully for sense, and any typographic or other errors corrected. Images and captions can also be added during the editing process.

■ Interactive media

An interactive media product should contain all the elements that have already been mentioned in this section. Images, video and sound and text can all be an integral part of a multimedia product.

The combination of the editing of these separate elements will contribute to the shape and form of the product

It can save valuable time in the editing process if you undertake an initial edit on paper. This can be used for all media products and involves making decisions before committing yourself to time on equipment and using resources.

Figure 4.15 is a paper edit that Media Productions did for the video elements of their interactive DVD.

Figure 4.16 is a schematic for Media Productions' DVD showing how it might work.

Media Productions (MP)
Video and New Media Production

Initial Paper Edit

Programme title: T34300
Client: GDA
Production Assistant: Alan Smithers
Producer: Chris Manchester
Director: Barry Norman
Date: 2 July 2007

Tape No.	Scene No.	Time Code In	Time Code Out	Description	Effect	Sound
2	12	00.01	00.09	L/S of school	fade in and cut to	atmos
2	13	00.26	00.35	M/S of school	fade to	atmos
2	1	00.37	00.55	L/S children in playground	cut to	atmos
2	2	01.16	01.25	C/U children playing	cut to	atmos
2	1	01.26	01.59	M/S children playing	cut to	atmos
2	1	02.46	03.59	interview with teacher	cut to caption (name)	live interview
2	1	04.00	04.50	L/S teacher and children	fade to	atmos & music
2	1	04.51	05.48	M/S teacher with children	fade to	atmos & music
2	1	05.49	07.35	interview with head	fade out caption (name)	live interview

Figure 4.15: Initial paper edit.

Media Productions (MP)
Video and New Media Production

Media Productions

Schematic for: T34300
Designer: James Smith

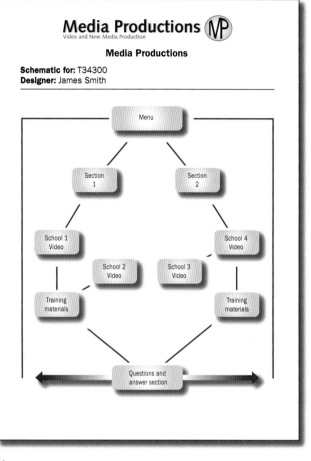

Figure 4.16: Schematic for an interactive DVD.

Case study

Media Productions

The last piece in the jigsaw for the Media Productions DVD was the authoring. This was the adding together of all the pieces of production into a final product.

The elements in this process were:

- video footage shot in schools
- text explaining what was happening in each scene
- text that formed the training elements of the DVD
- graphics needed to explain certain parts of the training

- interactive elements that took the viewer through the training
- menu that started the DVD and allowed the viewer to navigate through the DVD.

All of this work was undertaken by James, a new media and video graduate, who specialised in preparing material for DVD. He took all of the material and put together a plan of how the DVD interactivity might work.

Theory into practice 8

You should now undertake the production and post-production of your project.

You must do the following.

- Produce a production schedule that covers your production and post-production. **P3**

- Use the information in your production schedule to successfully record and edit your material. **P3**

- Keep careful records of the production and post-production processes. **M3**

- Identify any changes you have made to your production schedule. **M3**

- Review your edited material to ensure it is fit for purpose. **M3**

- Keep a production diary of all your work. **M3**

Grading tip

To reach Distinction level, you should show that you have worked independently when undertaking your production and post-production work. This should show that you are able to undertake these activities with little help from your teacher or colleagues and show you have creativity and flair and that you have a professional approach to your production and post-production work.

Relationship with client

Throughout the production process you must keep in touch with your client. They will need to be kept up-to-date with the progress of your production and post-production work. You may be able to arrange a face-to-face meeting, write them a letter or send them an email. In response to their ongoing feedback, you may have to revise aspects of the production as you go along.

It is important to keep good relations with your client, but you must also be realistic and tell them honestly if things they have requested are not possible or if things have gone wrong. If you keep detailed records you will be well-placed to deal with any complaints or other problems that may arise.

When you come to the post-production process you may want to invite the client to sit in on the shaping process. They might be able to offer advice on some aspects of their production process or on their product. Remember: effective communication with your client is essential if you are to produce a quality media product.

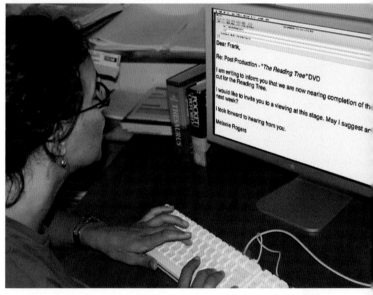

▲ **Figure 4.17: You must keep in regular communication with your client.**

Knowledge check 4.3

1. Apply your planning to production with some help from your teacher. **P3**

2. Show that you have used imagination in the application for production with only a little help from your teacher. **M3**

3. You will be able to show creativity and flair in the application of your production skills. **D3**

4. Your work will reflect professional practice when working independently. **D3**

Records and reviewing

It is vital to be able to review the processes you went through in your production. This is useful not only to be able to solve any disputes about the process, for instance if something went wrong, but also for your own personal development. You can see where things went well or badly, and learn from this for the next task.

Keeping a log or diary

You should keep a comprehensive diary or log of the work you have undertaken during the pre-production, production and post-production phases of your work.

This diary or log will help you to reflect on the work that you did and the help you had from colleagues. Consider the following points to include.

- How you thought of your idea.
- How you developed the idea into a proposal.
- How the proposal developed into a treatment.
- A breakdown of the primary and secondary research methods you used.
- Notes of meetings with team members.
- Notes on the way that your team members worked.
- Notes on the work you undertook for others.
- On-going notes of the skills you are developing.
- Reflections on the quality of your work.
- Notes on your time-management and leadership skills.
- An analysis of your media product compared to a similar professionally produced product.
- Understanding of the fitness for purpose of your own media product.
- Analysis of how well your media product meets the client's brief and audience needs.

All of these could be contained in a written diary or other appropriate format such as a PowerPoint presentation or a video/audio evaluation. Whichever method you use for your diary or log you should use appropriate media language.

Case study

Media Productions

Media Productions' producers always keep a comprehensive diary of their work. This may help when reviewing the finished product with their client.

It is not unheard of for the client to forget what they asked for in their initial commission. If this happens, and the producer has kept detailed records, he or she can always go back through the documentation and remind the client what was said and when. This can be useful if the client decides they do not want to pay for work that they think is not suitable.

Here is an example of a production diary used by a team member from Media Productions.

Media Productions MP
Video and New Media Production

Production Diary

Name: Chris Manchester

Production: T34300

Date	Action Taken
10th May	Met with client to discuss the location at St James school Client agreed to contact DGA to clear the location shoot
15th May	Met with cameraperson to discuss issues with camera safety when working in schools. Agreed that the camera and lighting must be secure as chilren will be involved and that this was the responsibility of the camera crew
16th May	Met with the director to discuss the location shoots. There was agreement on the length of time required for each location shoot – This was set at one day for each location.
4th June	Met with camera crew to brief them on the locations we would be using. Discussed the Health and Safety hazards when working in a school Each member of the crew took a Risk Assessment document and agreed to read and following the instructions on the form.
5th June	Location day at St James School – weather good. Camera crew arrived thirty minutes late at the location. The school were expecting us but were unsure just what we were doing. Contacted GDA to ask them to confirm with the school the nature of location shoot and what the footage would be used for. This was completed and confirmed by GDA senior management.

▲ **Figure 4.18: Production diary.**

It is important that you obtain feedback about your product from the client. If you are lucky, and you have provided them with what they want, they should really like the product. But what if they hate it? Before you present it, you need to ask:

- Does it meet the brief that you started with?
- Does it fulfill the client's brief?
- Has the client been consulted over any changes to the brief?

Case study

Media Productions

Media Productions held a meeting with the client for their interactive DVD product. At this meeting the Managing Director made some comments on some of the camerawork being a little wobbly. The director was annoyed by this comment but agreed to review this footage.

The Managing Director may not be an expert in video production but he knows about his audience and his products. He wants the best possible interactive product for this product.

The director changed the shot and the problem was solved.

It may be possible to get a number of people to see the finished programme and comment on it before you deliver to the client. Ideally it should be representatives from your intended audience who give you feedback on the effectiveness of your product.

If you want a greater range of feedback you should consider making multiple copies of your media product and sending it to a wide range of people. This might include finding a group from your target audience from another school or college who could give some feedback.

Be sure to include a stamped addressed envelope to ensure they return the product to you. You can focus their comments by including a questionnaire for them to answer about the product. It is much easier for people to complete questionnaires if they are simple to use, such as using tick boxes or just circling an answer. If you want more detailed feedback you could request short-sentence responses. It can be good practice to have tick boxes and short-answer questions in the same questionnaire.

In the case of multimedia websites you may be able to upload the pages onto the school or college website and ask for feedback.

Do not be disheartened by any negative views of your work. See them as a pointer to doing better next time. Maybe it is too short or too long, the sound may be indistinct, the pictures might be blurred, the interactivity does not work, roll-over buttons do not go anywhere. All of these things can be corrected if you know about them. If you have built in time into your post-production schedule you can re-edit the programme, re-record some of the material or fix your interactivity buttons before delivery to the client.

Sometimes it is good to sit down with an audience after a viewing of your product and ask for immediate responses. Their views could be recorded on video or audio tape and transcribed later. Some people will be more responsive in a face-to-face situation than in a written questionnaire. You can also ask questions back in response to their views.

Once you have obtained sufficient information, and made your amendments, what then? The information you received also needs to be analysed and recorded in a way that will show just what people think about your media product.

It is interesting to note that in feature films the distributors go to great lengths to obtain audience feedback. They will often have preview showings that ask for detailed audience feedback. In one of the *Star Trek* films, for example, there was a scene where the original Captain Kirk returns to fight alongside the new Captain, Jean-Luc Picard. The original scene showed Kirk dying a horrible death after an alien attack. The initial audience reviews showed that this scene was very unpopular, and in the end and the whole scene had to be re-shot with a more acceptable outcome.

Imagine the cost of doing this! But the producers obviously thought it was worth it. If the film was to be a success it was essential to keep the audience and film critics happy.

You may not have to go this expense, but it would be really good if everyone liked your media product. Getting feedback and acting on it is one way to help ensure they do.

Case study

Media Productions

Media Productions always undertake a review of their work with a client.

The DVD they were making for GDA was in the final stages of production. The client agreed to review the product with the director.

The original concept for the DVD work was for an interactive product with video footage, a voice-over, interviews and teaching materials in a text box over the pictures.

The director persuaded the client that in order to make the DVD effective it would be preferable to use new authoring software that allowed for the teaching materials to be tagged to the video material. This meant that as the relevant video material came up a window was opened that allowed the viewer to choose whether to see the teaching materials at this point or save them for later viewing.

The client agreed that this was appropriate and the DVD was produced in this form.

Sometimes it can be hard to balance artistic integrity with what the client wants. The client may have simply wanted to go with their original idea. Media Productions believe that the client is always right but can always be given an alternative!

Reviewing your work

It is essential that you undertake a comprehensive evaluation of your work on your media product. In order to do this you must consider the following questions:

- What did I do?
- What skills did I learn?

- What went wrong?
- What went right?
- What would I do if I could start again?

Remember to sell yourself in this evaluation. If you have done really good work then say so, and if you had problems identify them and say how you overcame these problems, or how you would do it differently next time.

If you have problems writing these down consider how you could record your thoughts in other ways.

Formats for reviewing your work

You may be able to review your work by producing a presentation for your teacher. The presentation should comprehensively cover all the aspects of your work. You should include examples of:

- your original ideas
- how the ideas were mind-mapped and then a final choice made
- discussions with your client
- documentation you used to produce your finished product
- analysis of the review of the product with the client and, where appropriate, with the target audience.

You may be able to produce an illustrated written report, a presentation using appropriate software, a video presentation or an audio presentation. Whatever style of presentation you choose, you should ensure that all the information the teacher needs is included.

Think it over 2

How can you get feedback on your product from an audience?

Could you organise a focus group?

Can you set up a meeting with your client and get some feedback from them?

What about asking your fellow students to look at your work and give you some feedback?

What will you do with the feedback you receive?

Theory into practice 9

You must review your work in an appropriate way and produce evidence that you have reviewed your work. Here are some guidelines. **P4**

- Be clear about what you have done. **P4**

- Use clear language when commenting on your proposal, treatment, production and post-production work. **M4**

- Use relevant examples to illustrate key points in your work. **M4**

- Provide an opportunity for your client to comment on your work. **D4**

- Provide an opportunity for a client/audience to comment on the quality of your finished product. **D4**

- Compare your finished product to your original idea – how closely does this match your original intentions? **D4**

- Describe how you managed the production and post-production process. **M4**

- Identify where and how you made changes to your work. **D4**

- Consider what you have learnt and how this might help you to find a job in the media. **M4**

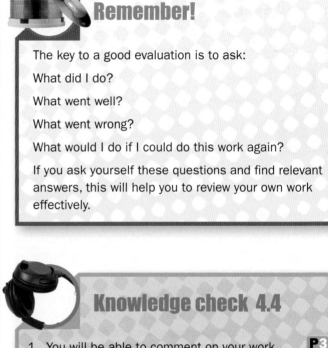

Remember!

The key to a good evaluation is to ask:

What did I do?

What went well?

What went wrong?

What would I do if I could do this work again?

If you ask yourself these questions and find relevant answers, this will help you to review your own work effectively.

Knowledge check 4.4

1. You will be able to comment on your work. **P3**

2. You will be able to use specific examples from your work to explain what you have done. **M3**

3. You will be able to use references to professional practice using fluent language and appropriate terminology. **D3**

Grading tip

To reach Distinction level, you should compare the work you have done with the work of professionals, how they have tackled working to a brief and how this influenced how you did your work. You should express this fluently using correct subject terminology.

End of Unit assessment

Preparation for assessment

A local charity that works with young people with a drug problem has asked for your help in redesigning their publicity material. They already have a brochure, a poster and a monthly newsletter. However, these were designed some time ago. The committee that runs the charity is concerned that the current publicity material does not reflect the work that the charity does.

The charity has asked you to come up with some ideas for new publicity material. They are willing to listen to your ideas about the style, content and design of the publicity material. They have asked that the material is carefully targeted to their client group. This has now been identified as 14–19 year olds.

Takecare
24 North Street
Littletown
GA47 1ZX

Date as postmark

Dear Colleague

Takecare is a local charity that works with young people. We try to inform our target audience of young people about the long term effects of drug abuse.

We have a variety of publicity material that we use in schools, youth clubs and nightclubs. This material is seen by our target audience as out of date. We would like you to think of some ideas for getting our publicity material out to our audience of young people.

Recent research has shown that our target audience is now the 14–19 age group. The material we are seeking must be aimed at this audience. We would welcome your ideas about the style, content and format of the publicity material. We really want to get to these young people and the material must get our message across.

Please send me your ideas so that I can discuss them with my colleagues. I will then arrange for you to visit us and explain your ideas in more detail.

Yours faithfully

Brenda Remington
Publicity Coordinator
Takecare.org.uk

Figure 4.19 Commissioning letter from Takecare.

End of Unit assessment activity 1

1. Identify the different types of briefs that you might find when working in the media industry.

   Produce a report, in an appropriate format, about the different types of briefs that you might find. Include some examples of these briefs in your report (your report could be a written illustrated report or a presentation using appropriate techniques).

2. Look through the letter that the charity has sent you (Figure 4.19). Answer the following questions:
   * What kind of brief is this?
   * Can you identify what the client wants you to do? If so, what is it?
   * How much scope is there for negotiation in what they want you to do?
   * How would you approach the client to suggest ideas for this commission? **P1**

   – To achieve a merit grade in this activity you must demonstrate that you have a competent understanding of working to a brief. This means that you have moved away from simply understanding to a clear consideration of how to work to a brief. You will use well-chosen examples in your work. **M1**

   – To achieve a distinction grade for this activity you must provide clear evidence of your thorough understanding through justification for the product you are suggesting to the client. You should also provide a wide range of examples that demonstrate your understanding of the range of briefs that you could be working to. **D1**

End of Unit assessment activity 2

Undertake initial ideas development for a media product that meets the needs of the client.

You must:

- Develop a range of ideas and then decide on one suitable idea (mind-map and select idea).
- Identify how this idea would meet the needs of the target audience.
- Prepare a proposal for your idea – think about how you will sell your idea to the client.
- Pitch your idea to the client (use an appropriate technique in presenting your pitch).
- Once the proposal and pitch have been successful you must produce a treatment. Present the finished treatment to the client for them to sign off before you move on to the production stage.
- The treatment must contain all the relevant documentation to support your production and post-production work. **P2**

Note: You may decide to work in a small group in this activity. If you do you must ensure that individual ideas, proposals and treatments are produced. You can meet as a team to discuss ideas and plan effectively but all the team members must produce appropriate documentation for their work.

- To achieve a merit grade in this activity you must demonstrate your competence in responding to a brief using imagination. You may still require some occasional guidance from your teacher. **M2**

- To achieve a distinction grade in this activity you will need to demonstrate that your planning is to near-professional standard. This is not saying that you will have to produce professional documentation without understanding why you are using them. You will demonstrate that you are thinking like a professional and planning in a way that reflects professional practice. You will have to show your independence in planning your work. This means you will think of ideas and work without being prompted. Your ideas should show that you thought creatively about your ideas and that they will work for the target audience. **D2**

End of Unit assessment activity 3

You have received an agreement from your client to start the production phase. They have seen your treatment and agreed to its contents. You must now do the following:

- Produce a production schedule.
- Ensure all your planning documentation is appropriate and effective.
- Undertake production work ensuring communication with your team and the client.
- Review your production works on an on-going basis and make changes, where necessary.
- Undertake post-production work, ensuring communication with your team and the client. **P3**

  - To achieve a merit grade in this activity you must demonstrate your competent application of practical work towards the realisation of the brief. You must use imagination and will require only occasional assistance from your teacher. **M3**

  - To achieve a distinction grade in this activity you will again have shown independence in the pre-production, production and post-production stages of your work. You will have worked in a way that reflects professional practice. Your planning, production and post-production work will show creativity and flair – you will not have just gone for the obvious choices but actively considered alternative solutions. **D3**

End of Unit assessment activity 4

You must review the work you have undertaken in this project. You must do the following:

- Review your time and resources management.
- Review your communications with your team and your client.
- Look at your finished product and compare it with your original intentions (from your proposal).
- Show your finished product to your client and an audience. Find a way of gathering information about what they think about your work.
- Analyse the feedback and make changes, where necessary.
- Ask yourself if the work you have produced has given you any thoughts about a career in the media. **P4**

  - To achieve a merit grade in this activity you must be able to explain clearly the work you have done to meet the brief. You will be able to provide examples to support your explanations and you will use appropriate subject terminology in your explanations. **M4**

– To achieve a distinction grade in this activity you must have undertaken a review of your work that compares and contrasts your planning, production and post-production work with that of a professional. You will have considered how your finished product compares with your original idea. You will have kept careful and effective records that you can use to comment on your work. Your will have expressed ideas fluently. Your review must use correct subject terminology. **D4**

Grading Criteria					
To achieve a pass grade the evidence must show that the learner is able to:	TiP	To achieve a merit grade the evidence must show that the learner is able to:	TiP	To achieve a distinction grade the evidence must show that the learner is able to:	TiP	Activity
P1 demonstrate understanding of the requirements of working to a brief	1 2 3 4 5	**M1** demonstrate competently understanding of the requirements of working to a brief with reference to well-chosen examples	1 2 3 4 5	**D1** demonstrate thoroughly understanding of the requirements of working to a brief with supporting justification and elucidated examples	1 2 3 4 5	End of Unit assessment activity 1
P2 plan a response to a brief, working within appropriate conventions and with some assistance	6 7	**M2** plan a competent response to a brief, showing some imagination and with only occasional assistance	6 7	**D2** plan a response to a brief to near-professional standards, showing creativity and flair and working independently to professional expectations	6 7	End of Unit assessment activity 2
P3 apply a response to a brief, working within appropriate conventions and with some assistance	8	**M3** apply a response to a brief competently, showing some imagination and with only occasional assistance	8	**D3** apply a response to a brief to near-professional standards, showing creativity and flair and working independently to professional expectations	8	End of Unit assessment activity 3
P4 describe and comment on own work to a brief, expressing ideas with sufficient clarity to communicate them and with some appropriate use of subject terminology	9	**M4** explain own work to a brief with reference to well-chosen examples, expressing ideas with clarity and with generally appropriate use of subject	9	**D4** critically evaluate own work to a brief with reference to professional practice, expressing ideas fluently and using subject terminology correctly	9	End of Unit assessment activity 4

Critical approaches to media products

Introduction

Working in the media can be both stimulating and rewarding and in this unit you will find a lot of information about the different media you can choose to study for this qualification. Unit 5 explains some important principles about the way the media industry works. Understanding how and why things happen will help you learn how to do things yourself.

Most media products are affected by the ways producers think about their target audiences. Media producers often share common understandings of how their products will be consumed and understood by those audiences. Some issues covered here relate to communication through 'mass' media that reach large numbers of people at the same time. Others are 'sector-specific', relating specifically to one particular medium, be it television, film, radio, sound recording, print, interactive media or computer games.

In the first part of this unit you will learn about the different ways media producers think about their audiences. For example, using research to judge what different audiences might be interested in. Gaining insights into the audience's tastes and consumption trends has become increasingly necessary in the highly competitive environment of the media industries.

Next you will learn about the ways in which media producers tailor their products to appeal to those audiences, shaping them according to their interests. Then you will learn how people within the audiences respond to the products – that is, how they take meaning from them and what they do with those meanings. The final part of the unit will show you different ways to develop a deeper understanding of media products that you see and hear.

After completing this unit you should be able to achieve the following outcomes:
- Understand how media producers think about audiences.
- Understand how media producers create products for specific audiences.
- Understand how media audiences respond to media products.
- Be able to develop responses to media products.

Think it over

The media industry has developed in response to a number of different factors, particularly advances in communication technology. **Mass media** enable the sending of messages to large and diverse audiences across the globe.

Audience demand changes in response to the choices available to them. When radio first became widespread it brought mass popular entertainment into the home. Whole families would gather around their one 'wireless' set to tune in to programmes. Music hall stars rapidly became radio stars, transferring their acts from theatres reaching just a few hundred people at a time, to a new national 'stage' on the radio, potentially reaching millions.

In turn, when television brought pictures into the home, many cinemas closed down. Initially, television was restricted to a small number of analogue terrestrial channels, but satellite, cable, and the development of digital terrestrial television – Freeview in the UK – has massively increased the amount of choice on offer.

The growth of the Internet and broadband, with its ability to provide fast download times as well as video and audio on demand, is challenging the traditional means of distribution. This breaking down of barriers between the original forms of distribution has made text, images and audio increasingly available through alternative, yet increasingly similar, platforms – a process known in the media industry as 'convergence'.

Defining audiences

In Unit 1 you learnt about a whole range of ways media producers find out about their audiences. This is called market research. The findings from this kind of research are used by media producers to get to know their audiences. They want to know what those audiences are like and what their likes, dislikes and interests are.

A lot of the work done in Unit 1 is very relevant to your work here. If you have completed section 1.1 you should refer to your findings wherever you can. If you have not, then you might find you can generate evidence for both sections at the same time by working on them together. But do not forget you will have to submit evidence separately for each unit.

Think it over 1

The people who run and work in the media industry think about their audiences in particular ways. When making media products of whatever kind, they have to think carefully about who will consume those products and make sure that their audience really will like them and want to keep coming back for more. As we have seen, if audiences do not want the products, the organisations that produce them will soon go out of business.

Imagine a newspaper that goes bust after a few months, a film that earns very little money at the box office, a television channel with very few viewers, or a radio station that hardly anybody listens to. Like a commercial website that rarely gets hits or an interactive media product that collects dust on retail outlet shelves before being returned to the distributor's warehouse, these are all disasters for the people who have produced them. They represent wasted investment and the eventual cost may well be bankrupt businesses and lost jobs.

In order to think about their audiences, media producers use audience data of the kind we explained in section 1.1. Audience data can be broken down into **demographic** groupings, so that different sections and sub-sections of the audience can be identified and catered for. The media industry uses the categories to distinguish between different groups of people. These include:

- socio-economic status
- interests and lifestyle
- sexual orientation
- gender
- age group
- location.

Most, or all, of these terms will already be familiar to you.

Media producers have to be careful that in making products to attract certain groups of people, they are not alienating or harming other groups. This includes making fun of characteristics apparently shared by people in certain groups. This is called **stereotyping** and can be damaging and hurtful as it makes people feel vulnerable.

Key Terms

Mass media are communications delivered over large electronic networks, such as radio, television and the Internet, aimed at reaching a very large audience.

Demographics relates to the way people can be grouped together and described based on different factors, such as age, gender and social class.

Stereotyping is a way of portraying a group of people that is used so often that it becomes very repetitive, and often a distortion of the truth. Eventually, this 'image' they are given can damage individuals within that group.

Think it over 2

Why do you think media producers want to identify differences between people? What are the advantages of them doing this?

How can stereotyping people be dangerous?

Socio-economic status

Socio-economic status refers to what is sometimes simply called social class. Social class is very difficult to define. As recently as thirty or forty years ago, it seemed perfectly appropriate in the UK to define people as upper, middle or lower class. Lower class was more politely called working class – not because people in the middle class did not work, but because the working class did the more manual, dirtier and more physically demanding jobs, such as mining or working in heavy manufacturing industries, including steelworks and shipbuilding. There was little movement between classes mainly because sons tended to follow their fathers into similar jobs, and many mothers and daughters did not work at all.

Now, many more women work and there is much more upward mobility through the class structure. This is due to greatly increased educational opportunities and a shift from heavy industry to a greater number of jobs in the service sector, banking and retail industries. This has led to children of working-class families growing up to more closely fit descriptions of the old middle class.

Key Terms

Socio-economic refers to both sociology and economics. Sociology is the study of society – how people live and relate to each other. Economics – or money matters – can affect how well people live, their lifestyles and how educated they can become.

Standard Occupational Classification is a detailed method of classifying socio-economic status based on profession.

■ Categories for describing socio-economic status

Today, the media industry uses a more detailed way of considering socio-economic status in its audience research. Devised in the 1950s this method categorises people according to the profession of the main earner in the household. Families are grouped into the categories using the labels A, B, C1, C2, D and E. Here A is considered more 'upmarket' than B, B than C1, and so on. See Unit 1 page 17 for more detail on these groupings.

This way of classifying people can be very useful for both media producers and advertisers. For example, Classic FM knows it attracts more ABC1s than C2DEs, and the businesses that advertise on the radio station know what kind of products this audience is most likely to buy. Classic FM also knows what kind of things its listeners will be interested in, so it also publishes a magazine, on sale through newsagents, with articles about music, concerts and other subjects of interest to ABC1 people. It also has a website.

Many other commercial radio stations that play more modern music know their listeners are more likely to be in the C2,D and E groups. People in these groups tend to buy tabloid newspapers more than broadsheets or compacts, so the presenters on these radio stations talk about stories in the tabloids, rather than classical musicians and composers. In 2007 the parent company of Classic FM, GCap Media, launched a new digital-only radio station for ABC1 people, called theJazz. They thought it would do for jazz music what Classic FM did for classical music in the 1990s.

Standard Occupational Classification is a newer way of classifying people according to social group. It is more complicated than the method described above, so media producers are less likely to use it.

Think it over 3

Some people are very surprised when they see which group the method puts them into. Of course, while the different categories relate quite closely to family income – the best-paid jobs tend to be in category A – some of the most 'prestigious' people are not the people we would most like to have around in times of need, for instance, when there is a leak or our house is on fire!

Interests and lifestyle

Another way of thinking about audiences concerns lifestyles. Lifestyle includes the way people live, but also the way they may choose to spend their time. As a way of classifying people, lifestyle is very closely related to occupation. This is simply because wealthier people have more money to spend on expensive hobbies and pastimes. A yachting magazine, for example, is more likely to interest people who have the money – and the time – to go yachting.

The advertisers who might want to advertise in a yachting magazine will be even keener to do so if they think the readers can afford to buy yachts, rather than just book an occasional mini-cruise on one. Wealthy people are more likely to be interested in lifestyle occupations and choices such as collecting antiques, consuming expensive organic food, yachting, eating out, investing in property and many other activities that media products can cover for them.

It is not just wealthy people who can afford to enjoy themselves, though. Other social groups spend time and money on leisure activities. Football is a big lifestyle indicator, for instance. Many C2DE men go to watch their favourite teams play, and so radio presenters aiming at this group will talk about football in order to interest

them. Sky Sport can sell advertising during and around its football coverage for products that appeal to men – such as beer and food. Beer drinking and watching football are closely related lifestyle activities that help media producers work out what some of their audiences like.

▲ Figure 5.01: It is very difficult to tell people's socio-economic status, or their interests and lifestyle, just by looking at them. Consider, though, where they are from, where they live and work and what they do in their spare time.

Key Term

Pink pound is a marketing term to describe the money spent by the gay communities on products aimed specifically to appeal to them.

Television programmes such as *Queer Eye for the Straight Guy* and films like *Brokeback Mountain* might appear to be aimed at a gay audience but hve a much wider appeal. Some media producers consider the **pink pound** to be a very attractive way of making money by serving an audience defined by its sexuality.

Theory into practice 2

Visit some specialist websites or read some magazines for particular interest groups. **P**

Explain (do not just describe) how some groups of people are more likely to be interested in information about cars, antiques or computers. **M**

Fully explain how different media products could be made to interest each group of people – and why. **D**

Sexual orientation

Some media products exploit differences between people's sexuality in order to attract audiences.

Today, negative portrayals are increasingly rare. Economic common sense shows that offending people who could be part of your audience will not help sales or ratings. In the TV programme *Little Britain*, for instance, the character Dafydd who is 'the only gay in the village,' can be understood as less of an attack on gay lifestyles than an attack on his hypocrisy, pretending to be something that he is not.

Targeting media products at members of the lesbian, bi-sexual and homosexual communities is quite common. A radio station called LBH Radio did just that – but it was set up by a straight man who had not done enough research into his target audience to fully understand it.

There are products aimed predominantly at the gay market in all media sectors. There is the newspaper *Gay Times*, magazines, such as *Out* and *Gay Parent*, the on-line Gay News Network and Planet Out website.

▲ Figure 5.02: The one thing you can be sure about people is that we are all different. Sometimes, though, stereotypes can be harmful.

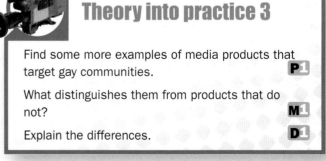

Theory into practice 3

Find some more examples of media products that target gay communities. **P**

What distinguishes them from products that do not? **M**

Explain the differences. **D**

Gender

We have already considered how gender can be a useful way of dividing people into likely audiences for products. Think again of the men who like football. Gender is a relatively simple way of classifying people because there are only two groups: male and female. Most people are obviously in either one or the other and most people do not object to saying which group they belong to in questionnaires, letters and emails (where you cannot actually see or hear them to determine their gender without asking).

Having only two genders to think about can be misleading, of course. It is far too easy to assume all men and all women think the same. This patently is not true, with many things being enjoyed or consumed equally by both men and women, by families and people of all ages. Media producers need to be sensible about targeting different audiences, and some wise media producers realise they might be able to double their audience if they can appeal to both men and women.

Age group

Planning content according to people's interests determined by their age is often a little easier. A whole generation of people who grew up at the same time will share memories and a feeling of nostalgia for certain moments in history, for instance milestone events such as the first moon landing or England winning the World Cup.

Radio stations that play 'oldies' from certain decades, such as the sixties, seventies or eighties, are trying to exploit that nostalgia by targeting particular age groups. So do television programmes that recreate particular eras, and books and magazines that feature particular events. Most older people do not like the latest chart sounds, and most young people do not want to listen to hits from the 1950s and 1960s. So Radio One and Saga Radio, which targets the over 50s, are certainly not competing for the same audience!

Case study

BBC Radio 1

Target audience

This radio station targets its core audience of 15–29 year-olds very carefully. While people outside this age range are welcome to, and do, listen in, the Radio 1 Controller is unlikely to worry if people outside the core audience do not like the programmes very much. On the other hand, he does have to start worrying if his core audience does not like the content.

Main product

The station concentrates hard on serving its core audience with a mix of mainly current and new music linked by presenters who are in touch with young listeners. Because of its public service obligations, Radio 1 supports a lot of new and UK acts and also there is a well-resourced news team providing regular bulletins, targeted specifically at the audience. It also produces documentaries on a wide-range of subjects. Radio 1 features some unsigned bands and session recordings in order to promote the development of new music and ensure that as a station it remains at the cutting edge of the music scene.

Associated products

The station's popular website features background information about the programmes, and audio downloads so listeners can listen again to certain programmes, or catch them on-line if they missed them on-air. There is also advice on the website about issues that concern the target audience.

The main network has to cater for a wide range of music tastes, but a second, sister, radio station, 1Xtra, is targeted at young listeners who are fans of contemporary black music. This niche audience has to access the station via digital platforms, because it does not have an FM transmitter network to broadcast from.

- **Do you know anyone outside the core target audience who listens to Radio 1 regularly?**

- **Why is there a second network, called 1Xtra?**

- **How is the news targeted at the core audience?**

All the different sectors of the media use age as a way of ensuring content matches the target audience's interests and expectations. In print there are magazines aimed at all age sectors, from toddlers to the retired. In television, BBC Three knows that its audience, being younger, is much more tolerant of bad language, whereas BBC Four is targeted at older, more culturally minded people. Both channels are able to plan their content intelligently as a result of this knowledge. The producers of every successful DVD, newspaper and website consider the age of their audience when planning content.

Location

Where people live or where they come from can have a fundamental effect on the way they think and what will interest them. Across the globe there are huge differences in the way people live. In parts of Africa, for example, getting safe drinking water can be one of the biggest issues in most people's lives. In other places ordinary people are caught up in a war or famine. Currently within the UK there are not such huge issues and contrasts, but there is still a wide range of issues affecting only certain sections of the community. For instance, issues of burning importance to rural communities are not of interest to urban communities. Availability of local transport, for instance, can be a major issue in the country, and when foot and mouth disease hit the farming industry in 2001, it was not just farmers who were affected, but the whole rural economy and community.

Planning media content by postcode – or at least by the region or the locality in which people live – can make that content much more relevant to the audience. Local newspapers and radio stations are able to cover news stories and provide information that are of real importance to people living in that area, such as road closures or local authority decisions. This is because people's own lives are touched by these issues in a very practical sense. Much more so than by many international news stories, which can seem of very little actual relevance to ordinary people's lives. In times of crisis, such as an unexpectedly big snowfall, it is often to the local radio stations that people turn in order to find out what is happening; whether their local school

is closed and perhaps where they might be able to get emergency supplies.

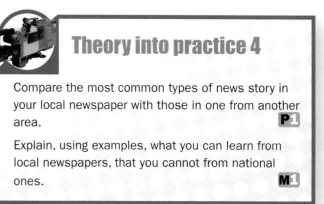

Theory into practice 4

Compare the most common types of news story in your local newspaper with those in one from another area. **P1**

Explain, using examples, what you can learn from local newspapers, that you cannot from national ones. **M1**

■ Geodemographics

You will need to demonstrate your understanding of this term. It refers to the way one area differs from another because of where it is. For example, a big city may have a higher percentage of people from lower socio-economic groups than a smaller city or town, simply because there are more poor areas in a big city.

Rural areas may have a high percentage of retired people, because after they have finished their working life, people have used their savings to retire to an area where they can enjoy more peace and quiet than in the inner city.

Key Term

Geodemographics is a way of thinking about the structure of audiences that is due to where people live.

■ Regional identity

In some regions, people have a greater sense of belonging than in others. In London, for example, as in many large cities around the world, there are many people in the population from other regions and countries. In other places it may be quite unusual to find people from elsewhere, simply because fewer people migrate into the area. These areas may have a very strong regional identity.

One example is Merseyside, in north-west England. Merseysiders are often nicknamed 'Scousers' and most of them do not mind this at all. In fact, they are mostly very proud of what makes them Scousers – the way they talk, the way they feel a strong sense of community, the way the rest of the country thinks about them, and the way they feel they all have their regional identity in common.

In areas with a strong regional identity, regional media products often do better than national ones. Radio City and Radio Merseyside, for example, are regularly the most listened to stations in Merseyside, because they know and deliver what their audience likes. Regional news is more likely to be popular in an area where people have roots in the locality and feel strongly about where they live.

▲ Figure 5.03: A local newspaper can be sure that its audience will be interested in local issues.

Types of audiences

We have identified a number of ways in which audiences can be identified. Not all media producers divide people up into small, easily identifiable audiences, though. Some want to reach as many people as they possibly can. Their products will be aimed at as many different people as possible, with lots of differences between them, but who *share* some common interests that unite them. These audiences are often described as mainstream.

■ **Mainstream audiences**

A very good example of this kind of audience is to be found in television. BBC1 is a channel that is targeted at the **mainstream audience** of people who want to be entertained, informed and sometimes challenged by a mix of comedy, drama, feature and documentary programmes. Of course, not everyone would enjoy every programme on the channel, but there are some that have very broad appeal. BBC1 and its main rival, ITV1, both run almost daily soap operas, *EastEnders* and *Coronation Street*, and they regularly achieve audiences of over 10 million each week. In our multi-channel world of hundreds of television and on-line sources of entertainment, that is very mainstream.

Often the BBC moves new series from its specialist channels BBC2 or BBC Three to BBC1, because they have proven they may have broader appeal than originally thought. *Little Britain* started out in this way, quickly demonstrating it had broad appeal, as all sorts of people, both young and old, began imitating the characters in it.

Theory into practice 5

Carry out some research to find examples of how different people fit into different categories, depending on how you classify them.

For example, select a number of friends, relatives, members of staff, fellow students and colleagues, if you have a part-time job.

Describe the categories of people they might fit in to. **P1**

Extension activity

Check through your work for section 1.1 of Unit 1 and compare it with what you have just found out. **P1**

What connections can you make between the work in the two units? **M1**

Key Term

Mainstream audience is a large audience made up of people who have a lot in common. Products for mainstream audiences are enjoyed by a broad range of people.

There are examples of products aimed at mainstream audiences in other media industries. Blockbuster movies, for instance, often have wide appeal. Some of the biggest earners at cinema box offices worldwide are shown in the box below:

Film	Gross earnings
Titanic (1997)	$1,835,300,000
Lord of the Rings: The Return of the King (2003)	$1,129,219,252
Harry Potter 1 (2001)	$968,600,000
Star Wars Episode 1 (1999)	$922,379,000
Lord of the Rings: The Two Towers (2002)	$921,600,000
Jurassic Park (1993)	$919,700,000
Shrek 2 (2004)	$880,871,036

Figure 5.04: High box office earners demonstrate the mainstream appeal of their content.

◼ Alternative audiences

Alternative audiences are the opposite of mainstream audiences. They are people who like new, striking or challenging media products. One problem with alternative audiences is that they tend to be small. These are people with unusual tastes, so there will not be many of them!

The radio station XFM began as an alternative commercial music station for London. Commercial radio stations need money from advertising to survive, and XFM's original audience was very small. Eventually, it was sold, and its new owners made it a bit more mainstream to attract a larger audience and more advertising, but without changing it so much that it would sound like any other station.

Think it over 5

How long can a media product remain 'alternative' if it proves to be very popular?

◼ Niche audiences

Niche audiences tend to be very specialised. Lots of magazines cater for niche audiences. They do not have a readership anywhere near as large as that of the national newspapers, sometimes printing only a few hundred thousand copies of each edition. Even smaller still are fanzines, which might run to only a few hundred copies, if that.

Because publishing on the web is so much cheaper than printing and distributing paper, the Internet has become very popular for websites that serve niche audiences. Even if they charged a subscription, they still would not make much money, because the audiences they are aimed at are so small.

Key Term

Niche is a specialised, and sometimes very narrowly defined market segment. The smaller the niche, the more difficult it may be to make money from it.

Lads' mags

One market niche that magazine publishers have discovered is young males. Magazines such as *Loaded*, *Nuts* and *Zoo* target this market with pictures of fast cars, gadgets and scantily clad young women. Until these came along, it was only the soft-porn magazines found on the top shelf in some newsagents that would use sexually provocative images to appeal to men. There is much less stigma, though, attached to reading a lads' mag in public, than there is to reading pornography.

A slightly different niche is the men's fitness market. *Men's Health* differs from more mainstream lads' mags by including content about getting and keeping fit, as well as more medically orientated health issues. Of course, men have always bought magazines specialising in such topics as computing, motoring, fishing, racing and football. However, until the arrival of the lads' mags in the 1990s there was no male magazine genre that could be described as an equivalent of the women's interest magazines, which range from *Woman's Realm* to *Cosmopolitan*.

Although some people disapprove of lads' mags and do not like to be stereotyped in this way, the product appeals to enough young male buyers to make money for the publishers.

▲ Figure 5.05: What will be the next niche market to be discovered?

Think it over 6

Why do you think media producers are interested in niche audiences? If they are very small, there may be very little money to be made from them.

Ethnicity

Some niche markets can be quite large, although they may never be as large as mainstream audiences, and they might be quite different in their interests. Often these larger niche markets are based on ethnicity, one of the ways of thinking about audiences that we have not yet thought about in much detail.

Ethnicity is not about lifestyle choices, or even about being able to move from one group to another through getting a good education and then a better job. Ethnicity is about our origins – where we come from, where our parents come from and where their parents come from. Even if we could change our skin colour or the way we speak, wear different clothing or adopt a different religion, we would still have origins in one or more ethnic groups. Even if ethnic groupings are useful ways of identifying what things groups of people may be interested in, it is important to remember that we should all respect people from every ethnic group, no matter how different they are from ourselves.

Ethnic groups can be divided in a number of different ways. We live in a society where many people have moved around the country, and even the world, before settling where they live now, so some people fit into more than one grouping.

In terms of ethnicity, we can group people by:

* skin colour
* country of birth
* race
* region of birth
* religion.

Theory into practice 6

Identify which ethnic groups are *most* likely to be the main audience for the following media products. Some will be easier to match than others, and you might need to use the Internet. **P1**

* *The Jewish Chronicle*
* *The Catholic Herald*
* *The Scotsman*
* B4U
* Sunrise Radio
* *In Britain*
* 1Xtra
* BBC Asian Network
* Pobol Y Cwm
* Ebony
* *The Tablet*
* *Searchlight*

Now research some more products from your chosen sector. **P1**

Grading tips

To reach Merit level, explain, rather than just describe, the connection between each product and the ethnic group/s most likely to be interested in it.

To reach Distinction level, in each case, fully explain their interest in the product by giving reasons why the content should appeal to them.

Audience research

How media producers think about their audiences depends on how well they know them. In Unit 1 we explained about the work of the data gathering agencies, and how they find out information about different audiences for media products.

■ Data gathering agencies

Each of these bodies tries to supply the most accurate information they possibly can about media audiences. One major problem, though, is that most of those audiences are invisible at the time of consumption.

Some audiences can be physically counted – attendance at a football ground, the number of people who pass through an art gallery or how many cars pass by an advertising billboard, for example. But we simply do not know how many people are tuned in to a television or radio programme, or how many people read a single copy of a newspaper. It may be bought and read by one person, and then dumped or recycled – or it may find its way into the waiting room of a doctor's surgery, and is then read by dozens of people through the course of a normal day.

Consumption of interactive media products can be measured up to a point, but once an item has been sold or downloaded from a website or over a mobile phone, it is difficult to detect any secondary use of it, that is by people it is passed on to, by whatever means.

The data gathering agencies include:

- BARB – the Broadcasters' Audience Research Board. Uses set-top meters in a sample of homes to measure what everyone who lives there watches on television,

▲ Figure 5.06: How many people will see these adverts in a typical day?

and for how long.
- RAJAR – Radio Joint Audience Research. Finds out what their sample audience listens to on the radio, and for how long.
- ABC – Audit Bureau of Circulations. Checks how many newspapers and magazines are *sold*, how many are given away free, and how many are returned unsold.
- NRS – National Readership Survey. Interviews a sample audience about what newspapers or magazines they have read (rather than just bought). The difference between ABC and NRS addresses the point made earlier about more than one person being able to read a single copy of a publication.

In Unit 1 you will find examples of their data. Most of the publicly available audience research is quantitative – that is it gives numbers of people in the audience. Sometimes the most useful research is qualitative – that is about what audiences actually *think* about the products. Some media producers market-test new ideas first, making sure they will appeal to the target audience.

■ Audience profiling

Once media producers think they have a pretty good idea what an audience is like, they often build up a **profile** of that audience. This is simply a way of understanding their audience more clearly. It is also a good way of telling other people what the audience is like, for example when selling advertising. Of course, even the BBC does this, because knowing their audience is the best way to give them what they want.

Think it over 8

How accurate do you think audience profiling can be? If a magazine editor imagines his target reader as a white male, aged thirty, who plays in a darts team, might he be missing out readers who do not play darts?

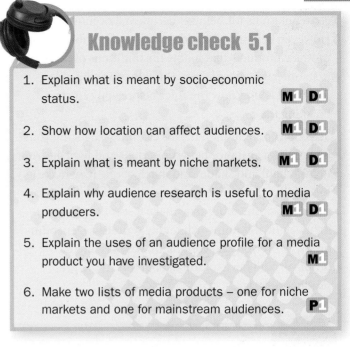

Knowledge check 5.1

1. Explain what is meant by socio-economic status. **M1** **D1**

2. Show how location can affect audiences. **M1** **D1**

3. Explain what is meant by niche markets. **M1** **D1**

4. Explain why audience research is useful to media producers. **M1** **D1**

5. Explain the uses of an audience profile for a media product you have investigated. **M1**

6. Make two lists of media products – one for niche markets and one for mainstream audiences. **P1**

5.2 Creating products for specific audiences

Addressing audiences

In the first part of this unit we explored how media producers think about their audiences. Now we turn our attention to the many ways they create products for specific audiences.

Selection of content

When choosing material to go in a product, media producers need to think first about the **genre** and the audience. They must ask the question, what does the audience want to see, hear or read about? To understand this, we need to understand the word genre. This just refers to a type or style – westerns, anime or romance can all be thought of as different genres. The genre of a media product is important because the audience will have certain expectations of a product in a particular genre. A news bulletin is one genre, and audiences will not, for example, expect to see a television newsreader doing a dance in the middle of a news bulletin. They might,

however, find it very funny if a newsreader appears on a comedy sketch show and then does a dance, because that is another genre.

Key Term

Genre is the French word for 'type'. In media studies it is used in a particular way, to group together all the media products of one type in order to help us to discuss and understand them. Genre categories might include situation comedy, current affairs and soap operas.

Media producers may also ask whether audiences want more of the same kind of material that they usually find in programmes of the same genre, or whether they want something a little different? Audiences may have expectations of a genre, but they can become tired of the same old material, and often welcome change if it is well thought out. That is why some media producers get reputations for being experimental or innovative. However, beginners would do well to show they can produce products that follow the traditions of the genre first, otherwise people may think they are not able to. You need to know the rules before you can start breaking them.

Selecting content often means carefully balancing your material, for instance between serious and light-hearted items – light and shade. Too much of one may make for a dull or upsetting programme or publication, while too much of the other may make it seem frivolous or lightweight and not worth taking seriously. Depending on the genre you are working in, you, as a media producer, will have to think about this in the pre-production stage.

Think it over 9

The BBC's first female television newsreader, Angela Rippon, may have been most famous for showing her legs in a dance routine on the *Morecambe and Wise Show*. How do you think the audience reacted to that very funny, but very unexpected scene? How can media producers keep audiences interested in their products without them growing stale?

Examples of content that media producers have to select in order to create their products are:

- Words – the way words are chosen and put together affects the meaning of the product, whether it seems believable and how interesting it is.
- Images – the choice of images can make a product attractive or dull, exciting or boring, interesting or tedious.
- Sound – can add to a visual medium, such as a moving image production or a website. Radio or audio products have only sound content.
- Sequences – the order that content appears in can alter meaning as well as affect the product's appeal to the audience.
- Colour – choosing attractive colours and having an effective colour scheme can make a product much more appealing to an audience.

- Fonts – the style and size of text can be very important, because they can make writing look **important**, serious, comic, educational or *fun*, depending on which ones are used.

Case study

The Hits

Target audience
This digital-only television channel secured a valuable slot on the surprise-hit platform Freeview, as well

Figure 5.07: The Hits is a Freeview success story.

as being one of a large number of music channels available on Sky and cable. Its prominence on Freeview enables it to reach a larger audience of young people than would be the case if there were lots more competitors on the platform.

Main product
The output is mainly current hits, chosen to form a playlist of videos that will directly appeal to the target audience. There are also interactive features designed to be popular with the market, such as dial-in requests, downloadable ringtones and on-screen text messaging, themed around relationships and dating.

Associated products
A radio station of the same name launched soon afterwards, using a similar playlist to target a similar audience via DAB radio, Freeview and the Internet. The parent company, EMAP, developed a range of other brands, including the Smash Hits television channel and radio station, which themselves drew from the popularity of the pop magazine of the same name.

- **Why are radio and television channels given the same names?**
- **Why is Freeview popular?**
- **What was the first media product to be named 'Smash Hits'?**

Target audience	Some of their interests	Product intended to address at least some of those interests
Young (perhaps single) men	Cars, having fun, daring activities, young women, weird phenomena	Bravo (television channel)
Young women	Celebrity lifestyles and gossip	Just 21 (magazine)
Middle-aged men	Rock music, going to gigs featuring classic rock artists	Planet Rock (digital-only radio station)
Middle-aged women	Real-life stories, cooking, fashion and beauty, health, soaps	Woman's Own (magazine)
Book buyers of all demographic groups	Buying books for study, entertainment and finding out information	Amazon.com (website)

▲ Figure 5.08: This table shows how different products single out particular interests within their target audiences, and aim to satisfy them. Some target audiences are very narrow, while others are very broad.

Theory into practice 8

Choose a range of media products and decide how the media producers have selected content to appeal to the target audience of each one. **P2**

Grading tip

To reach Merit level, keep records of your findings, explaining them as you work; you will be able to use them as assessment evidence later.

Construction of content

The way that content is constructed really does affect how much it will appeal to audiences. Most media products consist of a number of different content items. How they are put together can turn something rather dull into something very exciting.

Ways in which products can be constructed differently include:

- the order they are put in
- the size or duration
- how they combine with other elements.

■ Narratives

Most media products construct a **narrative** in one way or another. Telling a story – true or fictional – is constructing a narrative. It does not have to have a narrator – someone telling the story. Simply putting a number of images in a sequence could create a narrative. A particularly dramatic or descriptive piece of music can also suggest a narrative, even without pictures.

So, whatever the media product, a media producer is usually aiming to create a narrative. The more appealing the narrative to the audience, the more successful it is likely to be. We will look in more detail at the various different ways of constructing narratives in section 5.4.

◄ Figure 5.09: Each of these media products is aimed at a different audience, using different content to make them interesting to the targeted audience.

Key Terms

Narrative is the storyline, true or fictional, that underlies a media product. This can be anything from a film script to the content of a magazine or website.

Layout is the organisation of text and graphics in posters, websites, flyers and other printed media.

■ Layout

Media products, such as books, magazines and websites, that use images, fonts and framing elements, such as borders, boxes, headings and captions, use **layout** to appeal to their audiences. Layout is quite literally the way items are laid out on a page. By now you should have noticed that this book is laid out in such a way as to clearly separate different sections, while making the content look as lively and interesting as possible. Figure 5.10 explains some of the ways in which layout can be used to appeal to a target audience.

Elements	Type of element	Reason for use
Boxes, borders, typographical layout (font size, headlines, bylines), contents pages, hyperlinks, text (captions)	Framing	Divide up content, increase appeal to reader
Text (words), images, graphics	Content	Engage reader
Display ads, classified ads	Advertising	Earn income, inform readers
Contact details, response lines	Interactivity	Encourage response, increase income, provide service

Figure 5.10: Layout elements found in print products and web pages. How are they arranged?

Medium	Element	Type of element	Reason for use
Moving image (video, film, DVD)	Theme tunes, title sequences, credit sequences, scene changes, captions, narration, presentation, continuity announcements before and after programmes	Framing	Keep viewer watching, identify content, divide up content
	Images, music, words, actuality, sounds	Content	Engage listener
	Spot advertising, classified advertising	Advertising	Earn income, inform readers
	Menu selection, response lines, texting, phone-ins	Interactivity	Encourage response, increase income, provide service
Radio	Jingles, theme tunes, continuity announcements before and after programmes, signposting by presenter, trails, narration, presentation	Framing	Keep listener tuned in, identify content, divide up content
	Music, words, actuality, sound effects	Content	Engage listener
	Spot advertising, classified advertising ('Job slots' etc.)	Advertising	Earn income, inform readers
	Phone-ins, texting, email reponses asked for and read out	Interactivity	Encourage response, increase income, provide service

Figure 5.11: Layout elements found in other types of media products.

Think it over 10

The layout for a lively media textbook will not be appropriate for every kind of print product. Some textbooks are much more serious in their approach. Think what kinds of layout would suit other print products, such as a menu, a catalogue, a comic and the order of service for a funeral.

■ Captions and anchorage

One way of creating meaning in a media text is to add some extra information designed to make the audience understand it in a particular way. This is called **anchorage**. Throughout this book, for example, the images have captions underneath them. These have been added to explain their significance, or to make sure the image tells you something in particular in order to develop your understanding.

In many cases, changing the caption would change the way you think about the image – that is, you would have a different understanding of what the picture means. Consider the way the different captions for the image below alter the meaning of the same picture. Even though the picture is unchanged, the second caption encourages you to think about the image in a completely different way.

Now try and imagine other captions that could alter the meaning again. The possibilities are endless, because your imagination, and that of other people reading this, can range far and wide to bring an infinite variety of different ideas to the task. Because this can be quite good fun, newspapers and magazines often run caption competitions, inviting readers to suggest new captions for photographs that are already quite amusing. The funniest caption in the opinion of the Editor is the one that wins.

▼ Figure 5.12: Animal conservationists use zoo breeding-programmes to help endangered species to reproduce in safety.

▼ Figure 5.13: Life in captivity often causes distress and anxiety to wild animals.

Of course, different people find different things funny, so change the Editor, and perhaps somebody different would win the prize.

Many people find the front covers of *Private Eye* magazine amusing, because they normally feature a candid photograph of one or more politicians, with 'speech bubbles' added to it. By mischievously putting words into the mouths of the politicians, the meaning of the photograph can change quite dramatically, making an ironic or sarcastic point about them.

Key Term

Anchorage is a way of 'tying down' the meaning of some part of a media text.

■ Codes and conventions

When media producers create media products, they use several techniques to put meaning into them, all the time making sure they are appealing to their audiences. Often they do this using **codes** and **conventions**. To understand codes and conventions, you need to understand the term **signifier**. A signifier is simply something that creates meaning in a media product. Quite literally, it *signifies* something.

There are all sorts of ways a media text can make meaning. Just as a book could consist entirely of writing (as novels often do) relying on the words alone to tell the reader everything the author wants to encode, a radio programme could consist of only words all spoken in a flat monotone voice that does not really give anything away in terms of emotion, mood or action. A television programme could also feature a single person reading aloud from a book – and there have been very successful programmes that have done just that. Likewise, a print or an interactive media product could use only text to communicate to its audience.

Such unadventurous use of these different media would quickly become boring, and not very appealing at all. This is because the producers would not be exploiting the opportunities these media offer to the full. So, add a picture to a page, some emotion to a voice, and

moving images to a story reading, and not only does the text become more interesting, but the combinations of different **elements** within the text can start to work together to make meaning. By putting two elements together – like the picture and the caption – new meanings can be created and others become impossible.

Think it over 11

If the saying 'a picture paints a thousand words' is true, how many words does a moving picture paint? What about an interesting sound? Or a combination of the two?

For example, the sound of a lion roaring could make radio listeners think the action is taking place on the African plains, until they hear a loudspeaker announcement warning visitors that the zoo is about to close. A picture of a young man running towards an old lady might make television viewers think he is going to attack her, until another shot reveals that he is running to catch a heavy object falling towards her.

Remember the different fonts used earlier to add an extra layer of meaning to plain text? Well, choosing the right one for the type of headline or story involved can also add extra meaning.

Key Terms

Codes are systems of putting over a meaning to audiences without using words to explain what is going on.

Conventions are the accepted and expected ways of doing something.

Elements of a media product are the different parts of it which, when put together, make up the whole product.

Signifiers are elements which create meaning in a media product.

Codes

When signifiers work together, each one acts as part of a code – just as Morse code is a whole set of symbols that stand for letters, each symbol would be of little use without the rest. Without a complete set to work with, it would be impossible to spell out a word in Morse code, because several letters would be missing. In the same way, media texts rely on whole systems of signifiers working together to get their message across. Codes in media texts have developed over time, they were not created from scratch in one sitting.

The way news is presented on television is an example of how a media code develops over time. Many of the very first news broadcasts on television did not feature a newsreader on screen, but instead scripts were read out while still images or newsreel were shown. The newsreader's presentation manner had already developed on radio – sounding very formal because of the seriousness of news, occasionally sounding cheerier when reporting on a more light-hearted item.

Once newsreaders began to appear on screen, their dress, seating position and 'look' towards the camera all became important. The first audiences watching television newsreaders will have had to make sense of what they were being shown. Today we are all so used to the way television news is *normally* presented, that we subconsciously read those codes without having to think about them.

Think it over 12

Although the mass media can easily code meaning for audiences to decode using sight and hearing, it is rare for them to use touch, smell and taste. Scratch cards that release particular smells have been given away as a gimmick to cinema audiences, who were told which parts to scratch at different moments in a 'smellyvision' programme. Cinemas have also used devices beneath, and in front of, seats to move or spray people sitting in them at particular times – for example to give them an extra fright or a sudden sprinkling of water.

What do you think about these sorts of techniques?

We usually know we are watching a news programme the moment we tune into a channel. This is because the various signifiers working together to encode meaning into the programme do so immediately: we see a desk, one or two presenters, some on-screen headlines and perhaps a screen showing a reporter talking to the presenters. If we tune in before the programme begins, the opening title sequence tells us immediately what kind of programme is going to follow – the theme music is pacey yet important-sounding, and a series of images shows us glimpses of the world: people and places that are often in the news.

Even tuning-in to a foreign news programme has the same instant recognition factor – although we cannot understand what is being said, again it is the music, the use of images, the set design and so on that tell us what is happening. Similarly you would not need to look for very long at a foreign newspaper before you realised what it was! There are bound to be differences between newspapers from different countries, but the similarities between them are probably much greater.

We shall look at three particular categories of code:

- symbolic
- technical
- historical.

Symbolic codes – these suggest meaning through the choice of content – for example, using the colour red might suggest danger in a vampire movie, because it is the colour of blood. In another context, red can suggest passion, or love, and so an article about St Valentine's Day may have a red border or a red background. Facial expressions on actors in a drama, presenters, interviewees or contestants in a game show can also suggest the emotions they are feeling. Voices can portray emotion, too, and it is particularly important on radio, where faces cannot be seen and have to be imagined.

Technical codes – these include the use of graphics on screen and in print and multimedia products, the framing of an image, the use of soft focus to romanticise a scene or to hide someone's true age. Filters, lighting, camera angles, special effects and sound processing are other examples of ways in which technical aspects of a production can be put to work to create particular meanings.

Historical codes – some media products try to convey a moment in history. In order for the illusion to be convincing, all the different elements have to be right. The scenery or the backgrounds in any images have to reflect the time period. The costumes, tools, transport, buildings, what the people are doing and even the way they speak all have to seem authentic – otherwise there will be conflicting meanings in the text. If everything in the picture – and of course the sound – fits the time period, the most likely audience reading will be that the events shown are actually taking place then, rather than today. This is why film and television producers make great efforts to make sure there are not any television aerials or satellite dishes visible when they are shooting a scene from the days of Charles Dickens or Jane Austen.

Conventions

When producers and audiences have particular ways of doing things, these are called conventions. The signifiers we have just used to describe television news are all *conventions* of television news presentation. That is, they are the usual ways of encoding the same meanings into those texts. Until Channel Five launched in 1997 it had been usual for UK television newsreaders to sit behind a desk. Originally they had scripts, and more recently, keyboards or laptops on the desk. One of the

Theory into practice 9

Identify a range of different codes used in a number of media products of your choice. Include some that are symbolic, technical and even historical if possible, and say which category each set of signifiers fits into. **P2**

Explain how each code works – that is, what is it about each one that makes meaning? **M2**

Suggest alternative ways of encoding the same meanings into these texts. Explain how and why you think they would work. **D2**

more sensational aspects of *Five News* when it launched was the fact that instead of sitting behind a desk, Kirsty Young, the newscaster, moved around the studio and perched on the edges of desks while talking to the camera. This was done deliberately to imply a younger, more active 'feel' to their news, because Channel Five wanted to appeal to a younger audience. It would not have seemed so sensational in, for example, Germany or the United States, where television newsreaders have long stood up to deliver their bulletins.

▲ Figure 5.14: The conventions of television news presentation have changed dramatically over time.

When Channel Five began presenting their news in such a very different way from the convention, they were being groundbreaking: showing how something can be done differently without the media product losing its credibility with the audience. Innovation and creativity can be very good things. They can bring a breath of fresh air to that area of the media, and often one new idea is followed by another. Certainly, it is much more common now for newsreaders to get up and walk around the studios while presenting the news. So, what starts out as breaking a convention, sometimes becomes a new convention, as it is copied by others who also want to seem new, fresh and exciting. The way the broadsheet newspapers changed to compact size in a relatively short space of time is another good example.

When a comedy programme wants to satirise television news, it begins by taking the conventions of news presentation and then making something funny happen. In the same way, spoofs of different media products can also be made – for instance a spoof newspaper front page using many of the conventions of layout, language and image, but making it funny in some way.

Think it over 13

When do you think a new idea ceases to be a groundbreaking challenge to the usual conventions, and actually becomes a convention itself?

One of the best ways to understand conventions in the media is to ask yourself what would a media product be like if the producers did the *opposite* to the usual convention. For example, if the newsreader had his or her back to the camera while presenting the news, or was seen only in profile. What would audiences think if a serious newspaper had the sport on the first few pages, instead of the news? In the recent past, *The Independent* has broken with convention by printing just comment on the front page, instead of factual reporting.

Here are some more ways in which conventions could be broken:

- Placing captions above, instead of below images.
- Reading serious news in a light-hearted way.
- Beginning news bulletins with the 'funny' story and leaving the most important news until last.
- Allowing listeners to present radio programmes, while presenters sit at home.
- Playing music or music videos at the wrong speed.

Some of these examples of breaking conventions in the media would not be regarded as groundbreaking, challenging or innovative by their audiences. They would be thought of as mistakes – and even worse, if there were too many of them, the producers might even be thought of as incompetent or amateurish. That would bring about a loss of credibility, and the audiences for those products would decline.

There are plenty of examples of conventions being broken on purpose. Radio stations usually have news bulletins on the hour, but BBC Radio 1 has them on the half hour. That makes the station seem different from the rest, even though the reasons for it are historical: in the 1970s the station shared newsreaders with Radio 2, and they could not read different bulletins on different stations live at the same time!

New ideas often revitalise the print industry. *The Guardian* brought in a feature called 'Notes and Queries', in which readers provided answers to other readers' questions, instead of featuring an 'expert' who seems to know the answers to everything. Soon many other publications had similar features – although for copyright reasons they would be reluctant to admit they got the idea from *The Guardian*. Every clever idea has to have started being used somewhere – imagine people's surprise the first time a magazine stuck a free gift to each front cover, in order to increase sales. Now it is almost expected!

On the web, hyperlinks are usually images or text with underlining, but there is no rule or any technical reason why this should always be so. As developments in technology make the delivery of media products possible in more and more ways, the products themselves are likely to evolve as well. That means more conventions will be broken, and new ones will become established.

▲ Figure 5.15: Not all challenges to the usual codes and conventions are welcome.

Key Terms

Codes and conventions can be:

- **Linguistic** – to do with the style of language used (for example, is it formal or casual, does it sound like a news report or a fairy story?)
- **Visual** – to do with images (for example, how does the 'look' of the image affect meaning?)
- **Audio** – to do with sound (for example, is there a scary soundtrack to make a scene in a film more suspenseful?)
- **Symbolic** – suggesting something (such as red meaning danger)
- **Technical** – to do with the way a media product is made (for example how a director chooses to frame a shot)

Theory into practice 10

Choose a range of media products and show how they use a number of conventions. **P2**

Explain rather than just describe, what meanings they create, and how. **M2**

Explain the likely effect of doing the opposite of each of those conventions. **M2**

Explain how those conventions compare to others in the same products – for example, which are the most important and why? **M2**

Grading tip

To reach Distinction level, use well-chosen examples and explain them.

■ Modes of address

The way media products address their audiences can have a big effect on how audiences understand them.

This is important when planning a media product. For example, audiences today do not want to be spoken down to. Compare this with the way that fifty years ago public information films would tell them how to behave in the countryside, what to do in the event of a military attack or how to make scarce resources go further. **Modes of address** have changed over time. Until the 1980s all the serious programming on radio and television – and the continuity announcements before and after them – featured voices which spoke in 'received pronunciation', a kind of Home Counties English spoken in the most prosperous areas of the south-east. People in other regions, and even ordinary Londoners, rarely heard voices in the media like their own or their neighbours', unless they were being made fun of in comedies.

Today, as then, many people speak in a way that could be described as 'received pronunciation', but a wide range of other accents are also heard on radio and television in a variety of positive, authoritative roles.

However, mode of address is about much more than the way people speak. It is about the way a media product communicates with its audience – and that happens in a number of different ways, including the style of language used.

Language is not just about accent – it can also be about style, such as formal or informal. For example, a news article could be written in the formal style of a broadsheet or a compact newspaper, using long sentences and a wide range of vocabulary. Alternatively, it could be written in informal language as in a tabloid, with the words used often being simpler ones that a tabloid readership will find it easier to understand. That tabloid language would look very out of place in *The Times*, unless it was being used in a humorous way, perhaps to make fun of tabloid newspapers.

In film and in broadcasting, much of the language used is dialogue, but a different way of addressing the viewer or listener is used for documentaries, news reports and other factual programmes. This is more of a commentary or narration.

Modes of address also need to be changed for the age of the audience. The way most children's television presenters speak to their audiences is just right for children of the target age. Speaking to an adult audience in the same way would not be appropriate.

Language is also about **tone**. A media product that uses a friendly tone, can seem quite different from one that uses a very formal tone, or even a jokey one, and writers have to be careful to use the most appropriate one for the product – and the audience. Speaking softly or harshly can change the mode of address, just as writing in capitals in emails is considered to be shouting, and therefore, rather impolite.

Key Terms

Mode often means 'kind' or 'way'.

Mode of address is the way media products 'speak' to their audiences.

Tone refers to sentiment expressed, for instance stern, formal, friendly or angry.

Theory into practice 16

Choose a range of media products and explain the mode of address they use. **P2**

Select a number of media products and decide which ones are formal and which are informal in tone. **P2**

Explain how and why the language changes in some of them. **M2**

Explain a number of differences in the use of language to show your understanding. **D3**

Audience feedback

We have already investigated audience research used by media producers to understand their audiences and what those audiences want. Now let us consider the kind of feedback that producers can get from their audiences. They want feedback so they can understand if they are making their products as appealing as possible.

Producers can get audience feedback in a number of ways:

- Focus groups – made up of representatives of the target audience.

- Audience panels – members of panels provide feedback on a regular basis, perhaps at a regular meeting of the panel.
- Trialling and testing – samples of the audience give feedback on short 'pilot' extracts of what the complete product will be like.
- Reviews – sometimes, ordinary members of the audience provide reviews about new media products for newspapers, magazines and websites. There are also professional reviewers who write for newspapers: they can sometimes provide the cruellest feedback of all.
- Complaints – can be received directly from members of the audience, or they may complain to an official body, such as Ofcom for broadcasting, the ASA for advertising and the Press Complaints Commission for newspapers and magazines.

Theory into practice 12

Visit the websites of the following bodies: Ofcom, the ASA and the PCC. Search for their complaints pages and read through the feedback that has come to media producers in this way. Use your own words to summarise them, clearly identifying dates and sources. **P2**

Explain the reasons for the complaints being upheld or rejected. **M2**

Explain why those media producers risked getting complaints about these products. **D3**

Think it over 14

Sometimes media producers are happy to receive complaints about their work, especially if the publicity complaints can create lead to greater interest in the products. When a *Celebrity Big Brother* contestant, Jade Goody, was criticised for her treatment of fellow contestant, Shilpa Shetty, Ofcom received a record numbers of complaints. The audience ratings for the programme rose dramatically!

When do you think media producers should be worried about getting large numbers of complaints?

Knowledge check 5.2

1. Explain the word genre. **P2**

2. Explain how layout can be used in different ways in media products. **M2**

3. What is meant by anchorage? Give your own examples. **M2 D2**

4. Explain the terms code and convention, with your own examples of each. **M2 D2**

5. What is a signifier? Explain the term with examples. **M2 D2**

6. How do media producers use audience feedback? **P2 M2**

Audience responses

We have already spent some time investigating the way the media industry thinks about its audiences. Now let us consider what happens when audiences consume media products. That is, when audiences read, watch, listen to or interact with media products, how do they respond?

Media studies uses a number of key terms in order to understand what is happening when audiences make meanings from what they consume. For example, every media product is considered to be a **text**, in the same way that English lessons call a novel, a play or a poem a text. In media studies the texts are just as important as those studied in other subjects. Perhaps more surprisingly, in media studies consuming a text is often called **reading** it – even if it is a film, a DVD, a website, a radio programme or a television programme.

Key Terms

Text is any media product, when it is 'read', or consumed, by an audience. It may be written copy, or it may consist entirely of sounds and/or images.

Reading is the act of making meaning from a media text. For example, forming an understanding of what is happening in a radio play, or making sense of events described in a news report.

Audience understanding

If you have ever watched an obscure film and been unsure what it was all about, or simply argued with friends about the ending of a film and what it meant, you may have realised that meaning in media texts is not always the same for everyone. Some film directors set out to leave ambiguous endings, to force each member of the audience to think about what might happen next. At other times, media producers may try hard to make sure everyone in the audience understands the text in the same way.

Another way to explain this is to use a novel as an example. With perhaps only a single image on the front cover and the detailed description in the text for clues, every reader has to work quite hard to imagine what each character and every scene actually looks like. The more description there is of something in the novel, and the clearer that description is, the more likely it is that each reader will create images in their minds that are quite like the ones the author had imagined when writing the book.

If the descriptions are not very clear or detailed, the more likely it is that different readers will each form very different images from the same information. Each reader's version will be part of his or her very own reading of the text.

Now consider a radio play. As well as words, there are different voices speaking them out aloud, sound effects and perhaps music. Each sound in the play provides the listener with a little bit more information to use when building up a mental image of what is happening.

Think it over 15

In 1978 a radio play by Andrew Sachs was broadcast without any words at all. Consisting entirely of sounds depicting places and action, *The Revenge* (1978) was about a man on the run. Without any dialogue, listeners had to work out for themselves what was happening from start to finish. If you are able to listen to a recording of the play in class, preferably with the lights dimmed, it is interesting to stop the play occasionally and discuss what everything thinks is happening. Sometimes readings of the play are very different from one person to the next.

If the producer adds pictures, by putting the play on television, each viewer receives a lot more information about it. When they are *shown* images, they do not have to imagine them because they are already there.

Likewise, in other areas of the media industry such as print and multimedia production, audiences are given images to look at, and they have fewer gaps in their knowledge about what is happening to fill using their own imagination.

It follows that the more information is given to each member of the audience, (and so the less each one has to imagine), the more likely different people are to read a text in similar ways. Some media producers want individuals in their audiences to make different readings of a text, while others want them to understand the text in the same way. However hard producers may try to impose their own **preferred readings** on their audiences, they do not always succeed.

Key Terms

Preferred reading is the meaning the producer intended the audience to make from the text.

Oppositional reading is a meaning that is different in some significant way from the producer's preferred reading. The producer might think the audience has misunderstood.

Negotiated reading is the idea that meaning is created jointly by the text and the audience. Only when the two meet is meaning created.

Theory into practice 13

Identify and describe a number of different examples where media products could be read in different ways. For example, the start of a radio play where the opening is interesting but it is difficult to work out where it is set or whether it is in the past, present or future. **P3**

Ask other people what they think is happening – or about to happen – and compare their responses to each product. Explain why and how they might make different readings. **M3**

Extension activity

Look back at the section on anchorage. This is one of the many ways in which media producers try to impose their own meanings on their audiences. Without a caption, audiences are freer to interpret an image in their own ways. With a caption it is less likely that different people will 'read' the image in their own way.

Identify some examples of anchorage being used to impose preferred readings. **P3**

In each case, explain how the anchorage works. **M3**

Explain why anchorage works in those ways. **D3**

Participatory responses

Sometimes audiences respond to media products by wanting to become a part of the product itself. They might call a phone-in programme, send a text or an email in response to a question posed, a competition or a poll of the audience's opinions. Chat rooms and websites such as Wikipedia, MySpace and Blogger all use audience responses to actually create the product.

Usually there is someone moderating such sites, just as a producer would choose which texts should feature on a television or radio programme. Moderation in this context means deciding which strands in a chat room should be closed down, removing libellous or malicious

Figure 5.16: Different individuals are likely to make different readings of the same text, unless descriptions are very detailed and clear.

content, and ensuring that obscene material that breaks the law does not get included.

Many media producers find that when a debate gets heated or someone gets very emotional, their products get noticed more, and more members of the audience want to participate in some of the ways listed above. They may encourage callers who are distressed or members of a studio audience to contribute to the programme if they think that this will make it more interesting, exciting or simply more controversial for the rest of the audience.

Cultural competence

Individuals within audiences often 'read' media texts in ways that draw upon their previous knowledge and experience. Everyone has experienced certain aspects of life. As an example, we all know what it is like to feel hungry, or be cold, so we can understand what being hungry or cold feels like for someone shown in a media product. Other experiences are not universal. Only a woman who has given birth, for instance, can really know what this experience feels like.

The set of experiences that we each draw on in reading something depicted in a media product is called **cultural reserve**. It is knowledge that we possess that affects our own readings, so one person's cultural reserve may be quite different from another's, depending on what each has experienced in life.

Cultural competence is the extent to which someone can correctly understand something. To use the example of childbirth again, people who have not experienced childbirth can imagine the pain of childbirth because they have felt other kinds of pain, but they are not fully 'competent' to correctly imagine the pain of giving birth. Cultural competence is having the ability, through having experienced similar or comparable situations, to understand something depicted in the media that concerns a different way of life. For example, most judges do not have the cultural competence to understand what it is like to have to steal to survive. Nevertheless, judges are there to administer the law and a jury member may empathise.

Figure 5.17: Fan culture can be so strong that people react in extreme ways.

Key Terms

Cultural reserve is the understanding a person has of lifestyles, including popular culture, gained through experience.

Cultural competence is a person's ability to understand a particular culture or experience, as it is depicted in media products.

Think it over 16

Can cultural competence be learnt through the media? Even without experiencing at first hand what having a different lifestyle feels like, you might think you have a very good idea about it because you have seen it depicted on television, or another media product.

When you see war depicted in the media, how much do you really find out about what fighting or living in a war feels like?

When you read about celebrities in the press, how much do you really know about what it is like to live lives like theirs?

Fan culture

Media products can provoke such strong responses among their audiences that people become fans of the particular product. This could be a television programme, radio presenter, film star, newspaper columnist or even a website such as eBay. Media producers are usually pleased to provoke such strong responses from audiences, because fans are often prepared to buy associated merchandise, and so increase their profits. Merchandise, from *Postman Pat* shirts to fanzines, also act as an advert for the original media product, keeping the brand very visible and encouraging interest.

Audience theory

Not everyone who sees an advertisement or branding for a particular product will necessarily want to buy in to that product, but research has shown that young children are much more likely to respond to advertisements than teenagers or adults. Over the years, various theories have developed about the ways in which people respond to media products. There is no absolute agreement about these theories and some contradict each other. Therefore, they cannot all be correct, because they all say different things about audience responses.

Key Terms

Passive consumption is a theory in which audiences are believed to respond passively to media products. That is, the media tells them something, and they all respond in the same way.

Active consumption is a theory that states that audiences are made up of individuals who each respond in different ways, depending on their own opinions, experiences and personalities.

Hypodermic needle model

This is an early 'model' (or explanation) of audience response. It is so called because it compares audience response to the way a doctor might inject a stimulant into a human muscle. The same stimulant injected into any working muscle would cause it to respond in the same way. The model considers that the media 'inject' information into the human mind, and every human mind is likely to respond in the same way. This could be described as **passive consumption**.

Today, very few media academics think this explains very accurately how audiences actually respond to media products. Showing an image of a cuddly dog might make a lot of people say 'aaaah!' but plenty of other people will think of their allergies to dogs, their own pet dog who died the day before, or even the neighbour's dog who uses their garden as a toilet. In other words a proportion of the audience will have a negative response.

Proof that not everyone responds in the same way can be found in advertising. An advert may be considered a success if lots of people buy the product shown – but it is very unlikely that everyone who sees the advert will buy the product. No matter how good an advert for something mundane, such as washing powder, might be, for instance, it is unlikely, that everyone would rush out and buy it. Can you think of reasons why not?

Uses and gratifications theory

This model of audience behaviour is much more popular today. It considers individuals within audiences to be independent thinkers who respond in different ways to media products, depending on a range of different factors. These factors are:

- their experience
- their values (what they think is important and what is not)
- their understanding of what is being shown.

This response to advertising can be called **active consumption**.

We have already seen how individuals within audiences make different readings. Now consider how different individuals might want to *use* media products in different ways. Figure 5.18 contains some examples.

Type of person	Product
Commuter	Tunes in to a travel bulletin
Unemployed person	Finds a job hunters' website
Manual worker	Listens to radio for interest
Overweight person	Watches a slimming programme
Sports fan	Reads sport pages of the newspaper
Worried teenager	Reads agony column

▲ Figure 5.18: Different uses of media products by different people.

Individuals can also get gratification from media products. Here are some examples:

Media product	Gratification
Watching comedy	Has a good laugh
Reading novel	Enjoys escapism
Hearing play	Enjoys suspense
Visiting website	Buys a rare item
Posting comment on web	Gets anger off chest
Reading agony column	Feels better about a problem

▲ Figure 5.19: Different gratifications from media products.

The key to people's response is whether the media product is giving them what they want. People respond positively if the product is of use, gives them a sense of pleasure or satisfaction, or fulfils a need. Some products do all of these things.

Theory into practice 14

Carry out a reception study of a number of different media products. Find examples of how individuals could use them or gain gratification from them. **P3**

Grading tip

To reach Merit level, explain your findings fully in your own words.

Effects debates

Sometimes audience response to a media product can cause widespread concern. A particularly violent film or television programme, for instance, creates headlines in the news, and people discuss whether seeing violence on the screen encourages actual violence in pubs and clubs across the land. Sexual content can also spark controversy. This is because many people agree that exposing people – particularly children – to explicit sexual or violent content can have a harmful **effect**.

People who think audiences are easily influenced by content often call for greater **censorship**. On the other hand, people who think they are not unduly influenced by the media, or who think media influence does not matter, often demand less censorship. This is a debate that has raged since the development of print media, and although there is much more violent and sexual content in the media today than ever before, evidence is inconclusive about its effects, so this is a debate that may never go away.

There are strict rules about advertising on radio and television. For example, it would not be possible to show getting drunk in an advertisement as a good thing to imitate. There are debates about the use of advertising to influence children. Cigarette advertising has long been banned. Recently, concerns about obesity in children have led to calls for fatty foods and unhealthy fast foods to be banned from television advertising when children are watching.

Key Terms

Censorship is the removal of material regarded as unacceptably offensive, obscene, violent or otherwise inappropriate from a media product, or the restriction of that product's distribution. In some cases, censorship can mean the complete withdrawal of a product.

Effect is the impact of a media product on an audience. Some people think media products can have strong effects on their audiences, while others think such effects are very limited.

Think it over 17

Should violent and sexually explicit material be banned, or should it be allowed at certain times, or only in particular media products aimed at adult audiences?

How would you decide what should be allowed and what should be banned?

Who should watch all the risky material to decide which should be banned or what content should be cut out?

You may find you get some lively responses in class, and among older people, to these questions!

Extension activity

Look back through your work for Unit 1 about film classification. How has the work of the BBFC changed over the years as attitudes have changed? Use evidence to support your findings.

Knowledge check 5.3

1. What is meant by the media studies term 'text'? **P3**

2. Explain how audiences make 'readings' of different types of media text. Use examples to show your understanding. **M3 D3**

3. Show how media products can use audience participation. **P3**

4. What is the difference between passive and active audience responses? Explain your answer with examples. **M3 D3**

5. Describe an 'effects debate' over some thing or some issue shown in the media. **P1**

6. Explain how some people have argued that something in a media product has been copied and has been harmful to society. **M3 D3**

Critical approaches

In order to achieve the highest grades in this unit you will have to critically analyse a number of media products. This means studying them in a number of ways, which will be explained in this section of the book. If you just *describe* products, you will only be able to gain a pass mark. If you just *explain* them, you can only get a merit. Critical analysis, though, if done properly, could earn you a distinction. This section, on critical approaches to analysing media products, will tell you how to go about it.

We have discussed a number of ways in which audiences may respond to media products. Now it is your turn to respond to a number of such products. The work you have done in the previous section should help you, because now you are to become part of the audience for those products.

Content analysis

As you might expect, this means analysing the content of media products. This needs to be done in a careful, systematic way. Being systematic means you will analyse each product in a logical order, such as by:

- working from start to finish in a product, then moving on to the next one.
- comparing similar elements in a number of different products, for instance opening title sequences in a number of television dramas.

You should choose the approach that will suit you best. Think before you start what will work most effectively for the medium you wish to work with, and the aspects of that medium that you want to explore. Read on first, as the rest of this section could help you to carry out a successful analysis.

Key Term

Content analysis is a systematic study of the content of a product. This is best achieved by taking it apart and describing each individual element. Content analysis should also consider the structure and purpose of the product.

■ Content

When looking at content, try to imagine what the original proposal behind it would have been like. Ask yourself: what aspects of the subject matter would the professional media producers have emphasised in trying to get the go-ahead for this product? If your product is part of a series, then you will have to broaden your thinking to the whole series.

For example, if you were studying magazine programmes on radio or television, the edition of the professionally produced programme that you analyse may be the three-hundredth one to be broadcast, since the series was first proposed and commissioned. This could quite possibly be the case if it is broadcast daily. You would have to imagine what the original proposal would have been like – and also think about whether the product has evolved since it first appeared. The style and the content of the programme may well have changed a lot since it began.

Look at Figure 5.20 to see some examples. Because this book needs to cover all aspects of media products, the choice of medium is different for each example we have given, but if you make up a similar chart to begin your own study for this unit, you might only cover examples from one. The more description you can include about the content, the better.

Name of product (and genre)	Context for distribution	Target audience	Content
Look North (regional news magazine)	BBC1 early-evening regional optout slot	Adults	A range of news stories, hard and soft, from the local area
Kerrang! (glossy music magazine)	Newsagents – music magazine shelf	Teenagers to early twenties	News and feature items covering new rock music
Chris Moyles (radio sequence programme)	BBC Radio 1 at breakfast time	15–24 year olds	Current and new music, plus chat and humour
Our Town (interactive DVD)	Given away to visitors by tourist office and by post	Adults 35+	Features on places to visit, accommodation, festivals
Parlourhearth Ltd. (glossy four-page flyer)	Distributed by letterbox and in-store	Potential customers	Pictures and information about fireplace products
flogit.org (interactive website)	World wide web	People with IT equipment to sell	Lists details of IT equipment for sale, plus instructions on how to put item up on the site

▲ **Figure 5.20: Analysis of the content of several media products. Your own analysis should be of products from the same medium, and within the same genre.**

Once you have completed a table like the one in our example, you are ready to begin a content analysis of the range of products you are studying. Firstly, you should list the similarities between the subject matter, the topics covered and the kinds of angle the different producers have approached them from. In each case, find reasons why they are similar. These may relate to the target audience or the context for distribution – that is the method of delivery.

■ Structure

You can compare each product with the other examples you have chosen. It will help greatly to plan out on paper how each of the products is structured. That is, if you identify each part of each product in turn, listing them all in the order in which they appear, you will be able to identify and explain many of the differences and similarities between them. If you have chosen your examples well, you will have plenty of interesting points to make and comment on.

This stage is rather like planning a running order for a video, television or radio programme, or a film – but of course, you will be doing it *after* the product has been made. That does not matter too much, because this time you are just describing something you have chosen to study, rather than setting out to create something new.

If you are working with print or interactive media products, you will need to map out the content in a way that makes comparison straightforward. A site map for a website or a block diagram for a DVD would be useful here. List the various parts in each product, showing what they are, how long or large they are, and how they are placed in relation to other elements in the same product.

Theory into practice 15

Using the advice here decide how you are going to do your content analysis. It might help you to first discuss your approach with your teacher to make sure you are on the right track.

Select a range of products to critically analyse, labelling them clearly and keeping them safe until this unit has been assessed and verified. Choose products that are going to have a number of similarities and differences to explore.

Now use a table like Figure 5.20 to begin a systematic analysis of each of the products. **P4**

Grading tips

To reach Merit level, explain your findings with examples.

To reach Distinction level, make sure your examples are fully explained and that you use the correct terminology.

Key Term

Deconstruction is a method of analysis that depends on identifying the individual elements in a text, separating them from the others, and considering how they relate to the text as a whole, and to other parts of it.

Deconstruction

Content analysis often includes **deconstruction** – rather like children might pull something apart to find out how it is made and how the different parts of it work together. You should do this as part of your content analysis, being careful not to actually break anything, of course! The parts of media products can be called elements.

Some of the different types of elements found in different kinds of media products are listed below. You should look for each type of element in the products you are analysing, identify where they are placed in relation to other elements, and consider why they are used in this way. As you deconstruct your chosen examples, you may well identify more elements than are listed here. Because this example is multipurpose, some may not apply to your own choice of products.

Medium	Type of element	Elements	Reason for use
Print and web pages	Framing	Boxes, borders, typographical layout (font size, headlines, bylines), contents pages, hyperlinks	Divide up content, increase appeal to reader
	Content	Text (words), images, graphics	Engage reader
	Advertising	Display ads, classified ads	Earn income, inform readers
	Interactivity	Contact details, response lines	Encourage response, increase income, provide service
Radio	Framing	Jingles, theme tunes, continuity announcements before and after programmes, signposting by presenter, trails, narration, presentation	Keep listener tuned in, identify content, divide up content
	Content	Music, words, actuality, sound effects	Engage listener
	Advertising	Spot advertising, classified advertising ('Job slots' etc)	Earn income, inform readers
	Interactivity	Phone-ins, texting, email reponses asked for and read out	Encourage response, increase income, provide service
Moving image (video, film, DVD)	Framing	Theme tunes, title sequences, credit sequences, scene changes, captions, narration, presentation, continuity announcements before and after programmes	Keep viewer watching, identify content, divide up content
	Content	Images, music, words, actuality, sounds	Engage listener
	Advertising	Spot advertising, classified advertising	Earn income, inform readers
	Interactivity	Menu selection, response lines, texting, phone-ins	Encourage response, increase income, provide service

▲ Figure 5.21: Key structural elements to be found in different media products. You are bound to find most of these in the products you are analysing, and perhaps more – but how are they arranged?

■ Structuralism

This is a way of analysing media products on the basis of how they are structured. In fact, it is one of many approaches to content analysis. You have already begun a structuralist approach to your chosen media products, by beginning to examine how they have been structured.

We will be considering narrative structures soon – that is, looking at how the narratives in media products are put together and organised.

Theory into practice 16

Complete a table like Figure 5.21 for your chosen products. **P4**

Grading tips

To reach Merit level, instead of just describing them, explain for each product how the different elements are put together.

To reach Distinction level, be systematic in the way you carry out your analysis, explaining your reasons fully and clearly.

■ Semiotic analysis

Semiotics is the study of signs. You might wonder at first what this has to do with media products, but if you think carefully about your work earlier in this unit about signifiers, you'll soon realise that elements in media products that signify meaning are, in fact, signs! That means that analysing signifiers in your chosen media products would be a semiotic analysis of those products. The following Theory into practice activity will give you a chance to practise this.

Theory into practice 17

Look back through your work on signifiers. Use it to identify and list the signifiers in your chosen media products, then compare those findings with the information in Figure 5.21. **P4**

Grading tips

To reach Merit level, explain your findings with examples.

To reach Distinction level, make sure your examples are fully explained and that you use the correct terminology.

Genre

By now you will have noticed that certain media products have a lot in common, especially in the way they are constructed, the type of content, and much more. In many cases this will be because they are from the same genre. We looked at genre in Unit 3 and earlier in this unit if you want to remind yourself about it. Genre is used to make clear that we are talking about a particular type of product when we compare them. Producers also understand and use the word genre, so it is a very useful term.

The genre of a media product can depend on a number of factors. These include:

- the production technology used. That is, which medium is it? We can tell this from the production technology used.
- the distribution method used. Is it broadcast, shown in cinemas, sold in shops, posted on the Internet, or given away by hand? You'll find more information on the distribution of different media products later in the book.
- the codes and conventions used.
- the way genres have developed over time.

You'll probably find you already have a good understanding of genre, once you start to read through the examples in Figure 5.22.

Key Terms

Semiotics is the study of signs and symbols.

Genre analysis is a systematic study of the characteristics of products within a genre. Many products will share some of the same features, and it is often the presence or absence of these essential features which define whether the product is in the genre.

So, what makes a genre? A media text belongs to a particular genre if it shares a large number of characteristics with others in the same genre. That is, they use the same – or very similar – codes and conventions in order to make meaning. They tend to be structured in similar ways. For example, the whodunnit is a popular murder-mystery sub-genre of drama in radio and television, on stage and in film.

The following boxes list some of the most popular genres within the different areas of the media industry. These lists are not exhaustive – there are other genres and sub-genres that are not listed.

Genres in film with examples
Western *The Magnificent Seven*
Science fiction *Star Wars*
Comedy *Father of the Bride*
Road movie *Bonnie and Clyde*
Action hero *Indiana Jones*
Documentary *Fahrenheit 911*
Horror *The Exorcist*
Whodunnit *Murder on the Orient Express*
Fantasy *The Chronicles of Narnia*
Period *Pride and Prejudice*
Children's *Bambi*
Teen *Princess Diaries*
Comedy horror *Scary Movie*

Genres in television with examples
News programme *Channel Four News*
Documentary *Panorama*
Comedy sketch show *Little Britain*
Situation comedy *Two Pints of Lager*
Science fiction *Dr Who*
Reality TV *Big Brother*
Period drama *Bleak House*
Chat Show *Parkinson*
Soap opera *EastEnders*
Drama series *Waking the Dead*
Children's magazine *Blue Peter*
Teen magazine *T4*
Cartoon *Scooby Doo, Where Are You?*

Genres in radio with examples
News programme *Newsbeat*
Documentary *File on Four*
Comedy sketch show *Dead Ringers*
Situation comedy *Clare in the Community*
Science fiction *The Hitchhiker's Guide to the Galaxy*
Soundscape *The Twin Towers: A Memorial in Sound*
Period drama *Classic Serial*
Chat Show *Midweek with Libby Purves*
Soap opera *The Archers*
Drama series *Afternoon Theatre*
Breakfast show *Chris Moyles*
Children's magazine *Go For It*
Sequence programme *Steve Wright in the Afternoon*

Genres in print with examples
Compact newspapers *The Times*
Tabloid newspapers *The Sun*
News magazines *The Economist*
Freesheet *Metro*
Regional newspaper *Western Daily Press*
Local newspaper *Liverpool Echo*
Women's magazines *Cosmopolitan*
Lads' mags *Nutz*
TV listings *Radio Times*
Music magazine Smash Hits
Classified advertising *Exchange & Mart*
Special Interest *Boat Owner*
Fiction *True Romances*
Children's magazine *Bob the Builder*
Pre-teen magazine *Girl Talk*
Cartoon *Beyblades*

Genres in interactive media with examples
Website *amazon.co.uk*
DVD *Van Helsing*
CD-ROM *World Atlas*
Computer game *The Sims*
Game console game *Crash Bandicoot*

▲ Figure 5.22: Genre types. Can you think of other examples in each category?

Sometimes a media text will actually fit more than one genre. This may be because a suitable genre label has not yet been thought of to describe it adequately. You may find genres that seem to have quite different texts within them. For example, the label 'reality TV' is given to programmes that follow people around in what are supposedly their everyday lives – such as *Airline*. However, these programmes are very different in style, content and purpose to other reality programmes like *Big Brother*, *I'm a Celebrity, Get Me Out Of Here* and *Fame Academy*, in which groups of very different people are put together in a confined location, observed constantly through live feeds, voted in, voted out and voted winner.

▲ Figure 5.23: The marketing of a media product often reveals a lot about its genre.

Genre	Signifier	How does the signifier create meaning as part of a code?	Why is it used?	Is the signifier also a convention?
Special-interest magazine	Page 4 has a box with text within it, a lightly tinted background and a different typeface.	It divides this particular text from the rest, and gives it a particular significance. Readers are likely to understand the text as related, but supplementary material.	To add interest to the page, to separate out the supplementary text and to provide the reader with further information.	Yes, it is often used in newspapers, magazines and on web pages, and particularly in this genre.
Tabloid Newspaper	Front page has a large headline 'MURDER IN THE HOUSE'	It anchors the meaning of the picture below it and raises expectations of the story as being an important, topical and exciting one.	To get regular, occasional and even new readers to buy the newspaper.	Yes, and it is expected of newspaper front pages.
Compact newspaper	Front page has teasers highlighting feature items inside.	They act like a contents page, and raise readers' expectations that by turning to those inside pages, they will find those features.	To get regular, occasional and even new readers to buy the newspaper.	Yes, and it is expected of newspaper front pages.
Informative website	Home page has a column of buttons with text labels.	It acts like a contents page, and uses visitors' expectations that by clicking on each button, they will be taken to another page.	To divide up content in a clear way and to invite visitors to explore the site further.	Yes, and it is expected of home pages.
Informative website	Pages have underlined words.	Identifies those words as hyperlinks to other material that is not yet visible.	To invite visitors to explore the site for further information.	Yes, and it is expected of web pages.
Radio sequence programme	The programme has a jingle featuring a car horn before the traffic and travel bulletin.	The car horn suggests traffic, and its repeated use before the regular traffic and travel feature means it becomes associated with the type of information to follow.	To divide up content, alert listeners to the information that follows and to make the programme sound more interesting.	Yes, and because the car horn is so widely used, it may be becoming a cliché.
Radio news bulletin	Newsreader's tone of voice is serious.	It makes the listener feel that this is a serious piece of information, not to be ignored.	To make the news seem authoritative and to be trusted.	Yes, because serious news stories should not be funny.
Feature film	At 9 mins 10 secs a new establishing shot features a caption showing a date and time.	It sets the following events in a particular moment in the narrative, distancing it from the scene immediately before it.	To divide up content, explain the passage of time and to introduce the new location.	Yes, but it is not always used in feature films – its use depends on the style of the film and how important the change of time and location is to the narrative.
DVD of a television series.	The menu page has several selectable images and some text.	It acts like a contents page, and uses viewers' expectations that by selecting each image, they will be taken to different feature on the DVD.	To provide easy access to the different episodes and to invite viewers to explore the extra features.	Yes, viewers would expect this feature to be available on the DVD.
Television news bulletin	Whenever on screen, the news presenter looks straight at the camera while reading the script (off an autocue that the viewer does not see).	It appears to each viewer that the newsreader is looking them in the eye and talking personally to them. They are probably not aware of the autocue that enables the newsreader to do this.	To draw viewers into the programme and make them feel that that they are important enough to be engaged by eye contact.	Yes, it is such a widely used and long-standing convention that most viewers would assume there had been a technical breakdown if the newsreader started looking away from the camera to read the script off paper or a computer screen.
Television drama	At 20 mins 14 secs a cutaway of an actor's shocked expression while another character is telling some shocking news.	It allows viewers to see how the other person is reacting to the news and tells viewers that what has happened is shocking the second character.	To draw viewers into the programme and feel empathy with the second character, perhaps even responding in the same way.	Yes, viewers will not be surprised at all to see the second character for a moment, and they are very likely to understand what they are being shown as the second character's reaction.

▲ Figure 5.24: The use of signifiers in media products. Which elements in the products you are studying are also conventions?

Theory into practice 18

Define which genre your chosen media products belong to. **P4**

Now analyse the use of signifiers in your chosen products, using a grid like the one in Figure 5.24.

Extension activity

Look back through your earlier work on codes and conventions. Analyse the use of codes and conventions in your chosen products and add you findings to those for Theory into practice 16.

Grading tips

To reach Merit level, explain the use of codes and conventions, rather than just describing how they are used.

To reach Distinction level, use detailed explanations and the correct terminology.

Changes over time

By now you should have a very good idea of how your chosen products compare to a number of others in their genres. Genres have all developed over time – nobody sat down in the early days of each mass medium and made a list of possible genres within which to work. In most cases, a media producer simply made a product that was different in some way from everything that had gone before it, without realising that many more media producers would follow it with versions of their own.

It is that spark of an idea that one day may lead to you creating a whole new genre for others to follow. Remember that most media products are produced entirely within conventional expectations and surprise nobody at all with their approach. That does not at all mean that they are not worthwhile: some of the most successful genres and styles have been in existence for many years. The most enduring products – famous national newspapers, like *The Sun* and *The Daily Mail*, have undergone little real change in many decades. Other examples are the popular television and radio soap operas, *EastEnders*, *The Archers* and *Coronation Street*. Often, media producers are very wary of changing successful formulae – because they are afraid of pushing away their regular audiences, who might object to change.

Change does occur, though, and most often it is because technology advances. Changes are most obvious in the style of media products within a particular genre. Some examples of styles within different genres are shown in Figure 5.26.

Key Term

Soap operas are continuing dramas that could, in theory, run for many years. A number of different storylines (or 'narratives') run through each episode. New narratives begin from time to time, replacing older ones that come to an end.

▲ Figure 5.25: Content analysis of print products has to be as systematic as for audio-visual ones.

Genre	Style
Crime drama	Fast-paced action
	Slow-paced, whodunnit
Soap opera	Social-issues based
	Teen lifestyle
Documentary	Fly-on-the-wall/reality TV
	Investigative reporter-led
	Opinionated, partial approach, taking one side in a controversy
Sit-com	Centred on a location – a family's front room, a bar or a canteen
	Different locations in each episode
Western	Macho cowboys womanising and fighting Indians
	Gay cowboys being sensitive and challenging stereotypes
Tabloid newspaper	For a national audience
	For a local or regional audience
Informative website	Tribute site
	Authoritative news and information site
	Promotional

▲ Figure 5.26: Different styles within media genres. All of the above genres could also be done in a spoof style, sending up the genre for fun.

Think it over 18

Identifying different styles within your chosen genre may involve some wider research. For example, the products you have chosen to compare with your own so far may all have similar styles. So, by looking at some very different styles within the same genre you will be able to improve your critical analysis.

Theory into practice 19

Identify how some of the genres among your chosen products have changed over time. **P4**

Find reasons for those changes, and explain them in your own words, using examples. **M4**

Narrative structures

We began to look at structure earlier in this section. Now we shall look at how narratives are structured.

Narrative types

Each fictional or non-fictional product is organised according to one of the following **narrative structures**, depending on how the content is arranged or in the case of a story, the order in which it unfolds:

- open
- multi-strand
- non-linear.
- closed
- linear

Key Term

Narrative structure is the way in which a storyline or thread is put together. There are a number of common narrative structures, each of which can be found in different examples of media texts in many different genres. The drawings in Figure 5.27 show some key differences between different types of narrative structure.

■ Open narratives

An **open narrative** structure leaves matters unresolved at the end, with more content to follow – such as the next episode of a series, or the replay of a football match that has ended in a draw. A news article might end with the suggestion that there will be more to report the next day, after some more events have unfolded.

Closed narratives

A **closed narrative** structure is one in which the key issues are resolved at the end – when, for example, a criminal in a news story is brought to justice, or the final whistle has been blown and the football coverage ends with the final score and a definitive win.

Multi-strand narratives

A **multi-strand narrative** is typically used by soap operas and long-running serials, which do not use the more conventional approach of beginning/middle/ending, because several storylines run at the same time, some ending while others are just beginning. Importantly, there is no obvious end point to the story, when viewers, listeners or readers could stop following it without missing anything. This keeps people coming back to see what happens next.

Linear narratives

A **linear narrative** is organised in a simple sequence of beginning, middle, ending. The story is usually chronological, that is following the actual sequence in time, not moving around with flashbacks and flash forwards. This type of narrative could be plotted on paper along a straight line (hence linear). Compare this with non-linear narratives.

Non-linear narratives

A **non-linear narrative** is one that is more complicated than just beginning, middle, ending. Think of a story plotted along a straight line, then think of a flashback, when suddenly the narrative goes back in time to show something that happened in the past. On paper that might look like a loop back to somewhere near the beginning of the line, or even to a time before the line began.

Most people understand what is happening when they are shown a flashback in a narrative. Some other narratives tend to be much more difficult for audiences to enjoy because they are more challenging and perhaps jump about through time, without offering a clear sense of direction from a beginning to a middle and then an ending. Audiences can find these very difficult to follow.

Finally, there are media products that are simply not meant to be followed from start to finish. Encyclopaedias and dictionaries, websites, CD-ROMs and DVDs are good examples. Internet radio stations are also regarded as non-linear. Through on-screen interactivity, they permit listeners to choose the sequence of what they hear. Encyclopaedias and dictionaries are for dipping into, depending on what the reader is looking for, and so are CD-ROMs and DVDs. Consumers see or hear something that interests them, and perhaps go to different entries or follow the hyperlinks to find more information somewhere else within the product.

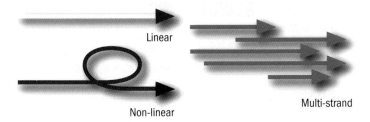

▲ Figure 5.27: Graphical representations of different narrative structures.

Key Terms

Some of the key elements in a narrative:

Enigma is where something in the story is unknown – to the cast, to the audience or both. When a movie ends with the audience having to guess what happens next, that is called an enigma. There may be an enigma within a narrative, too, if there is some great mystery that has not been explained.

Climax is a point in a narrative, usually at the end, or just before it, when everything comes together. In fiction all the action or interest in the narrative appears to be building towards this point. Perhaps it is a great chase scene, or the final duel between the hero and the villain, or even the point where a detective solves the mystery and confronts the criminal with the evidence. This is also called the denouement.

Equilibrium is the point in a narrative where the story is more or less over and all the disruption caused by the enigma and the climax has been resolved. The mystery is solved, good has triumphed over evil or everything is back in its place – being 'balanced' again.

Theory into practice 20

Investigate narrative structure in your chosen products by plotting them on paper. Identify what kind of structure each one has. For example, an episode of a serial would have an open, linear structure. **P4**

Grading tips

To reach Merit level, cover as many of types of narrative structure as you can.

To reach Distinction level, fully explain your findings and give clearly worked out reasons for them.

Representation

Representation in the media is an important issue for media studies and for producers. How someone is portrayed in the media can affect how people think about him or her. Positive portrayal can bring big benefits, but being portrayed negatively can cause great harm.

Often the media build up celebrities with lots of positive coverage, then knock them down again when they are caught doing something wrong or because they are simply out of favour.

Representing social groups

The media represent social groups in many different ways. Sometimes these representations are fair, and sometimes unfair. Often, the only way to know how unfair such representations are, is to belong to such a group, or to know someone very well who does.

This is important because it is very common for people to develop attitudes to others through what they see, read and hear in the media. In some parts of the United Kingdom it is still possible to hardly ever meet people with a skin colour other than white. A white person living there may have difficulty separating misleading media representations of people with different backgrounds from the reality they would find for themselves if they travelled more.

In many ways the media industry has grown up a lot in the past twenty to thirty years. Attitudes towards women and ethnic minorities have improved a lot. For instance women are no longer mainly depicted only as housewives and it is no longer acceptable to poke fun at people just because of their ethnic origins. In fact, forty or fifty years ago even sounding like they were from 'The North' made some comedians appear hysterically funny in the minds of producers and audiences alike. Sit-coms such as *The Clitheroe Kid* were hugely successful on radio and television in the 1960s, but the humour was derived mostly from the way characters were befuddled by everyday events and made to sound stupid.

■ Attitudes to race

Examples of racial stereotyping were once very common, and it was very unusual to see or hear people from ethnic minorities in any positive roles. In the 1960s, the BBC's *Black and White Minstrel Show* featured white dancers with their faces blacked-up by make-up, in a crude stereotyping of black people. It would now be found very offensive.

Although the representation of minorities has improved considerably, some people consider there to still be room for improvement. In 2001 the Director-General of the BBC described the Corporation as 'hideously white', meaning that non-white people were still under-represented. This can lead to misrepresentation of minority groups. The tone of some of the press coverage after the London suicide bombings of 2005, for instance, gave rise to concerns that it might provoke revenge attacks on Muslim communities.

News coverage of natural disasters elsewhere in the world does little to help the image of black people. Africans are rarely shown unless they are suffering from famine, drought, or disease. In addition they are not shown as active in such images. Instead, they are shown as sick, hungry or dying victims, rather than as merchants, farmers, doctors or in other more positive roles.

Think it over 19

Imagine how it must feel to be the only person who is different from everyone around them in some very noticeable way. Now imagine also being surrounded by negative images in the media of people that share that difference with you.

■ Pornography

The Internet is still awash with pornographic depictions of straight and gay women that many consider to be demeaning to the female gender because they characterise women as objects whose only use is for sexual gratification. Although the *Daily Mirror* abandoned topless photography some time ago, *The Sun* and, to a far greater extent, the *Daily Sport* still use images of near-naked women to sell their product to men.

Figure 5.28: The Internet is widely used to sell and distribute pornography; this is degrading to women and some of it is illegal.

■ What is normal?

The whole concept of 'normality' is a difficult one because today it is much more widely accepted that being different may in itself be normal and not really an issue. Another problem with criticising today's media too strongly is that you could argue that many of the 'normal' people shown are in fact gay or lesbian, but because the context is not one in which anyone's sexuality is discussed, you simply cannot tell who is gay and who is not. This applies to other demographic categories, too, such as religion. Unless someone is wearing religious clothing or insignia, it may be difficult to tell that they are fundamentally different in their religious beliefs from anyone else or from the mainstream.

■ Selection and representation

You could argue that people are only newsworthy when their lives are disrupted by some very dramatic change to their circumstances – such as when disaster strikes. Editors and producers throughout the media actively choose the stories they cover and the material they use to illustrate them, and it is rare for them to choose 'good' news stories from certain parts of the world.

It is these selection processes that most directly affect the representation of different social groups, that means both the selection of material for inclusion in media products *and* the selection of people to work in the media. There are now laws preventing discrimination against people on racial or gender grounds, as well as because of any disability they may have. These laws are to stop barriers being put in the way of people having equal opportunities in life, simply because they come from a minority – or, in the case of women, because they may need at some time to take a break in their careers in order to have children.

Theory into practice 21

Investigate the representation of social groups in your chosen products. You can use a table like Figure 5.29 to do this. **P4**

Make a list of how positive and negative representation occurs then report on your findings, explaining why certain groups may have been represented more positively and/or more often than others. **M4**

Explain how the representations you have studied might have been made fairer OR what the producers have already done to represent social groups fairly. **D4**

Social group	Positively represented	Negatively represented
White males		
Old people		
Women		
People with an obvious disability		
Lesbians, gay men, bisexuals		
Working-class men		
Non-white people		
People born in other countries		
People from UK regions other than the south-east		
People wearing religious clothing or insignia		

▲ Figure 5.29: Checklist for monitoring the representation in the media of people from different social groups. Some people represented may fit more than one description, so you will need to tick more than one box for them.

Representing social issues

The media do not only represent people in their products, they also represent issues that matter to us all.

■ Balance and bias

It follows that as well as sometimes misrepresenting people, the media can also misrepresent issues. One aspect of regulation that applies to the broadcast media – radio and television – is **impartiality**. Put simply, that means the media should report in a **balanced** fashion and not be biased one way or another when there is a controversial issue under discussion. Sometimes broadcasters are accused of showing **bias** towards one political party or another – but some issues do not belong to political parties alone, and there can be all manner of pressure groups wanting to have their own say.

Unlike broadcasters, the press and multimedia sectors are not regulated in this respect at all. The owners of newspapers and magazines can decide to use them to support political parties if they wish, and nobody can prevent them from doing so. Their only sanction is if readers and customers or web users stop consuming their products because they object to the bias.

Key Terms

Balance is giving equal emphasis to all sides of an argument, so no one side has an advantage over the others.

Bias is slanting the coverage of an argument in order to give one or more sides an advantage over other sides.

Impartiality is being unbiased.

Propaganda is material designed to persuade people that one or more sides of an argument are correct. This often involves slanting the truth, or selecting only information that promotes one particular cause. Propaganda is often regarded as being misleading or dishonest.

Political parties and pressure groups can and do set up their own websites, where they can put across their own points of view on almost any issues they like. They can also make and distribute tapes, DVDs and CD-ROMs to help promote their message. Politically inspired leaflets and posters are almost as old as the printing press itself. They are a very effective way of getting a message to an audience without journalists 'mediating' or altering it in any way – by asking awkward questions or putting across alternative points of view, for example.

Think it over 20

When do you think it is OK to put across two sides of an argument without saying either one is right? When is it better to take sides with one view over another?

▲ Figure 5.30 Political party literature can come in all shapes and sizes, for different purposes.

The biggest political parties have a right to free airtime on the main television channels and radio stations. Some is only allocated to them during election periods, but they may also choose to schedule a small number of Party Political Broadcasts at other times in the year. In some other countries, such as the United States, they must pay for advertising on radio and television, just as they can buy advertising space in newspapers, magazines and other organisations' websites here.

Case study

Political influence of the media

When John Major was re-elected Prime Minister of a Conservative Government in May 1992, *The Sun*'s headline was 'It is The Sun Wot Won it!'. Five years later, when it changed its support to Labour, the newspaper's headline was 'It is The Sun Wot Swung It'. Many political commentators agree that *The Sun*'s support was crucial on both occasions. Others think the newspaper was just reflecting a change of mood in the country.

- **Do you think newspaper owners or editors should decide who runs the country?**

- **If no, how would you prevent this from happening?**

There are all sorts of social issues represented one way or another in the media. A good argument – or, more politely, a heated debate – over an issue lots of people feel strongly about can make good listening or viewing on radio or television. Chat shows and phone-ins do just that, on a daily basis. Newspapers and magazines also like to print letters, emails and texts from readers. Bulletin boards, blogs and podcasts are the Internet's contribution to this type of material.

Media producers know that their own audiences will agree with some of the comments sent in and disagree with others – perhaps enough to send in their own. A full postbag, a busy telephone line to a radio studio or a large text or email response can indicate that a programme or a feature is very popular, and is getting the audience's attention. Some topics crop up time and again, either because there is something happening in the news that suddenly makes them topical again, or just because producers know they are perennial issues that will always provoke a response.

Smoking

Every year a group called Action on Smoking and Health (ASH) promote a National No Smoking Day. There are clear health reasons for not smoking that have been demonstrated in medical studies many times. Smoking damages the lungs of the smoker, and makes lung and heart disease more likely, as well as cancer. It is also important not to smoke near others, because secondary smoking (inhaling someone else's smoke) can be almost as harmful, particularly to children, as actually smoking. The popular entertainer, trumpeter and television presenter, Roy Castle, died from lung cancer, despite being a non-smoker. He had too often filled his lungs in smoky venues in order to play his trumpet, and the smoke he inhaled from other people's cigarettes killed him.

Yet, for some people, smoking is about personal freedom, and a rival organisation, the Freedom Organisation for the Right to Enjoy Smoking Tobacco (FOREST) is a pressure group that puts across very forcibly the view that people have the right to smoke if they wish. So, on National No Smoking Day, media producers regularly pit ASH members against FOREST members in interviews, written features, chat shows and other staged confrontations designed to produce emotive products that will interest their audiences.

Think it over 21

The way a subject is treated in the media is not always the correct way. Often, subjects are represented in ways that are irresponsible or morally wrong. Even worse is exploitation, where someone is wrongly treated so the media can make money.

This is a kind of 'balance', when each side has an equal chance to express its point of view, because each argument is made in turn and the audience can make up their own minds on the issue. In other ways, giving both sides equal time on this issue could be regarded as unfair, because the medical evidence overwhelmingly supports one side of the debate.

In recent years this issue has become topical when bans on smoking in public places have been imposed by politicians, when people have sued tobacco companies for damage to their health, and when tobacco advertising and sponsorship has been banned in some sports and not others.

The MMR vaccine

In this case, overwhelming medical evidence that a triple vaccine against measles, mumps and rubella, given to very young children was safe was 'balanced' repeatedly in the media with the views of a very small number of experts who thought it was not. Most of the medical community, including the Government's Chief Medical Officer and the National Institute for Clinical Excellence, considered MMR to be safe, and many of them repeatedly said so, starting when the controversy began in 1998.

Because one researcher claimed the vaccine could cause autism in children, many worried parents began to demand that the vaccines were given separately, instead of combined, even though this did not give as good protection against these three potentially dangerous diseases. Several doctors began offering separate vaccines, either because they began to have doubts themselves, or because it was better to vaccinate children in this way than not to vaccinate them at all.

So very soon there were lots of people for the media to interview on both sides of the debate – even though there still was not any actual evidence linking MMR to autism, just a lot of suspicion. It quickly became widespread practice to give both sides equal coverage, even though there was no medical evidence to justify the concerns.

Racism

'Balancing' the views of a racist with a reply from somebody strongly against racism might seem like another subject that would be likely to provoke some lively debate and a strong response from audiences. However, in Britain a law called the Public Order Act 1986 made it illegal to incite other people to racial hatred – and that is what media organisations would risk doing by allowing racist views to be openly promoted in their products.

Some people may feel this is a restriction on freedom of speech, normally something we hold dear. However, violence and bullying happens against people from ethnic minorities anyway, simply because they are perceived as 'different', and the law recognises that allowing further incitement to racial hatred is very likely to cause more distress and physical harm to innocent people.

Gun crime

When an activity is illegal, it is difficult for the media to portray one side of an argument as acceptable. This is especially so with issues such as violence, bullying, drug-taking, spreading graffiti, stealing or carrying illegal weapons. For example, the growth of gun crime in recent years has been a cause for concern for police, schools, parents and, of course, victims. Yet, some young people say they carry illegal weapons because they feel unsafe, and they need them to protect themselves.

This subject may be attractive to media producers, because it appeals to people's fear – both of danger to themselves or the possibility of becoming innocently caught up in someone else's fight. Some parts of the media would want to appear 'cool' rather than siding with the police on matters such as this. That may actively encourage those who already break the law to carry on and other people to join them.

▲ Figure 5.31: Issues can be portrayed in many different ways, depending on the way the producers decide to represent them.

How illegal acts are treated in the media can bring complaints of irresponsibility. After all, many media producers go home to very safe neighbourhoods when they finish work, and the dangers they show in other people's neighbourhoods may not trouble them at all. Some critics of the media will say that rising levels of violence over the past forty years are a direct result of the glorification of violence on television and in the lyrics of rap songs.

■ Issues are everywhere

It is not just in news and documentary programmes, and on the news pages of websites that you will find issues being represented. Like the guns in film and television drama, controversial issues such as the ones we have explored here can crop up almost anywhere in the mass media.

Some promising places to find such issues being mixed in with other, less controversial material, include:

- soap operas on radio and television
- problem pages in magazines
- feature films and film shorts
- local talking newspapers for the blind
- web pages
- presenter links in radio programmes
- interviews with celebrities
- music videos and song lyrics
- blogs and podcasts
- drama series and serials
- sport reports.

Knowledge check 5.4

1. Explain how deconstructing a media product can help you to understand it. **P4**

2. Explain why marketing material usually tells audiences about its genre. **M4**

3. Describe a number of different narrative structures. **P4**

4. Explain the differences between them, using examples. **M4 D4**

5. Why is representation important in media products? **P1**

6. Explain how stereotypes can be harmful. **M4**

7. Explain what is meant by 'balance' in media products. **M4**

8. When is it acceptable for a media product to be unbalanced – or 'biased'? **D4**

Theory into practice 22

Identify a range of social issues, such as the ones discussed above, that are represented in the area of the media you have been studying. **P4**

Explain fully each of the different ways in which they are covered. **M4**

Is this representation fair or unfair? Explain clearly how fairly or unfairly you think these issues have been covered. **D4**

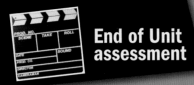

End of Unit assessment

Preparation for assessment

You should now be ready to produce the pieces of work for assessment that will go towards your final grade for this unit.

Your work can be presented in either written or oral form and be accompanied by appropriate notes, logs and diaries, as well as examples of research material that you have studied.

Whether producing a written or oral report, you should ensure that you use appropriate subject terminology correctly and express your ideas clearly and fluently.

There are guidelines with each activity telling you what need to do to gain a Pass, Merit or Distinction.

End of unit Assessment activity 1

For this assessment task you need to think carefully about the ways in which media producers think about audiences. Use your work for the learning activities in this section to help you.

Then, in your own words, describe and explain these different ways. Wherever you can, you should illustrate the points that you make with appropriate examples.

– To achieve a pass grade for this learning outcome you need to describe how media producers think about their audiences. The descriptions should be accurate and relevant and include some appropriate use of subject terminology. **P1**

– To achieve a merit grade you will also need to include with your explanations a number of well-chosen examples. Be very clear, too, and use a lot of appropriate subject terminology. **M1**

– To achieve a distinction grade you will need to fully explain everything and justify what you say by using supporting arguments, evidence and detailed examples. You should also use technical and specialist language correctly and fluently. **D1**

End of unit Assessment activity 2

For this assessment task you need to think carefully about the different ways media producers create media products for their audiences. Use your work for the learning activities in this section to help you.

Then, in your own words, describe and explain these different ways. Wherever you can, you should illustrate the points that you make with appropriate examples.

– To achieve a pass grade for this learning outcome you need to describe how media producers create products for their audiences. The descriptions should be accurate and relevant and include some appropriate use of subject terminology. **P2**

– To achieve a merit grade you will also need to include with your explanations a number of well-chosen examples. Be very clear, too, and use a lot of appropriate subject terminology. **M2**

– To achieve a distinction grade you will need to fully explain everything and justify what you say by using supporting arguments, evidence and detailed examples. You should also use technical and specialist language correctly and fluently. **D2**

End of unit Assessment activity 3

For this assessment task you need to think carefully about the different ways in which media audiences respond to media products. Use your work for the learning activities in this section to help you.

Then, in your own words, describe and explain these different ways. Wherever you can, you should illustrate the points that you make with appropriate examples.

- To achieve a pass grade for this learning outcome you need to describe all the different ways in which media audiences respond to media products. The descriptions should be accurate and relevant and include some appropriate use of subject terminology. **P3**

- To achieve a merit grade you will also need to include with your explanations a number of well-chosen examples. Be very clear, too, and use a lot of appropriate subject terminology. **M3**

- To achieve a distinction grade you will need to fully explain everything and justify what you say by using supporting arguments, evidence and detailed examples. You should also use technical and specialist language correctly and fluently. **D3**

End of unit Assessment activity 4

For this assessment task you need to think carefully about the different ways in which media products represent different social groups and social issues. Use your work for the learning activities in this section to help you.

Then, in your own words, describe and explain these different ways. Wherever you can, you should illustrate the points that you make with appropriate examples.

- To achieve a pass grade for this learning outcome you need to describe all the different ways in which media products represent different social groups and social issues. The descriptions should be accurate and relevant and include some appropriate use of subject terminology. **P4**

- To achieve a merit grade you will also need to include with your explanations a number of well-chosen examples. Be very clear, too, and use a lot of appropriate subject terminology. **M4**

- To achieve a distinction grade you will need to fully explain everything and justify what you say by using supporting arguments, evidence and detailed examples. You should also use technical and specialist language correctly and fluently. **D4**

Grading Criteria

To achieve a pass grade the evidence must show that the learner is able to:	TiP	To achieve a merit grade the evidence must show that the learner is able to:	TiP	To achieve a distinction grade the evidence must show that the learner is able to:	TiP	Activity
P1 describe how media producers think about their audiences, expressing ideas with sufficient clarity to communicate them and with some appropriate use of subject terminology	1 2 3 4 5 6 7	**M1** explain, with reference to well-chosen examples, how media producers think about their audiences, expressing ideas with clarity and with generally appropriate use of subject terminology	1 2 3 4 5 6 7	**D1** fully explain, with supporting arguments and elucidated examples, how media producers think about their audiences, expressing ideas fluently and using subject terminology correctly	1 2 3 6 7	end of Unit assessment activity 1
P2 describe how media producers create products for specific audiences, expressing ideas with sufficient clarity to communicate them and with some appropriate use of subject terminology	8 9 10 11 12	**M2** explain, with reference to well-chosen examples, how media producers create products for specific audiences, expressing ideas with clarity and with generally appropriate use of subject terminology	8 9 10 11 12	**D2** critically evaluate, with supporting arguments and elucidated examples, how media producers create products for audiences, expressing ideas fluently and using subject terminology correctly	9 10 11 12	end of Unit assessment activity 2

Grading Criteria						
To achieve a pass grade the evidence must show that the learner is able to:	TiP	To achieve a merit grade the evidence must show that the learner is able to:	TiP	To achieve a distinction grade the evidence must show that the learner is able to:	TiP	Activity
P3 describe how media audiences respond to media products expressing ideas with sufficient clarity to communicate them and with some appropriate use of subject terminology	13 14	**M3** explain, with reference to well-chosen examples, how media audiences respond to media products, expressing ideas with clarity and with generally appropriate use of subject terminology	13 14	**D3** fully explain how media audiences respond to media products, with supporting arguments and elucidated examples, expressing ideas fluently and using subject terminology correctly	13 15 16 17 18 20 21 22	End of Unit assessment activity 3
P4 describe media products, expressing ideas with sufficient clarity to communicate them and with some appropriate use of subject terminology	15 16 17 18 19 20 21 22	**M4** explain media products with reference to well-chosen examples, expressing ideas with clarity and with generally appropriate use of subject terminology	15 16 17 18 19 20 21 22	**D4** critically evaluate media products, with supporting arguments and elucidated examples, expressing ideas fluently and using subject terminology correctly	15 16 17 18 20 21 22	End of Unit assessment activity 4

Understanding the media industries

Introduction

The media industries have grown enormously over the last few years with many media companies expanding from national into multinational organisations. There are many more people working in the media than ever before. As the growth continues, and new ways of delivering the media are developed, industry-trained media people will be much in demand.

The media industries cover a wide range of activities from television and film through to web design and print-based products. The range of skills required to create these products is growing rapidly.

Alongside this expansion in the media industry is the debate about how the media is regulated. Who is really in charge of what we see and hear?

In this unit you will see how the media industries are structured, and investigate the ownership of media companies. You will be able to explore employment opportunities and job roles and learn about the ethical and legal constraints that affect media production. You will also learn about the ways in which media industries are regulated.

This unit will help you to develop a real understanding of the media by focusing on one company, Media Productions. This is a production company that originally worked in video and film production but is now moving into new media technology. Media Productions produce interactive CD-ROM and DVD products as well as designing web-based material. They create their own print products using graphic design software and the latest printer technology. They also market and distribute their own, and other people's, media products.

After completing this unit you should be able to achieve the following outcomes:

- Understand the structure and ownership of the media industries.
- Know about employment opportunities and job roles in the media industries.
- Know about ethical and legal constraints relevant to the media industries.
- Know about regulation of the media industries.

Think it over

It is essential that as a media professional you have an understanding of the structure of the industry you are working in. You need to know who owns what so that you can target them effectively when job hunting or looking to sell your services.

It is important for media professionals to understand the nature of this industry, make contacts within the industry and use a network of contacts to find work.

There is significant growth in the number of people employed on a freelance basis in the media. This means that the traditional 'job for life', that was often a major deciding factor in working for a company such as the BBC, no longer applies. Staff are often recruited for a single project, and once this is completed they move on to another job. Freelance writers will write an article or script for a fixed fee and many media professionals, including producers and directors, may work on several projects at the same time.

The media are constrained by ethical and legal issues that you have to take into account at all times. There have been several high-profile cases where people have been successfully sued for breach of privacy or defamation of character. Codes of practice are in place for media professionals to follow and work to. Regulators, such as Ofcom and the ASA, provide a standard-of-conduct framework for media companies to observe and conform to.

Industry sectors

The media industry as a whole is made up of a number of sectors as illustrated in Figure 6.01.

The media sectors are made up of different companies that specialise in producing particular media products. Figure 6.02 gives some examples of media sectors and products produced in these sectors.

▼ Figure 6.01: Sectors in the media industry.

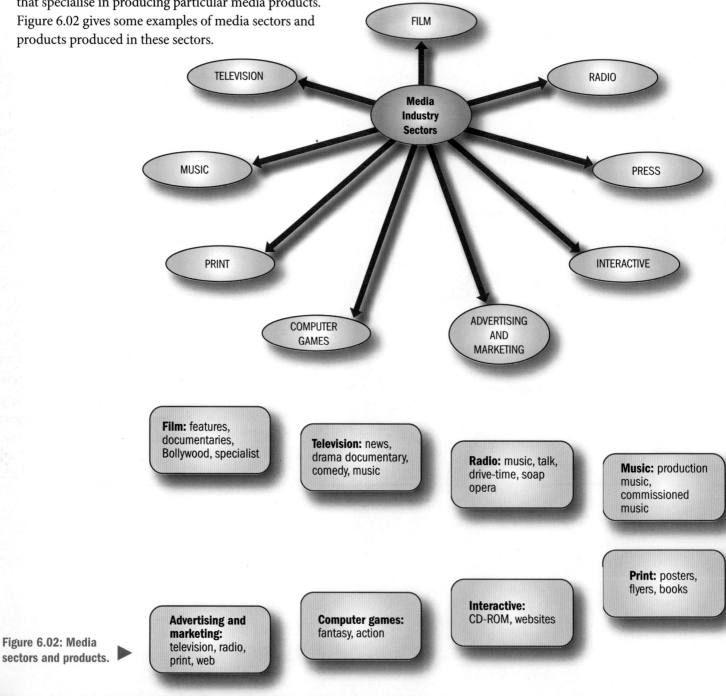

Figure 6.02: Media sectors and products. ▶

Film: features, documentaries, Bollywood, specialist

Television: news, drama documentary, comedy, music

Radio: music, talk, drive-time, soap opera

Music: production music, commissioned music

Print: posters, flyers, books

Advertising and marketing: television, radio, print, web

Computer games: fantasy, action

Interactive: CD-ROM, websites

Here are some examples of media companies that work in each of the main sectors.

Sector	Company
Film	Sony Paramount Buena Vista International Disney MGM
Radio	Classic FM BBC Emap Virgin
Television	Carlton BSkyB ITV Channel 4 Five
Print	Emap Dennis Publishing Newsquest Centaur Media Johnston Press
Interactive	Windfall Digital Illumina Digital KMP
Computer games	Climax Eurocom Revolution Software Team17
Advertising and marketing	Emap McCann Erickson
Music	Emap Zomba Music Carlin Production Music Conrad Productions
Press	News International Trinity Mirror Pearson Emap Johnston Press

▲ Figure 6.3: Representative companies in media sectors.

You will see that one name appears again and again in these lists. This company is Emap.

Case study

Emap

Emap started life as a local newspaper company in 1947. Since then it has grown and diversified into several media sectors. It now describes itself as 'a media company whose purpose is to create must-have entertainment and information which can be delivered to every home and business within defined communities'. It divides its business up into Consumer Media (magazines and TV), Radio, Communications and Advertising. Visit the Emap website at www.emap.com and follow links to 'History' from the 'About us' page. The timeline here will give you an idea of how a company can grow and diversify over time.

Do you think this is typical of the ways in which companies in the media industry diversify into new markets? Give reasons for your answer.

What does this example tell you about the media industry in the UK?

However, the media industry is not just about large companies like Emap. There are many independent producers in all areas of the media. But you should think about how important large companies are in controlling the media and what role smaller companies have to play.

Think it over 1

Is the media industry controlled by a small number of companies?

Is the media industry controlled by companies outside the UK?

See if you can find the names of the major companies that operate in the UK media industry.

Media Productions

Media Productions is a company that works across a number of media sectors. This is not uncommon in the media industry. Companies have to adapt to market forces and produce products that clients need.

Media Productions originally worked exclusively in film, but as the need for film products reduced it moved into video production. The market is once again changing and the company now distributes almost all of its products on DVD.

Media Productions is typical of many media companies in that it adapts in response to client needs. If the client wants an advertising campaign Media Productions can produce a DVD, an interactive CD-ROM, a website, posters, flyers and a radio commercial. In order to be able to do this, Media Productions has a range of media professional contacts it can call on, rather than permanently employing people across the whole range of expertise. These contacts can supply the skills and experience needed to make the various products when required. In addition Media Productions might hire specialist equipment to make certain products.

There is a core of staff at Media Productions that provides the administration and support for all the production process the company is involved in. These include:

Managing Director: runs the company and manages the business

Creative Director: oversees the creative elements of the company business

Producer: controls the production process in a range of projects, hires freelance staff, controls resources

Office Manager: ensures that the administration of the company is carried out, e.g. payment of invoices

All of these people have a vital part to play in the successful operation of this media company.

Structure and ownership

There are many types of companies working in the media industries. They range from large public companies to independent producers. The one thing they have in common is that they produce media products for an audience.

Ownership

Here are some definitions of ways in which media companies are owned.

Private ownership: generally accepted in the UK to be a company that is owned by an individual or group. Private companies are able to operate with only limited information being available on their operations to competitors. Private ownership includes people operating on their own, such as freelance writers as well as partnerships and limited liability companies.

Public company: generally accepted in the UK to be a company that has shares publicly traded on the stock exchange. PLCs have to report on their business operations to their shareholders and to **Companies House**.

Public service media: companies owned by national, regional or local government.

Multinationals: companies that work across a number of countries. Examples of this would be News Corporation and Viacom.

Independents: companies that work on their own without the benefit of belonging to a larger company. Media Productions is an example of this type of company Independents are generally owned by an individual or a small group of investors.

Conglomerates: are mergers of companies made in order to form some kind of **synergy** between them. Generally they comprise companies that seem to have no obvious link between them.

Key Term

Structure is the way that the media industries are grouped together and form media sectors.

Key Terms

Ownership refers to who owns companies or groups of companies in the media industries.

Companies House is an organisation that oversees the business of limited companies. It examines and stores company information, incorporates and dissolves limited companies and makes this information available to the public.

Synergy is the combination of two or more factors (or companies) which together are more effective than those factors would be on their own.

Company organisation

■ Vertical and horizontal integration

Vertical integration: this describes a group of companies that are linked through a hierarchy with a common owner. The companies can co-operate to produce the materials needed for production, undertake the production process and distribute the end product. This provides a reliable workflow with increased profits for the company. An example of this would be Apple Inc. who design their computer hardware, operating systems and much of the software used in their products. Since 2001 they have also introduced Apple stores for retail sales and the Apple iTunes on-line store.

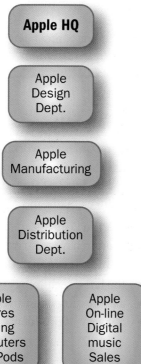

Figure 6.04: Apple Inc. has a vertical integration structure.

Horizontal integration: this is the term applied when media companies own producers of products in one area. An example of this would be EMI who are the world's largest independent music company. They own record producers and music publishing companies.

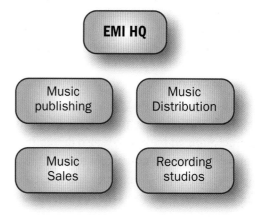

▲ Figure 6.05: EMI has a horizontal integration structure.

Theory into practice 1

Find examples of a vertically integrated media company and a horizontally integrated media company. **P1**

For each one prepare an illustrated report that highlights how each one of these operates in the media industry. Try to find examples of their products and how these might be affected by their integration structure. How is their distribution affected? **M1**

Present your report in an appropriate way to the rest of your class. **M1**

Grading tip

To reach Distinction level, you should show that you can fully explain the structure and ownership of the media industries, making relevant and well supported points, expressing this fluently and using correct subject terminology.

■ Mergers and takeovers

Media companies merge with each other and in some instances take over a rival company. The reason for this is generally to provide growth for a company and to use the technology developed by a rival company.

This provides new sources of income and growth in the customer base. It also allows for companies to diversify their product range. For example, a company might have always worked in live-action film but after taking over an animation studio can now can work in animation as well.

All of this is driven by the need to make a profit and produce products that an audience wants to buy, usually within a pre-determined budget. It is also driven by the constant need for media companies to be at the cutting edge of technology. Companies aim to create their products in a way that meets the **organisational objectives** of the company.

Not all mergers are seen as acceptable. They may be regarded as creating a situation where one individual or company has undue influence over audiences. Political issues could be aired for one particular party or products from one manufacturer could be favoured over another. In a recent example the government stepped in when BSkyB acquired 17.5 per cent of the shareholding of ITV plc. The Department of Trade and Industry decided that this merger might not be in the best interest of the consumer.

Company objectives

■ Research and development

Research and development is an important element of many media companies' corporate plan. It is essential to move on and develop new products that meet the needs of their audience. It can be expensive to hire researchers in order to find the next big audience-grabbing media product. However, if they are successful, the pay off will be worth it. Media companies are constantly looking, for instance, for the next *Big Brother* or *Deal or No Deal*.

Media companies do not just have to come up with novel programming ideas, they are also finding in recent years that their products need to be delivered in a different way. The viewing habits of their target audience are changing and they have to adapt to meet this change.

Case study

Media Productions

Media Productions started life working in film production. They had experience of producing 16mm film and supplying this in a variety of forms to their clients.

The company then realised that there was a movement towards new media formats, particularly in the VHS video format. They immediately reviewed the market and saw that they could move rapidly into this new area by delivering their film products on video cassette.

It was not long before the company identified that there would be savings if they could produce their original material on the video format. This meant moving away from shooting on film to shooting on video. Staff needed to be retrained and equipment purchased but the competitive benefits were sufficient to make this cost effective.

In the past three years the company has seen the growth of digital formats, and again they have responded quickly, moving from tape-based operations to digital acquisition and editing. This has involved them in further costs for equipment and retraining, but it has also kept the company at the forefront of technology, giving them a competitive edge.

■ Competitors

All companies are working in a market place and this means they will have **competitors**. In the media industry this is no different from Tesco having competition from Sainsbury's, Asda and Morrisons.

In order to keep ahead of their competitors media companies have to strive to consistently offer their clients something better than their rivals. This might be:

- the latest technology
- a professional but friendly atmosphere
- delivery of products on time and on budget.

Key Terms

Organisational objectives are the aims set by a company to be achieved in a certain timeframe.

Research and development is where companies spend money on looking at new products and product delivery or developing existing products.

Competitors are other companies in the market place selling the same or similar products or services. These companies are in competition with each other for custom.

■ Customers

Whatever you do as a media producer you must always remember that there is someone out there waiting to take on your customers. Without customers, your company will fail, so keeping their needs in mind and ensuring their continued satisfaction is an essential company objective.

Case study

Media Productions

Media Productions staff are always aware of the need to communicate with their customers. They see this as a way of ensuring that their competitors do not steal their clients.

Media Productions company policy is to treat clients as friends rather than just business acquaintances. This helps to foster trust between the company and its clients. Many of the clients are on first name terms with staff and they feel they can always ask questions and get straightforward answers.

Theory into practice 2

Prepare an in-depth, illustrated report on one media sector. You will need to:

- identify the sector   **P1**
- describe the range of products produced by this sector   **P1**
- identify at least five companies working in this sector.   **M1**

You then need to think about the most appropriate way to present your report and make the presentation to your teacher or the rest of the class.   **M1**

Grading tip

To reach Distinction level, you should show that you can fully explain the structure of one sector of the media industries, making relevant and well-supported points, expressing this fluently and using correct subject terminology.

■ Companies working in the media sector

There are many companies working in the media industries. Some of them may be surprising as you might know them better as producers of other products.

▲ Figure 6.06: Sony is best known as an electrical manufacturer, but it has diversified within the media industries.

Sony was originally a manufacturer of electrical and electronic products. They diversified into ownership of media products such as film, television and music production.

▲ Figure 6.07: Virgin started life as a producer of student newspapers.

Virgin began as the brainchild of Richard Branson and was originally a producer of student newspapers. It then began selling and producing records. The company now has interests in air, train and coach travel, mobile phones and financial services. It has recently moved into the cable market with the acquisition of NTL and Telewest.

▲ Figure 6.08: Viacom and CBS have merged and demerged in their combined history.

Viacom is one of the world's largest media companies. You may not have heard of the name but you will have seen their films produced under the Paramount banner.

▲ Figure 6.09: Paramount operates under the Viacom umbrella.

Viacom owned, until recently, the Blockbuster chain of video and DVD rental stores. They also owned one of the largest roadside poster distributors in the world. They still own major brands that you will recognise, such as MTV and DreamWorks.

What do you notice about Sony? Like many media companies today, it developed a market for product and then used its skills to move into media.

Theory into practice 3

Undertake research into a well-known media company, such as News Corporation. **P1**

Produce a diagram of the companies they own and the products they produce. **M1**

Identify if they are a horizontally or vertically integrated company. **M1**

Grading tip

To reach Distinction level, you should show that you can fully explain the structure of one company in a sector of the media industries, making relevant and well-supported points and expressing this fluently using correct subject terminology.

Case study

Media Productions

Media Productions is an independent producer and has no links to other media companies. The company buys materials, for example blank DVDs, from other companies working in media sales. Media Productions is able to take on jobs that it really wants to do rather than jobs it is told to do by a parent company.

However, Media Productions must be financially stable as it does not have a big company behind it to bankroll it. Media Productions has to compete with other production companies for work and has to be competitive in its quotes and costings.

Knowledge check 6.1

1. Find examples of three vertically integrated companies. **P1**

2. Find examples of three horizontally integrated companies. **P1**

3. Prepare an illustrated report on one media sector using a range of examples. **M1**

4. Use an example of a media company and identify their products, what they produce and if they are vertically or horizontally integrated. **P1**

6.2 Know about employment opportunities and job roles in the media industries

Employment opportunities

There is a great range of employment opportunities in the media industries. These fall into a number of categories, which can overlap. For instance, you can have a full-time, permanent job that involves you working shifts, or a part-time, temporary job with a fixed number of hours per week.

Work categories

Work tends to be categorised by how secure it is. Full-time work, with a permanent contract is the most secure, whereas casual and freelance work are the least secure.

■ Full-time

A **full-time** job is where you work all the time for one company. Often this involves a set number of hours per week, but in the media industries there tends not be a regular pattern of working hours.

Case study

Media Productions

Working hours in the media industries can be long and unpredictable. On a recent commission the crew at Media Productions were employed to film a short news item for national television.

The crew started out at 6.00am to travel to Yorkshire and arrived at the location at 9.00am. They filmed a short sequence and then had to travel to Manchester to film an interview. They were then directed back to Yorkshire as the main person they wanted to film had returned home unexpectedly.

The crew had a short break for lunch (20 minutes) before heading off again to another location. Their final interview of the day was at 10.00pm again in Manchester. They arrived back at their office at 1.00am.

■ Part-time

In a **part-time** job you work for part of a day or week for one employer. Depending on the hours, it is possible to have two or more part-time jobs at the same time.

■ Freelance

Many people working in the media industries work as **freelances**. This means they effectively work for themselves, hiring themselves out to various employers for particular jobs or projects. They move from project to project offering their skills as prospective employers need them. There is no job security in freelance work as you have no fixed income and no benefits, such as paid holiday, sick leave or use of company facilities. You may also be unlucky enough to find yourself with no work for long periods. However, you can develop lots of new skills by moving between companies, and the flexibility of not being tied down to a full-time job might suit your lifestyle. You can make lots of useful contacts as a freelance that might result in a permanent job someday if that is what you want. Many freelances enjoy the freedom to pick and choose who they work for, when they work, and the roles they undertake.

Case study

Media Productions

Media Productions employ freelance staff for their particular expertise or if a crew is shorthanded. On a recent production the location recce and risk assessment highlighted the need for extra crew as they were filming in a school. Someone had to be on-hand at all times to ensure that no children were injured by the lights and camera equipment. A freelance production assistant was hired to do this.

■ Shift work

This is working a set number of hours at a particular time of the day to ensure a job is covered for 24 hours. This might be working early morning until the afternoon, afternoon until late evening or even working throughout the night. Many broadcasters have staff on **shift** patterns to maintain equipment or ensure a broadcaster stays on the air.

▲ Figure 6.10: If equipment needs to be in full working order 24 hours a day, you need to ensure there is always someone available to repair it if it goes wrong!

■ Permanent

A **permanent** job is one with a contract that has no fixed end-date. It is the most secure job option, with both worker and employer having to give notice before ending the employment contract. Permanent jobs often have benefits such as a pension scheme, membership of a health scheme, a company canteen and company-organised social events. Many media jobs used to be permanent but this is not cost effective today for many media companies.

■ Temporary

A **temporary** job can be full- or part-time but is only short-term. You will have a fixed number of days or weeks to work until the job is completed. There is generally no guarantee of further work once the temporary job finishes.

■ Voluntary

Working on a **voluntary**, or unpaid, basis is how many media graduates start out gaining experience and making contacts. Although the work is unpaid, you might receive expenses. One way of gaining voluntary experience in the media is to work for hospital radio. These are radio stations run on a closed loop in hospitals. Many well-known broadcasters started their careers as volunteers in hospital radio.

Maybe you could work for a student newspaper. Remember the example of Richard Branson who founded the Virgin empire with a student magazine.

■ Casual work

Some companies will employ **casual** labour to meet particular needs. People might be taken on just for a day or two. This is sometimes hourly paid work – where you are paid according to the amount of time worked (excluding breaks) or piecework – where you are paid per item of work completed, such as developing films or duplicating DVDs.

Case study

Media Productions

Media Productions employs staff on a casual basis when it has a major duplication and distribution job. For example, it had to duplicate and distribute 5,000 DVDs across the UK. A number of casual staff were employed to undertake the duplication and packaging work.

Recruitment

Media workers can be recruited in a number of ways. Your school or college careers adviser can give you details of media jobs in your area. There may be advertisements in national and local newspapers. The trade press carries adverts for jobs as do trade websites. You may be able to use personal contacts to find a job or investigate an agency that specialises in media appointments.

Think it over 2

Mark was a learner on a National Diploma in Media course. He wanted to work in the media industry so he tried to arrange work experience. He wrote to a local film crew producing a soap based on a country veterinary practice. He received a response that said they would consider his application, but not this year.

Mark then discovered that a friend of his mother's knew the person who trained the animals that appeared in this soap. His mother rang her friend who rang the animal trainer. She then contacted the soap's producer and recommended Mark to him.

Mark received a call from the producer offering him some work experience on the set. Mark did his work experience and worked hard. At the end of the experience he was asked if he had any plans once he finished his course, and was offered a job on the crew for the next series of the soap.

Why do you think Mark's application was refused first time round?

Do you think it is fair that Mark eventually got the job through his contacts?

What can you do to improve your contacts in the media industries?

Do you think this might eventually help you to get work?

Sometimes you just have to persevere. You may have to write lots of letters and not be put off by rejections. This is a competitive industry and there may be hundreds of people going for the same jobs. Sometimes you hear about jobs through word of mouth. If so, follow this up as quickly as you can, as getting an application in early could work in your favour. Remember, personal recommendations can be a great help.

You can also consider moving to higher education and gaining more qualifications to improve your job prospects. Many universities offer media production degrees or Higher National Diplomas that allow you to develop high-level skills. A lot of employers in the media industry welcome graduates with qualifications. You are best placed to get a job if you can offer a good combination of qualifications and experience.

Many media companies use the services of specialist recruitment agencies. These agencies will advertise media jobs in the press or on-line. They keep details of media job hunters and are able to match the job seekers with companies looking to recruit. They will charge the companies for this service, but some think it is worth it to get good recommendations of suitable candidates.

Job roles

In the media industries job roles tend to fall into one of eight main categories. Some jobs may include elements of several categories. For instance, although being a producer is regarded as a managerial role, producers should also be creative and have technical expertise, as well as financial and legal knowledge.

- **Creative**: roles in developing and producing creative media products, e.g. graphic designer, director
- **Technical**: roles using technology to support the creative process, e.g. sound engineer, cameraperson, video editor
- **Editorial**: controlling the style and content of a media product, e.g. director, sub-editor, picture editor
- **Marketing**: involves researching the market and organising a selling strategy for a media product and then implementing this strategy
- **Managerial**: overseeing a team of people and ensuring that a product is produced on time and to budget, e.g. producer
- **Administrative**: a vital role in the smooth running of any company. This involves producing documentation, booking resources and keeping records, e.g. production assistant
- **Legal:** Some media companies employ legal staff to check that the material they are producing will not break laws and will meet the requirements of a media regulator
- **Financial:** Media companies employ staff to ensure that invoices are produced, budgets are monitored and bills are paid.

Presentation for employment

When applying for media jobs you will need to demonstrate to a potential employer what you can do. This is referred to as presentation for employment, and for this you could produce:

- a portfolio of your design work, and print material
- a showreel of all your moving image products
- an interactive CD or DVD with examples of your e-media or games-development work
- a personal website that the employer could access to see your web design and other media work.

Applying for a job

■ Curriculum vitae

You should produce a Curriculum vitae that outlines your qualifications, skills and interests. It is a good idea to modify your CV for each job you apply for. For instance,

if you are applying for two jobs, one in television and one in radio, adapt your CV to emphasise your relevant experience in each of these areas.

■ Covering letter

Most job applications will also ask for a covering letter. This is your opportunity to state the most important things about you, why you want the job and why you are a good candidate. You can direct the employer to the most relevant part of your CV in your covering letter. Some employers will not even bother to look at your CV if your covering letter does not impress them enough to want to find out more about you, so make your application letter really count.

On page 204 is an example of a letter of application for a media job.

Curriculum Vitae
Michael A. Foan
28, Chalk Pit Lane
Oldtown, OT3 8NN

Personal Details

Name:	Michael Allen FOAN	**Tel:**	01234 543210
Date of Birth:	17.11.1980	**Mob:**	07777 345762
Place of Birth:	Oldtown, UK	**e-mail:**	mikeafoan@email.com

Summary
Recently qualified media professional with experience in radio presenting and a particular expertise in music and sports broadcasting and writing.

Educational Qualifications

BA (Hons) Media Production (Radio and Television) 2/1	2006
Advanced GCE Media (A)	2003
Advanced GCE English (A)	2003
Advanced Subsidiary GCE History (C)	2002
GCSE English (A), Maths (C), History (A), French (C), Geography (B)	2001

Employment History
June 2006–Present
Oldtown FM. Presenter of evening show.

September 2003–June 2006
Oldtown FM. Station assistant working on Saturday morning sports and music show.

August 2003
Oldtown FM Work experience.

January 2002–August 2003
Bestco Supermarket Shelf-filler.

Educational History

University of Sunderland	2003–2006
Oldtown Comprehensive	1996–2003

Skills and Interests
Music, sport and writing. I have written four magazine articles for the music press as well as my first novel (currently available for publication).
Computing: (Mac and PC) Microsoft Word, Quark XPress, DreamWeaver
I hold a full, clean driving licence (since 1998)

Other Experience
Duke of Edinburgh Award (Silver)
Oldtown Orienteering Club member since 1999

Referees

Mr John Jameson	Anna Smith
Headteacher	Programme Co-ordinator
Oldtown Comprehensive	Oldtown FM
George Street	FM House
Oldtown OT7 8KM	High Street
john-jameson@oldtowncomp.ac.uk	Oldtown OT1 6YH
01234 987655	01234 765432
	annasmith@oldtownfm.com

▲ Figure 6.11: Your CV should be short and to the point – giving essential information about you at a glance.

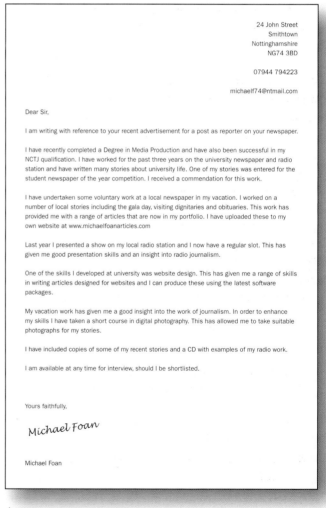

▲ Figure 6.12: A covering letter allows you to state why you think you are right for the job, and to direct the employer to the most relevant experience on your CV.

Theory into practice 5

Find an example of an advertised media job. Prepare a CV and letter of application for this job. **P2**

Remember to include in your CV:

- Your name
- Date of birth
- Your previous experience
- Address
- Your qualifications
- Your interests.

Your covering letter should say why you are interested in this job. **M2**

Grading tip

To reach Distinction level, your covering letter and CV should demonstrate that you have a thorough understanding of employment opportunities and job roles.

■ References

You should be able to provide an employer with names and addresses of people that can provide a **reference** for you. This might be your teacher or head teacher. It may be someone that you have worked for in a part-time capacity. It could be someone that knows you from one of your outside interests, such as a scoutmaster or a netball coach.

An employer will want to form a picture of you before they go ahead with an interview. If your CV and letter have provided them with sufficient information to ask you for interview then you have made the first step. Follow this up with a range of good references.

Self-presentation

You have sent in your CV and letter of application and have been asked to attend an interview. How you present yourself at your interview will be crucial to getting the job. Even if you look great on your CV, if you do not come over well in the interview, you are unlikely to get the job. First impressions are critical. No matter what your normal personal style, you will be expected to present a professional image at an interview. How you dress, your hair, your general tidiness and even for women the appropriateness of your make-up, will all be judged in the first few seconds.

Think it over 3

What kind of things should you consider when attending an interview? Think about the following.

Do you dress in torn jeans?

Do you talk to the interviewer in street jargon or in dialect?

Do you give the interviewer a big kiss when you meet them?

Here are some basic guidelines about how to approach an interview.

- Dress smartly.
- Greet the interviewer when you enter the room.
- Do not speak too fast, and keep to the point.
- Keep eye contact with the interviewer during the interview.
- Think through your responses before you jump in to answer questions.
- Have some questions of your own to ask the interviewer – this shows you have thought about the job you are applying for.

Think it over 4

A study in *The Times* newspaper stated that media graduates were more successful than any other graduates in finding a job after graduation. However, this may not necessarily be in the media industry. Media graduates are good at being interviewed. They have good communication skills developed by undertaking a media qualification!

How can you impress a potential employer? Why not consider using a presentation as part of your interview. Inform the employer that you require a data projector for your interview. This will show them that you have thought about the interview. Why not put together a PowerPoint presentation to demonstrate your skills in communicating with an audience or client.

These are some examples of slides that you could use to start your presentation.

▲ Figure 6.13: Presentation slides will help the interviewer remember you and your qualifications and experience.

Further slides could highlight your qualifications, personal skills and interest. If you were really clever you could bring in to your presentation an example of your work. This could be a video clip, a sound clip or some graphics from a website.

You should remember to use appropriate media language when talking to a prospective employer. This will demonstrate that you have a working knowledge of the media.

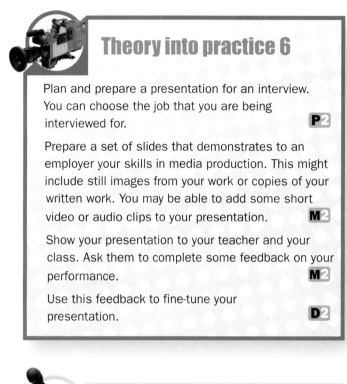

Theory into practice 6

Plan and prepare a presentation for an interview. You can choose the job that you are being interviewed for. **P2**

Prepare a set of slides that demonstrates to an employer your skills in media production. This might include still images from your work or copies of your written work. You may be able to add some short video or audio clips to your presentation. **M2**

Show your presentation to your teacher and your class. Ask them to complete some feedback on your performance. **M2**

Use this feedback to fine-tune your presentation. **D2**

Grading tip

To reach Distinction level, your presentation should demonstrate thorough understanding of employment opportunities and job roles in the media industries.

Professional development

No matter where you are on the career ladder, you should always consider updating and developing your skills. This is called **professional development** and can include anything from finding work experience while you are studying for your BTEC National, or doing a post-graduate degree in screenwriting.

Case study

Media Productions

Media Productions holds regular staff meetings where issues about current productions are discussed. Matters relating to staff development can also be talked about and information handed out to staff.

The company has a policy of supporting staff who want to learn new skills. This can include financial support for attending college.

Every year staff are invited to attend an industry event, Broadcast Live, in London. This gives staff an opportunity to see the latest technology and meet with supply companies. It is also a good day out, which contributes to team-building within the company.

Sources of information

You can find information about professional development from a number of different sources. College and university prospectuses give details of media courses offered, and there are independent sources of information too.

▲ Figure 6.14 Skillset aims to ensure that all media professionals are well-trained. It also offers free career advice.

The Skill Sector Council for the audio-visual industries is Skillset. It is both industry- and government-funded, and its aim is to ensure that there are sufficient skilled people available to work within the media industries. It does this by providing information and funding. It also publishes research and undertakes consultation work. It identifies challenges facing the industry and suggests strategies to overcome those challenges. It is particularly

useful for media students and industry professionals as it also offers careers advice online, face to face and over the phone. It also actively supports continuing professional development for media professionals.

There are other organisations that support media professionals.

Figure 6.15 BECTU has a strong commitment to helping its members develop professionally. ▶

BECTU (Broadcasting, Entertainment, Cinematograph and Theatre Union) is a trade union for people working in broadcasting, film, theatre, entertainment, leisure, interactive media and related areas, who are primarily based in the United Kingdom. It will negotiate with employers on pay and conditions, advise members on employment issues and mediate in disputes between employers and employees. It also represents freelance workers. BECTU publishes *Stage and Screen* magazine which has useful articles and advertisements for media professionals.

BECTU also provides information on appropriate rates of pay for a variety of roles in the media. They work with Skillset in providing professional development for staff.

Think it over 5

Imagine that you have been working as a production assistant for a year. You have seen the production and post-production process in operation and want to move on in the industry. You need to develop new skills and would like to learn how to edit. What do you do?

Key Terms

Professional development is the further stages of education a media professional might undertake in order to build on and update their skills.

Work experience is the opportunity for students, usually still in full-time education, to work for short periods (normally without pay) in the industry, to experience what it is like to have a media job.

Theory into practice 7

Think about the media industry you would like to work in. Try to find out about professional development courses in this area of the media. **P2**

If you want to work in the newspaper industry try searching for courses such as NCTJ or post-graduate courses.

Make a list of professional development courses. **M2**

Grading tips

To reach Merit level, you should use well-chosen examples to support your understanding of professional development opportunities.

To reach Distinction level, you should use a wide range of examples and explain why these are relevant to your understanding of professional development opportunities.

Education and training

You can study for additional qualifications on a part-time or even a full-time basis. A number of universities and colleges offer a range of development programmes for media professionals in all aspects of the industry, from management to web design. If you are considering

some sort of professional development, check out your local college and see if there are any appropriate evening classes. It is also worth finding out if your employer will pay for you to attend college or go on a short course. Many employers are keen to develop their people, and some might even run in-house courses or training on the job.

Case study

Media Productions

Media Productions values staff members and provides opportunities for them to develop their skills.

John, a production assistant, is going to part-time classes at a local college. He is learning to edit using the latest software.

Paula is a production secretary who is studying business skills on a BTEC National Diploma in Business on a day release programme.

Ahmed, the office manager, really wants to learn about using media production equipment. He wants to make his own programmes and learn how to make his holiday videos look good. He is being mentored by Dave, one of the senior camera operators, and uses equipment at work in his lunchtime and after he finishes work.

Every year Media Productions provides two work experience placements. There are offered to local schools and colleges. Applicants for these placements are asked to provide a letter of application and a CV. In the past some of the work experience students have found employment with the company.

Work experience

You may decide to undertake some **work experience** in the media industry. If so then you will need to consider what job you would like to do and where you would like to do it. It is never easy to find work experience placements, so you are going to have to be persistent.

Record of employment history and skills

We looked at how to put your CV together in the
previous section. But you might also consider keeping
a more detailed record of your skills and employment
history. This is useful both for you to keep an eye on
how your career is progressing, and as evidence of your
professional development to show new or prospective
employers. Evidence can be presented in any media
format, such as a website, a showreel or a DVD.

Professional behaviour

Is important for you as a media worker to behave in a
professional manner. The following is a list of attributes
you must have in all your work dealings.

- **Reliability**. If a media worker cannot be relied upon
  to do their job as expected they will eventually be
  recognised in the industry as someone who cannot
  be trusted.
- **Punctuality and attendance.** A producer would
  find it impossible to work with a staff member who
  is constantly late for meetings or location shoots. If
  you cannot be relied on to turn up for work you can
  affect the success or failure of a shoot and cost your
  company a lot of money.

- **Commitment**. A staff member who does not take
  their job seriously, who constantly disagrees with
  their manager or is easily distracted from the task
  will not progress in this industry.
- **Communication**. It is vital to discuss issues with
  the team and client and be aware of all the activities
  being planned. Keeping up a dialogue with a client
  will help to ensure the successful production of an
  appropriate media product.
- **Efficiency and time management**. Employers do
  not want staff who are constantly struggling to keep
  up with their work. Staff who take long lunch breaks,
  spend time on private phone calls and Internet
  use, and take long coffee/cigarette breaks can be a
  problem for a manager.
- **Personal responsibility**. Everyone working in the
  team must be able to review their own roles in the
  team and take responsibility for their own work and
  behaviour. They must be able to consider how they
  might improve their performance or learn new skills.

Grading tips

To reach Merit level, you should use well-chosen examples to support your understanding of professional behaviour.

To reach Distinction level, you should use a wide range of relevant examples and explain why these are relevant to your understanding of professional behaviour.

Knowledge check 6.2

1. Identify a range of media jobs, **P2**

2. Identify the elements of these jobs such as pay, contracts offered, etc. **M2**

3. Using an example of a media job that you have seen advertised, prepare a CV and application letter. **D2**

4. Prepare a presentation that you would use for a job interview. Plan this carefully. **D2**

5. Think about your chosen media career – make a list of the professional development opportunities there are for your chosen career. **D2**

6. Write a report on the professional codes of practice and behaviour expected in your chosen career. **D2**

6.3 Ethical and legal constraints

As a media worker you will come across both **ethical** and **legal constraints** in the course of your career. You need to be aware of these issues, and the codes of conduct and legislation that surround them.

Key Terms

Ethical constraints refers to the considerations that media professionals have to make when working in the media industries, for instance privacy and codes of conduct.

Legal constraints refers to the issues that media professionals have to consider regarding the law, for instance copyright law and race relations law.

Ethical

Codes of conduct

People working in the media need to follow **codes of conduct** in order work to ethical standards. These codes of conduct or codes of practice suggest certain standards of behaviour, for instance how journalists should conduct themselves when reporting on news stories.

Codes of conduct help media professionals to work in an ethical way. For instance, there are ethical considerations when reporting on someone's private conversations. Journalists must be aware of the consequences of recording a private conversation or invading someone's private correspondence.

Think it over 7

Go to the website of the National Union of Journalists www.nuj.org.uk and find their code of conduct. This code sets out the main principles of British and Irish journalism and has been in existence since 1936. If you join the union you must sign an agreement saying you will try to stick to these rules.

What are the main principles that the code is based on?

Do you agree with all the points? If not, why not?

If you were a journalist would you find it easy or difficult to stick to this code of conduct?

This is purely a voluntary code, it is not binding by law. Do you think any of it should be made law?

Figure 6.16 The NUJ has a strict code of conduct that it expects its members to adhere to. ▶

Think it over 8

You have met a friend at a restaurant to discuss your latest business idea. This idea will be revolutionary in the world of IT. Your friend agrees to help you to put your plans into practice.

The next day you see an article in a newspaper about the very same idea that you had discussed with your friend. It appears that a reporter had been sitting on the next table and had overheard your conversation.

Do you think the reporter acted ethically?

What would you do?

You could complain to the newspaper but your idea has already been exposed to a wide audience. Do you think the reporter should be reprimanded by his editor for invading your privacy?

Case study

Media Productions

A researcher approached Media Productions about a programme idea. This was a new and interesting idea that would make a good programme for broadcast television.

The creative director rang a number of contacts in the industry to see if anyone had been approached with a similar idea. She discovered that another production company had been approached by the same researcher with the idea and had been paid a sum of money to develop the idea further.

Media Productions politely informed the researcher that they knew about this, and also informed him that they had alerted other companies to this potential scam.

Representation

It is important for the media industries to represent people in the right way. There should, for instance, be no intention to misrepresent people because of the colour of their skin, their religion or their sexual orientation.

Television and radio producers have to be sensitive to representation issues in their programme making. The BBC, like many organisations, has a series of guidelines for producers to follow in their programme making. These are intended to help producers deal with difficult editorial decisions. This does not mean that the BBC wants to avoid contentious issues, nor that it does not make controversial programmes, but its guidelines are there to help producers make such programmes effectively and ethically. It reviews its guidelines regularly and they are approved by the BBC's board of governors. You can read the guidelines at: www.bbc.co.uk/guidelines/editorialguidelines

Think it over 9

In the 1970s it was seen as acceptable to represent people in a way that would not be allowed today.

A comedy programme *Love thy Neighbour* was aired on commercial television in a prime-time slot. In the programme the white neighbour of a black family referred to the black father as 'sambo' and in turn the black neighbour called the white family 'white honkeys'.

A well-known comedian of the same era, Dick Emery, regularly adopted the character of a camp homosexual character. His mannerisms were intended to raise a laugh at the expense of gay people.

There were also a number of comedy programmes that made fun of religion and religious figures.

Do you think it is acceptable to make fun of people's race, sexuality or religion?

Do you think these programmes could still be made and find a broadcaster today?

Do comedians today still use religion, race and sexuality as the butt of humour?

You must be certain that you take into account ethical issues when planning and producing your work. Your approach to these issues also says something about the way that you work as a media professional.

Case study

Media Productions

The management at Media Productions have taken ethical issues into consideration in the way they run their business. With regard to environmental issues, for instance, they have put the following procedures into place.

1. All materials are sourced, wherever possible, from sustainable resources.

2. Paper used for printing, DVD covers and labels is from recycled sources.

3. The company strives to decrease its carbon footprint by reducing electricity consumption by using low voltage light bulbs in offices and not using standby mode in its editing suites and studio operations.

4. Wherever possible the company uses shot footage from other countries from local producers so decreasing the use of airline flights.

5. All company vehicles are powered by dual fuel technology.

The measures taken by Media Productions may seem very small in the light of the effects of global warming. However, the company is seeking to make its contribution to minimising its effect on the planet's resources. The company ensures that the message gets out to all its clients by including a statement in its literature, on its website and on its products about global warming.

◀ **Figure 6.17 You must be fully aware of legal and ethical issues when making a media product.**

Legal

There are a number of legal statutes that affect the media industries. Here are some examples.

Race Relations Act 1976: This act makes it unlawful to discriminate against anyone directly or indirectly on racial grounds.

A new body, the Commission for Equality and Human Rights, came into existence in 2007. The commission identifies equality as a concern for all of us, and identifies equality, diversity, and respect for the human rights and dignity of all citizens as core British values. You can find out more about CEHR by visiting its website at www.cehr.org.uk

As a media professional you would have to take note of this and ensure that any material you produce follows these guidelines.

Human Rights Act 1998: This is a far-ranging act that covers many aspects of what you might do as a media producer. You should read this act carefully. It states that (amongst other things):

Everyone's right to life shall be protected by law. No one shall be deprived of his life intentionally save in the execution of a sentence of a court following his conviction of a crime for which this penalty is provided by law.

No one shall be subjected to torture or to inhuman or degrading treatment or punishment.

No one shall be held in slavery or servitude.

No one shall be required to perform forced or compulsory labour…

How would you react if you were faced with filming someone working in forced labour? Would you be able to film this in a dispassionate way or would you want to intervene?

Licensing Act 2003: This act provides information on the licensing of premises to be used for the showing of films.

Privacy Law: This law is all about protecting and preserving the privacy rights of individuals. Everyone has a right to privacy whether it is from newspapers wanting pictures of a celebrity on holiday to someone appearing in court. The Information Commissioner's Office (ICO) is an independent public body in the UK that protects personal information by making rulings on cases where people's privacy has been invaded. It also promotes access to official information for both companies and individuals. You can find out more about the ICO at: www.ico.gov.uk

Copyright Law: Copyright law is all about protecting the rights of a person who has created something, such as a book, an article, a piece of music, an image or a website design. You can find out more about copyright in Unit 2.

There are several organisations that deal with copyright, such as the Authors' Licensing and Collecting Society that represents the interests of UK writers. The ALCS works to make sure writers are paid for any of their work that is copied, broadcast or recorded. There is more information about ALCS at: www.alcs.co.uk

In the UK the Intellectual Property Office is a government body that is responsible for granting IP, or Intellectual Property, rights. You can see from their website www.ipo.gov.uk that copyright can have far-reaching consequences for a media producer.

Libel: Libel is the attacking of a person's good character in a fixed medium – such as print or film. Media producers have to take great care to ensure they do not libel anyone. Libel can exist in cyberspace as well as in a printed magazine or on a broadcast programme.

Libel law is there to protect individuals or organisations from untruthful attacks on their reputation. A person is libelled if a publication has a detrimental effect on their lives, for instance by casting a slur on their good name, causing them to be hated, shunned or ridiculed, or adversely affecting their business or how they make their living.

Key Term

Libel is a harmful statement in a fixed medium, especially writing, but also a picture, sign or electronic broadcast.

As a media producer you will have to consider what you say about an individual or organisation before you commit this to words or images.

Official Secrets Act: This is an act that prohibits current or former government employees, or anyone given access to sensitive information, from telling anyone else about their work. This includes newspapers or television stations. Any journalists who are told information covered by the act and then repeat it in print or broadcast it can be prosecuted.

Obscene Publications Act 1959 & 1964: This act set out what is regarded as obscene and unfit for publication in England and Wales. It enforces the censorship of obscene materials.

Protection of Children Act 1978: This legislation provides protection for children against abuse. It makes it an offence, for instance, for indecent images of children to be taken, shown or distributed in the United Kingdom. It is also an offence to possess such images.

Media producers must take extreme care when using images of children under the age of 18 in their media products, that they do not unwittingly breach the provisions of this act.

Video Recordings Act 1984: This act came about because of the growth of so-called 'video nasties', usually explicitly violent videos that came to be seen as corrupting young people. Its aim was to ensure that all video recordings available in the UK were approved by a recognised authority. This authority was the British Board of Film Classification, which now has statutory powers over video and DVD recordings.

Knowledge check 6.3

1. Produce a list of legal issues that might affect your work as a media producer. **P3**

2. Identify how media producers have been affected by some of these issues. **M3**

Theory into practice 9

Make a list of ethical and legal issues that might affect your work as media producer. **P3**

For each of the ethical and legal issues find examples of how media producers have been affected by these issues. You will need to use a range of research techniques to find this information. **M3**

Present your list and examples to the rest of your class using an appropriate presentation technique. **M3**

Add any extra examples your classmates may have found to your list. You will find this list useful when you are making your own media products.

Grading tip

To reach Distinction level, you should use a wide range of relevant examples and explain why these are relevant to your understanding of ethical and legal issues.

Regulatory bodies

There are a number of **regulatory bodies** that you need to be aware of. Their work could have an impact on what you produce as a media professional. These bodies could also have an effect on what you produce as part of this course.

Key Term

Regulatory body is an organisation that oversees the running of a business or sector of the media industry, such as Ofcom, BBFC and PCC.

Remember!

The following are regulatory bodies we looked at in Unit 2. Go back to that unit and refresh your memory.

British Board of Film Classification (BBFC)

Office of Communication (Ofcom)

Press Complaints Commission (PCC)

Advertising Standards Authority (ASA)

Theory into practice 10

Make a comprehensive list of the regulatory bodies for the media industries. **P4**

For each regulatory body:

- find their postal address, telephone number and Internet address **P4**
- identify the area of the media they regulate **P4**
- note down how this regulatory body might have an impact on media products that you produce. **M4**

Grading tips

To reach Merit level, you should use well-chosen examples to support your understanding of regulatory bodies and their impact on your work.

To reach Distinction level, you should use a wide range of relevant examples and explain why these are relevant to your understanding of regulatory bodies and their impact on your work.

Regulatory issues

Without regulation, producers could present all manner of inappropriate material at whatever time of day they chose.

This could have serious implications for groups of consumers. Children could have access to violent or sexually explicit material, racial groups could be offended by inappropriate subjects or content, people could be hounded or defamed with impunity.

Regulatory bodies and professional organisations exist to ensure that listeners, viewers and readers have access to appropriate material. They produce regulations and codes of conduct to protect audiences.

Think it over 10

You will have to consider these issues when you make your own media products.

How would you feel if you were doorstepped by a reporter or photographer?

What if the paparazzi recorded your every move? What if someone tapped your phone and reported your private conversations in a newspaper?

Some people may say that they have been denied access to something they want or that choices have been limited.

In the press, journalists follow a self-regulatory code that ensures they all work in a professional way. However, there are always pressures from editors to get that big story before the competition.

In the recent past there have been incidents where editors have printed stories and photographs without checking their authenticity.

In May 2004 the *Daily Mirror* published photographs it said were of prisoners being mistreated in Iraq. The newspaper said that it published the photographs in good faith, genuinely believing them to show British soldiers abusing an Iraqi prisoner. However, the pictures were proved to be fakes and the editor of the paper, Piers Morgan, was sacked for allegedly refusing to apologise over this mistake.

Figure 6.18 It is vital to check your sources to make sure what you publish or broadcast is true – a lesson the Daily Mirror learned the hard way with this false story about Iraqi prisoners.

Case study

The Hitler Diaries

In 1983 the German magazine, *Stern*, started to publish the alleged diaries of Adolf Hitler. They are said to have paid nine million marks, about four million pounds, for these diaries. *Stern* also sold the diaries to *The Sunday Times* but it was demonstrated at the last minute that the diaries were forgeries. In the rush to publish the diaries no one had tested them for authenticity. A scientist then proved that the paper and ink used were not available until after the end of the Second World War.

Imagine the embarrassment of the newspaper and reporters having been duped into printing extracts and selling newspapers on the back of them.

What should the newspapers have done to confirm the diaries' authenticity?

What do you think should have happened to the editor of *Stern*?

Hans Booms holds up a volume of the alleged Hitler diaries at a press conference on 6 May 1983 in West Germany.

Censorship

Television producers work to guidelines that allow certain things to be broadcast on television after the **watershed** (generally 9.00pm). This will be adult content and not suitable for children to view.

Many people see this as government **censorship** as they feel they have the right to see what they want and when they want. However, this has to be balanced with the rights of children who are likely to be watching television before 9.00pm to be protected from violent or sexually explicit images.

Key Terms

Watershed is the time (usually taken as 9.00pm) after which it is allowable to broadcast material with adult content, such as sex and violence. This material is not deemed appropriate for earlier in the evening when children may be viewing.

Censorship is the cutting or altering of material that is deemed unsuitable in a media product. The material could be of a sexual or violent nature, or in some totalitarian regimes, could express undesirable political views.

Some films have caused concern but have not been ultimately censored. Harry Potter books and films, for instance, were received enthusiastically by children, but teachers and religious leaders warned against children being indoctrinated into accepting the occult as fact rather than fiction.

Regulation and ownership

The Communications Act 2003 requires Ofcom to review the media ownership rules at least every three years. This is to ensure that there is a range of available sources for the public to receive news, information and opinion. It is also important for companies to be able to invest in the UK in order to expand their activities.

The changing landscape of the media industry demonstrates the importance of regulation in ensuring that no one company controls all the media.

At the start of this unit you looked at Emap. This company owns a range of media production companies. It could be seen that they control what you see and what you hear.

News Corporation is an organisation that owns companies such as *The Sun* newspaper, BSkyB, HarperCollins Publishers and 20th Century Fox.

It may be necessary for Ofcom to ensure that this company's increasing control over television and newspapers does not provide a platform for one person's views.

▲ Figure 6.19 What would it be like if one organisation or individual controlled all of the media?

Earlier in this unit you will have seen that media producers have to address issues such as taste and decency, access to information and codes of conduct on a daily basis.

You will have to address these issues in your media production work. When you start to plan your media products you must ask yourself the following questions:

- Is this product suitable for the target audience?
- Will the product infringe someone's copyright?
- Will I be invading someone's right to privacy by making this product?
- Will I be libelling someone when making this product?
- Will I be making this product in a professional, ethical and legal way?
- How can I ensure that the work I have produced meets a professional standard?

Take into account all the issues raised in this unit and consider them when planning and producing your media products.

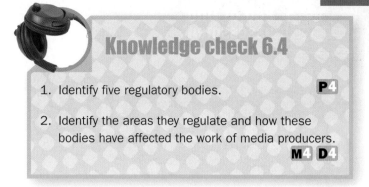

Knowledge check 6.4

1. Identify five regulatory bodies. **P4**

2. Identify the areas they regulate and how these bodies have affected the work of media producers. **M4 D4**

Preparation for assessment

You must produce an illustrated guide to working in the media industries.

This guide will be produced in the most appropriate format.

The guide will help when you start working in the media industries.

In order to produce this guide you will undertake research into the media industries, the employment opportunities available, the ethical and legal issues you will encounter and the regulatory issues you may have to take into account.

The guide can be produced in any media format you choose. It must, however, be accessible for anyone to read or view.

End of Unit assessment activity 1

You must explain the structure and ownership of the media industries. You should use appropriate illustrative methods to explain clearly how the media industries are structured. Consider using diagrams and charts to show how the media industry is structured. **P1**

– To achieve a merit grade you must explain, with reference to well-chosen examples, the structure and ownership of the media industries. Your examples will help to explain clearly the ownership and structure of the media industries. Express your ideas with clarity and with generally appropriate use of subject terminology. Your use of subject terminology will help to demonstrate that you have a really clear understanding of structure and ownership issues. **M1**

– To achieve a distinction grade you must fully explain the structure and ownership of the media industries,

justifying points made with supporting arguments and elucidated examples, expressing ideas fluently and using subject terminology correctly.

To do this you must provide clear examples of the media industries and explain how and why media companies work in the media sectors and why they sometimes work together. You should consider how you can demonstrate this – maybe through a presentation using examples of the media products the companies produce. **D1**

End of Unit assessment activity 2

You must produce evidence of your understanding of employment opportunities and demonstrate that you understand the different roles in media employment.

Produce a CV and showreel.

– To achieve a pass grade you must demonstrate that you understand how you can undertake further development of your media skills.

Record, in an appropriate way, your professional work on a number of production roles you have undertaken. **P2**

– To achieve a merit grade you must demonstrate competently your understanding of employment opportunities and job roles in the media industries with reference to well-chosen examples. You will be able to talk about the range of employment opportunities available and be able to describe how this might affect your career opportunities. You will have a clear understanding of a range of job roles and be able to explain what these roles involve. **M2**

– To achieve a distinction grade you must demonstrate a thorough understanding of employment opportunities and job roles in the media industries with supporting justification and elucidated examples.

To do this you must provide a range of examples of employment opportunities. You could link these employment opportunities with the media sectors you have identified in Activity 1. You must be prepared to justify your choice of examples and give reasons why some roles are appropriate for the employment contract associated with them. You should demonstrate your ability to prepare a professional CV and portfolio or showreel. **D2**

End of Unit assessment activity 3

Produce evidence that you understand the ethical and legal issues surrounding the production of a media product. **P3**

- To achieve a merit grade you must demonstrate competently your understanding of ethical and legal considerations relevant to the media industries with reference to well-chosen examples. You will be able to discuss how these affect your own work and how this might affect your career in the media industries. You will have provided relevant and appropriate examples to illustrate the points you discuss. **M3**

- To achieve a distinction grade you must thoroughly demonstrate an understanding of ethical and legal considerations relevant to the media industries, with supporting justification and elucidated examples.

To do this you should consider carefully the ethical and legal considerations you must make in each of the media industries. You should be able to link these to real media products and demonstrate how these products might have ethical and legal issues. You may be able to link this to media products you have planned or produced. **D3**

End of Unit assessment activity 4

Demonstrate your understanding of the regulatory issues when working on a media product. **P4**

- To achieve a merit grade you must explain, with reference to well-chosen examples, the regulatory issues affecting the media industries. You must express your ideas with clarity and with generally appropriate use of subject terminology. You will be able to discuss how regulatory issues affect your own work and how this might affect your career in the media industries. You will have provided relevant and appropriate examples to illustrate the points you discuss. Your use of subject terminology will help to demonstrate that you have a really clear understanding of regulatory issues. **M4**

- In order to achieve a distinction grade you must fully explain the regulatory issues affecting the media industries, justifying points made with supporting arguments and elucidated examples, expressing ideas fluently and using subject terminology correctly.

To do this you must consider what regulatory issues affect media industries and justify why these are in place. You may be able to link this to work that you have undertaken on a media product – what did you have to consider about regulation when you planned your product? Remember to use correct subject terminology and write fluently. **D4**

Grading Criteria

To achieve a pass grade the evidence must show that the learner is able to:	TiP	To achieve a merit grade the evidence must show that the learner is able to:	TiP	To achieve a distinction grade the evidence must show that the learner is able to:	TiP	Activity
P1 describe the structure and ownership of the media industries, expressing ideas with sufficient clarity to communicate them and with some appropriate use of subject terminology	1 2 3	**M1** explain, with reference to well-chosen examples, the structure and ownership of the media industries, expressing ideas with clarity and with generally appropriate use of subject terminology	1 2 3	**D1** fully explain the structure and ownership of the media industries, justifying points made with supporting arguments and elucidated examples, expressing ideas fluently and using subject terminology correctly	1 2 3	End of Unit assessment activity 1
P2 demonstrate understanding of employment opportunities and job roles in the media industries	4 5 6 7 8	**M2** demonstrate competently an understanding of employment opportunities and job roles in the media industries, with reference to well-chosen examples	4 5 6 7 8	**D2** demonstrate thoroughly an understanding of employment opportunities and job roles in the media industries, with supporting justification and elucidated examples	4 5 6 7 8	End of Unit assessment activity 2

Grading Criteria						
To achieve a pass grade the evidence must show that the learner is able to:	TiP	To achieve a merit grade the evidence must show that the learner is able to:	TiP	To achieve a distinction grade the evidence must show that the learner is able to:	TiP	Activity
P3 demonstrate understanding of ethical and legal considerations relevant to media industries	9	**M3** demonstrate competently an understanding of ethical and legal considerations relevant to the media industries, with reference to well-chosen examples	9	**D3** demonstrate thoroughly an understanding of ethical and legal considerations relevant to the media industries, with supporting justification and elucidated examples	9	End of Unit assessment activity 3
P4 describe the regulatory issues affecting the media industries, expressing ideas with sufficient clarity to communicate them and with some appropriate use of subject terminology	10	**M4** explain, with reference to well-chosen examples, the regulatory issues affecting the media industries, expressing ideas with clarity and with generally appropriate use of subject terminology	10	**D4** fully explain the regulatory issues affecting the media industries, justifying points made with supporting arguments and elucidated examples, expressing ideas fluently and using subject terminology correctly	10	End of Unit assessment activity 4

Appendix

Introduction

This appendix is intended to highlight the different aspects of employment and regulation issues you might find in each area of the media. After completing this appendix, you should be able to achieve the following outcomes:

Unit 7: Understanding the television and film industries
- Know about media ownership and organisational structures in the television and film industries.
- Know about job roles in the television and film industries.
- Understand contractual, legal and ethical obligations in the television and film industries.
- Be able to prepare personal career development material.

Unit 8: Understanding the sound recording industry
- Understand organisational structures and ownership in the UK radio industry.
- Understand job roles, working practices and developing technologies in the UK radio industry.
- Understand how to prepare for employment in the UK radio industry.
- Understand contractual, legal and ethical issues relevant to the UK radio industry.

Unit 9: Understanding the sound recording industry
- Understand organisational structures and ownership in the UK recording industry.
- Understand job roles, working practices and developing technologies in the UK recording industry.

- Understand how to prepare for employment in the UK recording industry.
- Understand contractual, legal and ethical issues relevant to the UK recording industry.

Unit 10: Understanding the print and publishing industries
- Understand organisational structures and job roles within the print and publishing industry.
- Understand working practices and employment contracts commonly used in the print and publishing industry.
- Understand financial issues and market trends affecting the print and publishing industry.
- Understand legal, ethical and professional obligations in the print and publishing industry.
- Be able to prepare personal career development material.

Unit 11: Understanding the interactive media industry
- Understand organisational structures and job roles within the interactive media industry.
- Understand financial issues and current market trends affecting the interactive media industry.
- Understand contractual, legal and ethical obligations in the interactive media industry.
- Be able to use project management techniques commonly used in the interactive media industry.
- Be able to prepare personal career development material.

Thinking points

Whichever media industry you want to work in, there are similar things across all of them that you need to know. Unit 6 has dealt with a lot of these, such as organisation and structure within the industry, job roles, contractual, legal and ethical considerations and preparing personal career development material.

Project management techniques are similar across the industry and these have been examined in Unit 3 Production management project.

This appendix to Unit 6 will provide a background for you to consider how you might work in each of the identified media industries.

The television and film industry has undergone many changes over the past few years. Television has entered the digital age with information transmitted not just from large land-based transmitters via a housetop aerial, but also by satellite via a dish or by cable.

This change to digital technology has prompted a rise in television channels that cater for the tastes of a wide viewing audience.

News, music and entertainment can be seen twenty-four hours a day. Images of the latest big news story can be instantly beamed across the world. Viewers can pay to see top-notch sports fixtures using technology that allows them to freeze live television and watch again. Football matches can be seen from a number of different camera positions by simply pressing a button and selecting the angle.

The film industry is going through massive changes as delivery is now being undertaken through computers and down telephone cables. Films can be distributed on mobile telephones and consumers are looking for new ways to view their favourite films.

All of this has an impact on the way that the film and television industry is structured and owned.

Here is an example of just one company operating in the world of television.

You can see from this diagram that one company has interests in lots of organisations.

As a media professional you will need to know who owns what and who produces which media products.

The following case study looks at the career development of someone working in the television and film industry.

Case study

Sarah Urban

Sarah Urban studied for four years at university doing a Media Production degree. Although her main interest was radio, the varied nature of the course enabled her to develop knowledge and skills in a number of different areas of the media.

Because she did regular work experience for several independent television production companies on reality TV shows, when a first job as a runner came up, she took it immediately and found it very interesting and enjoyable.

Sarah is developing contacts and gaining valuable experience on a temporary contract, while watching out for further opportunities to develop her career.

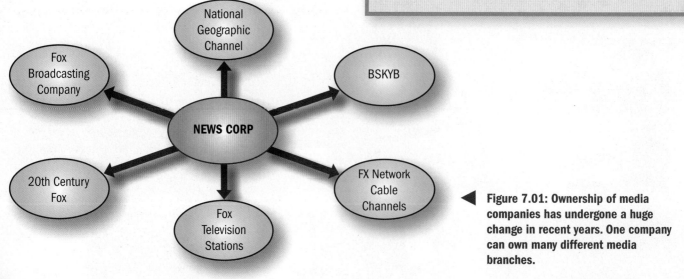

Figure 7.01: Ownership of media companies has undergone a huge change in recent years. One company can own many different media branches.

7

Not everyone undertaking a National Diploma in Media qualification ends up behind the camera. Lucy Kite is an example of a student who went on to work in front of the camera.

Case study

Lucy Kite

Lucy started her career in media by taking a National Diploma in Media at a college in the East Midlands. Lucy developed her skills in media production and learned about how to film and edit her own programmes. However, she felt that she wanted something different from her career and decided to undertake a Degree in Broadcast Journalism at Nottingham Trent University.

It was here that Lucy developed her skills in journalism that lead to her job as Entertainment Correspondent at Central Television East.

Lucy spends her time interviewing celebrities and finding suitable stories for the local East Midlands News. She has presented items from the USA as well as in Nottingham and Derby.

Lucy's qualification in media production provided her with the skills to understand the needs of television production. The broadcast journalism degree gave her the skills to find appropriate stories, to write copy and then present it to camera.

Here you can see Lucy working with her cameraman on a story for Central News.

Theory into practice 1

This activity is in four stages and will help you to produce material for the assessment criteria for **Unit 7: Understanding the television and film industries**.

You must produce a *Student Guide to Working in the Television and Film Industries.*

Stage 1
Produce a section on the television and film industries. Include the following in this section:

- how these industries are structured
- the technology used in these industries
- who owns what in these industries
- how the industries are funded. **P1**

Stage 2
Produce a section on job roles in the television and film industries.

- Describe the working patterns in these industries.
- Identify developing technologies in the television and film industries. **P2**

Stage 3
Produce a section that highlights contractual issues, contracts of employment, employment legislation, and ethical and legal issues in the television and film industries. **P3**

Stage 4
Produce a section that helps you and the reader to prepare a personal career development plan. **P4**

The *Guide* can be in any media format you choose. Think carefully about how you might present this work. Will it be a presentation using PowerPoint, a DVD programme, an audio piece or a printed booklet?

Grading tips

To reach Merit level, you should use well-chosen examples to illustrate the points you are making. You should be clear in your explanations and use appropriate media terminology and language.

To reach Distinction level, you should use appropriate examples that illustrate and clarify the points you are making. You should use fluent, appropriate media language and the correct subject terminology. You should fully explain your points.

Radio is one of the fastest growing media industries. At the present time there is a large number of radio stations in the UK providing a wide range of broadcasts for equally varied audiences. As the radio industry develops new ways of reaching new audiences so the opportunities for working in this industry increase.

You will need to understand how the radio industry is structured if you want to work in this sector. One of the major players in the radio industry is the BBC. You can see here how BBC Radio is structured:

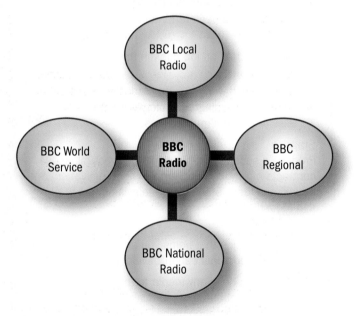

▲ **Figure 8.01: How BBC Radio is structured.**

You will need to understand the different ways in which radio stations are funded. Commercial radio companies are funded by the advertisements they carry or sponsorship from commercial organisations.

Working in the radio industry requires a commitment to unsociable working patterns, such as an early shift to work on the morning drive-time show or the late night shift to work on a talk show or specialist programme.

Theory into practice 2

Identify how the BBC is funded. **P1**

Explain how the following contribute to the funding process:

- regional and local radio, world service and other radio activities
- other revenue streams
- links with other organisations. **M1**

Identify commercial organisations working in the radio industry.

For each organisation:

- Find the names of the radio stations that they own
- Identify from your research how these radio stations are funded. **M1**

Grading tip

To reach Distinction level, justify your points and use clear examples. Express your ideas fluently and use subject terminology correctly.

The case study on the next page gives an example of a media student who now works in the radio sector.

When looking at the radio industry you should remember that there are also organisations that promote not-for-profit radio access. These can include hospital radio, restricted-service licences and community radio.

8

Case study

Katy McDonald

Katy McDonald is a radio journalist. She studied for a Media Production degree at the University of Sunderland, and stayed on there for a further year to complete a post-graduate course – an MA in journalism.

As a student she did some work experience at Sky Television, and then talked her way into Metro Radio in Newcastle, where she began by working for free. After a short while she was being paid to do the technical operation on the Saturday afternoon sports programme and a five-nights-per-week phone-in on Metro's sister station, Magic 1152.

As soon as she got her qualifications in journalism – including the National Council for the Training of Journalists (NCTJ) certificate – Katy got a full-time job on the news desk, where she quickly became morning news editor, compiling and presenting bulletins on Metro and Magic.

Think it over 1

You will find that much of the information you need about job roles, working practices and preparing for employment has been covered in Unit 6.

Check out Unit 6 to see if there is information you can use in your work.

Theory into practice 3

This activity is in four stages and will help you to produce material for the assessment criteria for **Unit 8: Understanding the radio industry**.

You must produce a *Student Guide to Working in the Radio Industry*.

Stage 1
Produce a section on the structure of the radio industry. Include the following in this section:

- how this industry is structured
- the technology used in this industry
- who owns what in this industry
- how the industry is funded
- identify not-for-profit radio organisations. **P1**

Stage 2
Produce a section on job roles in the radio industry.
- Give examples of working practices in this industry.
- Identify developing technologies in the radio industry. **P2**

Stage 3
Produce a section that helps you and the reader to prepare a personal career development plan.

- Identify how people are recruited to the radio industry.
- Identify professional bodies in the radio industry. **P3**

Stage 4
Produce a section that highlights contracts of employment, employment legislation, and ethical and legal issues in the radio industry. **P4**

The *Guide* can be in any media format you choose. Think carefully about how you might present this work. Will it be a presentation using PowerPoint, a DVD programme, an audio piece or a printed booklet?

Grading tips

To reach Merit level, you should use well-chosen examples to illustrate the points you are making. You should be clear in your explanations and use appropriate media terminology and language.

To reach Distinction level, you should fully explain your points. Where appropriate, use examples that illustrate and clarify the points you are making. You should use fluent, appropriate media language and the correct subject terminology.

The sound recording industry has seen many changes over the last few years. The move to digital production techniques means that equipment used for recording and editing sound has not only shrunk in size but also in cost.

You will need to understand the technology used in the sound recording industry and the way in which you would be part of a team.

It is important to understand the types of recording studios that operate in this sector and the type of work that they undertake.

A sound recording studio could be employed across a range of activities, such as recording a live band, mixing a soundtrack for a television programme or film or recording the soundtrack for a video game. Whatever project the studio is working on, the same principles of teamworking apply to its employees.

This is an example of a small recording studio.

Figure 9.01: Turtle Studios is a small company but its multi-tasking staff offer a comprehensive sound-recording service.

You can see from this example that this recording studio offers a range of services and its engineers are also musicians. In a larger organisation you might find that there are a range of job roles. These might be creative, technical or managerial roles.

This is an example of a larger recording studio based in London.

▲ Figure 9.02 Tin Pan Alley Studio offers a wide range of services and jobs.

Think it over 2

You will find that much of the information you need about job roles, working practices and preparing for employment has been covered in Unit 6.

Check out Unit 6 to see if there is information you can use in your work.

9

Theory into practice 4

There are several sound recording industry organisations that you should know about. List the following organisations and identify their roles in the sound recording industry. **P1**

- Association of Professional Recording Services (APRS)
- Music Producers Guild (MPG)
- Association of Post-Production Studios (APPS)
- Joint Audio Media Educational Services (JAMES)
- Audio Engineering Society (AES)
- Professional Lighting and Sound Association (PLASA)
- Music Industries Association (MIA)
- British Phonographic Industry (BPI)
- Association of Independent Music (AIM)
- Commercial Radio Companies Association (CRCA)

You could take one organisation each or in pairs. Other learners could do the same until each organisation is researched.

Once you have all the information, put together a presentation or illustrated report that you can share with the whole class. **M1**

Grading tips

To reach Merit level, you should use well-chosen examples to illustrate the points you are making. You should be clear in your explanations and use appropriate media terminology and language.

To reach Distinction level, you should fully explain your points. Where appropriate use examples that illustrate and clarify the points you are making. You should use fluent, appropriate media language and the correct subject terminology.

Theory into practice 5

This activity is in four stages and will help you to produce material for the assessment criteria for **Unit 9: Understanding the sound recording industry**.

You must produce a *Student Guide to Working in the Sound Recording Industry*.

Stage 1
Produce a section on the structure of the sound recording industry. Include the following in this section:

- how this industry is structured
- the technology used in this industry
- who owns what in this industry
- how the industry is funded **P1**

Stage 2
Produce a section on job roles in the sound recording industry.

- Give examples of working practices in this industry.
- Identify developing technologies in the sound recording industry. **P2**

Stage 3
Produce a section that helps you and the reader to prepare a personal career development plan.

- Identify how people are recruited to the sound recording industry.
- Identify professional bodies in the sound recording industry. **P3**

Stage 4
Produce a section that highlights contractual issues, contracts of employment, employment legislation, and ethical and legal issues in the sound recording industry. **P4**

The *Guide* can be in any media format you choose. Think carefully about how you might present this work. Will it be a presentation using PowerPoint, a DVD programme, an audio piece or a printed booklet?

The print and publishing industry, like many other media industries, is going through a period of change. Many of the traditional print techniques have now been replaced by digital print technology.

This has meant that people working in this industry have had to adapt to change. New technology requires people with understanding of this technology and the skills required to produce quality print publications.

In order to understand the structure of the print and publishing industry, look at the following material about one publisher.

▲ **Figure 10.01: Harcourt is a large educational publisher that publishes both print and electronic media.**

Think it over 3

You will find that much of the information you need about job roles, working practices and preparing for employment has been covered in Unit 6.

Check out Unit 6 to see if there is information you can use in your work.

Case study

Dan Walker

Dan left school with a love of drawing, colour and graphics. He had done well in his GCSEs and his careers officer suggested a career in printing. Dan started as a trainee print manager at a local print company and attended college on a full-time basis for three years. He then spent two years on day release at college while working for the print company and learning skills on the job.

Now Dan runs a multi-million pound digital printing press that prints a wide range of products. He has to work to tight deadlines and accurate colour tolerances. His everyday work includes printing posters and tour books for bands such as Coldplay, DVD box set covers for films such as *Lord of the Rings*, cartons for packaging and leaflets for major companies.

Dan uses his skills to colour-match exact customer requirements for a print product. He has ultimate responsibility for ensuring that the print product he produces matches the design provided by the graphic designer. Dan's skills have been developed through working on a wide variety of print products and training both on the job and through his college course.

There are many other job roles within the print and publishing industry. One of these is in photography.

A photographer could take photographs for a newspaper or magazine, for posters and brochures or the images for this book.

10

Case study

Stuart McIntyre

Stuart studied for a National Diploma in Media. On this course he learned the skills of photography, video production and sound recording. He enjoyed his photography work and decided to take a Higher National Diploma in Photography. After completing this course he started his career as a professional photographer.

While studying for his HND, Stuart met a local photographer who was producing portraits of celebrities for magazines, such as the *Radio Times*. Stuart was able to work as his assistant and gained valuable experience while still studying.

Stuart has his own studio in the East Midlands and takes on a wide range of work for a variety of clients. He has further developed his skills in portrait photography as well as magazine work, packaging shots, architectural photography and fashion photographs.

Stuart used his time on the National Diploma in Media to try out a range of media work and to find out what he really wanted to do.

Theory into practice 6

This activity is in four stages and will help you to produce material for the assessment criteria for **Unit 10: Understanding the print and publishing industries**.

You must produce a *Student Guide to Working in the Print and Publishing Industries*.

The *Guide* can be in any media format you choose. Think carefully about how you might present this work. Will it be a presentation using PowerPoint, a DVD programme, an audio piece or a printed booklet?

Stage 1
Produce a section on the structure of the print and publishing industries. Include the following in this section.

- how this industry is structured
- the technology used in this industry
- who owns what in this industry
- how this industry is funded. **P1**

Stage 2
Produce a section on job roles in the print and publishing industries.

- Give examples of working practices in this industry.
- Identify developing technologies in the print and publishing industries. **P2**

Stage 3
Produce a section that identifies financial issues and market trends in this industry.

- Include examples of sources of income and expenditure.
- Identify products and services and how these might change in relation to national and international trends.
- Explain how convergence in media might affect these industries. **P3**

Stage 4
Produce a section that identifies legal, ethical and professional obligations. Include examples of all of these. **P4**

Stage 5
Produce a section that helps you and the reader to prepare a personal career development plan.

- Identify how people are recruited to the print and publishing industries.
- Identify professional bodies in the print and publishing industries. **P5**

Grading tips

To reach Merit level, you should use well-chosen examples to illustrate the points you are making. You should be clear in your explanations and use appropriate media terminology and language.

To reach Distinction level, you should fully explain your points. Where appropriate, use examples that illustrate and clarify the points you are making. You should use fluent, appropriate media language and the correct subject terminology.

The interactive sector of the media industry is growing rapidly. The industry creates a wide variety of multimedia content for the Internet, computers, kiosks, mobile phones, DVD, CD, television, media players, set-top boxes and other emerging technologies.

People who work in this industry tend to be multi-skilled and are able to perform many functions. They can plan, produce and test products that they have developed from an initial idea.

Many people in this industry work as freelances, although some work as part of an in-house department.

An example of a large interactive media production centre is BBC Online. They provide web support for the BBC's range of radio and television programming.

The BBC website is one of the most visited websites in the world. However, not all websites have to be as large or as varied as this. Many companies now have a website to sell their products or services. Figure 11.01 is the website of a media production company. You can see that they use this to promote their services.

As in all media industries there are regulatory bodies and organisations that set out a code of practice for their industry. You can find details of some of these in Unit 6.

Theory into practice 7

Identify the role that each of the following organisations plays in this industry:

British Interactive Media Association (BIMA)
British Computer Society (BCS)
British Film Institute (BFI)
British Web Design and Marketing Association (BWDMA)
Producers' Alliance for Cinema and Television (Pact)
British Academy for Film and Television Arts (BAFTA)
UK Film Council.

P1

Case study

Thomas Holmes

Thomas attended a college in Nottingham to take a National Diploma in Media. He was interested in computers, photography and video production. After finishing the National Diploma he went to university to complete a Bachelor of Arts degree in Media Production (Video and New Media).

Thomas now works as a freelance web designer, producing material for a wide range of clients. He works from his office at home and uses broadband technology to communicate with clients. He uses a wide range of hardware and software to produce high-quality web designs. He is also working in the area of DVD menu design and authoring for a DVD production company.

Now Thomas is developing his own web hosting facility, to ensure he has control of his web designs from initial design to integration into the worldwide web. His business is growing because clients have seen the quality of his work and recommended him to their colleagues. Thomas is considering taking further courses to keep his skills up to date with developments in technology and software.

▲ **Figure 11.01: PMH Productions uses its website to promote all of its services.**

Think it over 4

You will find that much of the information you need about job roles, working practices and preparing for employment has been covered in Unit 6.

Check out Unit 6 to see if there is information you can use in your work.

Theory into practice 8

There are many jobs in the interactive media industry.

Identify what each of these jobs involves:

Researcher	Graphic designer
Layout artist	Photographer
Journalist	Copywriter
Sub-editor	Editor
Printer	Production co-ordinator
Print finisher	Sales executive
Publisher	Coder.

Grading tips

To reach Merit level, you should use well-chosen examples to illustrate your points. You should be clear in your explanations and use appropriate media terminology and language.

To reach Distinction level, you should fully explain your arguments. Where appropriate, use examples that illustrate and clarify your points. You should use fluent, appropriate media language and the correct subject terminology.

Theory into practice 9

This activity is in four stages and will help you to produce material for the assessment criteria for **Unit 10: Understanding the interactive media industry**

You must produce a *Student Guide to Working in the Interactive Media Industry*.

Stage 1
Produce a section on the structure of the interactive media industry. Include the following in this section:
- how this industry is structured
- the technology used in this industry
- who owns what in this industry
- how the industry is funded. **P1**

Also produce a section on job roles in the interactive media industry.
- Give examples of working practices in this industry.
- Identify roles and responsibilities in the interactive media industry. **P1**

Stage 2
Produce a section that identifies financial issues and market trends in this industry. Include examples of: financial, market and industry trends **P2**

Stage 3
Produce a section that highlights contracts of employment, employment legislation, and ethical and legal obligations in the interactive media industry. **P3**

Stage 4
Produce a section that identifies the project management techniques commonly used in this industry. **P4**

Stage 5
Produce a section that helps you and the reader to prepare a personal career development plan.

- Identify how people are recruited to the interactive media industry.
- Identify professional bodies in the interactive media industry. **P5**

The *Guide* can be in any media format you choose. Think carefully about how you might present this work. Will it be a presentation using PowerPoint, a DVD programme, an audio piece or a printed booklet?

The games industry is the fastest growing sector of the media industry. It is a fast-paced environment where innovations in technology and gameplay result in significant financial reward for the developers. To work in the games industry you need to be adaptable and quick thinking and have the ability and desire to constantly update your skills.

Beyond the technical skills needed for a specific role, games companies look for employees with:

- original and innovative ideas
- creativity
- good communication skills
- problem-solving abilities
- team skills
- flexibility
- tenacity
- an awareness of the applications and possible applications of technology.

Games are produced by developers who may also be the distributors of the game. Here are some examples of companies working in this sector.

SCi Entertainment Group plc (SEG) is the UK's leading publisher of computer games and one of the world's leading developers and publishers of entertainment software. SEG was formed in May 2005 from the integration of two of the UK's two largest video games publishers, SCi Games and Eidos Interactive. The group now has a very impressive portfolio of intellectual property and a global distribution network.

The company's strategy is to maintain a strong presence and reputation as a publisher of successful games by owning and exploiting game franchises.

Game Republic – a not-for-profit company – was set up by a group of games software developers in Yorkshire. Game Republic has created an environment that allows the growth and development of studios producing games software in the Yorkshire and Humber region. It has established partnerships with local universities and with organisations such as Yorkshire Forward, Business Link, Screen Yorkshire, UK Trade & Investment and the Department of Trade & Industry to support its studios. Game Republic acts as a facilitator to support developers in whatever way it can.

Theory into practice 10

Identify at least four games development companies in the UK. **P1**

Identify games that each of these companies has developed. **P1**

Think it over 5

You will find that much of the information you need about job roles, working practices and preparing for employment has been covered in Unit 6.

Check out Unit 6 to see if there is information you can use in your work.

▲ **Figure 12.01 Game Republic supports small game-developers in the north of England.**

Theory into practice 11

Identify the role that each of the following organisations plays in this industry:

The Independent Games Developers Association (Tiga)
The Entertainment and Leisure Software Publishers Association (ELSPA)
The International Games Developers Association (IGDA)
Women in Games
British Academy of Film and Television Arts (BAFTA)
Mobile Entertainment Forum (MEF)

Theory into practice 12

This activity is in four stages and will help you to produce material for the assessment criteria for **Unit 12: Understanding the games industry**

You must produce a *Student Guide to Working in the Games Industry*.

The *Guide* can be in any media format you choose. Think carefully about how you might present this work. Will it be a presentation using PowerPoint, a DVD programme, an audio piece or a printed booklet?

Stage 1
Produce a section on the structure of the games industry. Include the following in this section:

- how this industry is structured
- the technology used in this industry
- who owns what in this industry
- how the industry is funded. **P1**

Also produce a section on job roles in the games industry.

- Give examples of working practices in this industry.
- Identify roles and responsibilities in the games industry. **P1**

Stage 2
Produce a section that identifies financial issues and market trends in this industry. Include examples of:

- financial trends
- market trends
- industry trends. **P2**

Stage 3
Produce a section that highlights contractual issues, contracts of employment, employment legislation, and ethical and legal obligations in the games industry. **P3**

Stage 4
Produce a section that identifies the project management techniques commonly used in this industry. **P4**

Stage 5
Produce a section that helps you and the reader to prepare a personal career development plan.

- Identify how people are recruited to the games industry.
- Identify professional bodies in the games industry. **P3**

Grading tips

To reach Merit level, you should use well-chosen examples to illustrate the points you are making. You should be clear in your explanations and use appropriate media terminology and language.

To reach Distinction level, you should fully explain your points. Where appropriate, use examples that illustrate and clarify the points you are making. You should use fluent, appropriate media language and the correct subject terminology.

Index

Pages in *italics* refer to illustrations and charts, those in **bold** type to key terms.